UNMASKING
AUTISM

UNMASKING AUTISM

Discovering the New Faces *of* Neurodiversity

Devon Price, PHD

HARMONY
BOOKS · NEW YORK

Copyright © 2022 by Devon Price

All rights reserved.

Published in the United States by Harmony Books, an imprint of
Random House, a division of Penguin Random House LLC, New York.
harmonybooks.com

Harmony Books is a registered trademark, and the Circle colophon is
a trademark of Penguin Random House LLC.

Library of Congress Cataloging-in-Publication Data is available upon request.

ISBN 978-0-593-23523-2

Ebook ISBN 978-0-593-23524-9

Printed in the United States of America

Editor: Michele Eniclerico
Cover Designer: Anna Bauer
Text Designer Andrea Lau
Production Editor: Serena Wang
Production Manager: Kelli Tokos
Composition: Scribe, Inc.
Copy Editor: Tom Pitoniak
Indexer: Stephen Callahan

10 9

First Edition

To all the Autistics I met online,
before I knew who I was.
Your friendship provided an oasis
when I was at my most miserably adrift.

CONTENTS

INTRODUCTION

Alienation

When I moved from Cleveland to Chicago in the summer of 2009, I had no idea I'd need to make friends. I was twenty-one years old, serious, and socially withdrawn, and I truly believed I did not need other people. I'd moved to the city for graduate school and figured I could pour all my energy into classes and research and think of nothing else.

Solitude had worked pretty well for me up to that point. I had excelled academically, and living a "life of the mind" kept me from worrying too much about my many problems. I had an eating disorder that had ravaged my digestive system, and gender dysphoria that made me resent how other people saw me, though I didn't yet understand why. I didn't know how to approach people or initiate conversations, and I didn't care to learn, because most interactions left me feeling irritated and unheard. The few relationships I did have were enmeshed; I took responsibility for others' problems, tried to manage their emotions for them, and lacked any capacity to say "no" to unreasonable requests. I didn't know what I wanted out of life, other than to become a professor. I didn't want a family, I didn't have hobbies, and I believed I was incapable of really being loved. But I was getting good grades and my intellect earned me a lot of praise, so I just focused on those strengths. I pretended all the rest was a meaningless distraction.

When graduate school began, I rarely went out with my new classmates. The few times I did, I had to get completely hammered to overcome my inhibitions and seem "fun." Otherwise I spent whole weekends alone in my apartment, reading journal articles and falling down strange internet rabbit-holes. I didn't let myself have hobbies. I barely exercised or cooked. I'd occasionally hook up with people if I wanted sex or even just a little attention, but every interaction was impassive and rote. I had no sense of myself as a multifaceted human being.

By winter of that year I'd turned into a lonely, isolated wreck. I'd spend an hour sitting in the shower while the hot water rained down on me, lacking the will to stand up. I had trouble speaking to other people. I couldn't think of any research ideas and lost all interest in what I was studying. One of my supervisors chewed me out for rolling my eyes at her during meetings. At night bone-shaking sobs of despair and overwhelm would overtake me, and I'd pace around my room, whimpering and striking myself in the temples with the heels of my hands. My solitude had somehow become imprisoning, but I was too lacking in social skills or emotional self-awareness to get myself out of it.

I couldn't understand how I'd gotten myself into that miserable position. How was I supposed to know I needed friends, and a life? How could I go about connecting with others, when every effort was so unsatisfying? What did I actually enjoy or care about? Around people, I felt I had to censor every natural reaction, and pretend to have interests and feelings that were normal. Plus, people were so overwhelming. They were all so loud and erratic, their eyes like painful laser beams boring into me. All I wanted to do was sit in the dark and not be bothered or judged.

I believed something was fundamentally wrong with me. I seemed to be broken in ways I couldn't explain, but which everyone else could see at a glance. I spent several more years languishing like this, working myself to the point of burnout, having emotional breakdowns, relying on romantic partners for social contact and a sense of worthiness, and googling things like "how to make friends" in the middle of the night. Through it all, I never considered asking for help or sharing with anyone how I felt. I lived by a very narrow set of rules, and remaining independent and invulnerable was chief among them.

Things finally began to change for me in 2014, when I was on vacation at Cedar Point amusement park in Sandusky, Ohio. My family went there every single year. We were a family that loved our routines. I was sitting in a hot tub with my cousin, who had recently gone away to college and found the transition very challenging. He confessed to me that he'd recently been assessed for Autism. I had just completed my PhD in social psychology, so he wanted to know if I had any knowledge about Autism Spectrum Disorder.

"Sorry, I really don't know about that," I told him. "I don't study people with mental illnesses; my research is on the social behavior of 'normal' people."

My cousin started talking to me about all the things he struggled with—how hard it was to relate to classmates, how adrift and overstimulated he felt. A therapist had floated Autism as a likely explanation. Then my cousin pointed out all the Autistic traits he'd noticed were common in our family. We didn't like change. None of us could handle talking about our emotions and mostly interacted using a surface-level script. Some of us had hang-ups about food textures and strong flavors. We rambled on and on about the subjects that interested us, even if it bored others to tears. We were easily overwhelmed by change and rarely went out into the world to have new experiences or make friends.

When my cousin told me all this, I felt dread. I didn't want any of it to be true because in my mind, Autism was a shameful, life-ruining condition. It made me think of people like Chris, an uncoordinated, "cringey" Autistic kid I'd gone to school with whom nobody had treated well. Autism made me think of withdrawn, prickly TV characters like Benedict Cumberbatch's Sherlock, and the *Big Bang Theory*'s Sheldon. It called to mind nonverbal children who had to wear big clunky headphones to the grocery store and were viewed as objects rather than people. Though I was a psychologist, all I knew about Autism was the broadest and most dehumanizing of stereotypes. Being Autistic would mean I was broken.

Of course, I'd already felt broken for years.

As soon as I returned home from that vacation, I threw my bags down, sat on the floor, propped my laptop up on my knees, and started obsessively reading about Autism. I inhaled journal articles, blog posts, YouTube videos, and diagnostic assessment materials. I kept this obsessive reading mostly hidden from my then-partner, the way I kept all my deepest fixations hidden from people in my life. I soon learned that *itself* was a trait common among Autistics; we tend to latch on to subjects that fascinate us and focus on them with a fervor others find weird. After being mocked about our passions, we become secretive about our *special interests*. Already I was thinking about Autism in terms like *we* and *us*; I saw myself clearly reflected in the community, a fact that scared and exhilarated me.

The more I read about Autism, the more things began clicking into place. I had always been overwhelmed by loud sounds and bright lights. I got inexplicably angry in crowds; laughter and chatter could make me blow up with rage. When I got too stressed out or became overcome with sadness, I found it hard to speak. I'd hidden all this for years because I was certain it made me a joyless, unlovable asshole. Now I was beginning to wonder why I believed such awful things about myself.

Autism was my newest obsession, a thing I couldn't stop reading and thinking about. But I'd had many other special interests in the past. I remembered being passionate about bat watching and horror novels as a child. Kids and adults alike had chided me for being too "weird" and "hyper" about those interests. I was "too much" in so many ways. To other people, my tears were immature tantrums and my opinions were condescending diatribes. As I grew up, I learned to be less intense, less embarrassing—less me. I studied other people's mannerisms. I spent a lot of time dissecting conversations in my head, and I read up on psychology so I could understand people better. That was why I'd gotten a PhD in social psychology. I had needed to carefully study the social norms and patterns of thinking that seemingly felt natural to everybody else.

After researching Autism privately for about a year, I discovered the Autistic self-advocacy community. There was an entire movement led by Autistic people who argued we should view the disability as a perfectly normal form of human difference. These thinkers and activists said our way of being wasn't wrong at all; it was society's failure to adapt to our needs that left us feeling broken. People like Rabbi Ruti Regan (author of the blog *Real Social Skills*) and Amythest Schaber (the creator of the *Neurowonderful* video series) taught me about *neurodiversity*. I came to recognize that many disabilities are created or worsened by social exclusion. Armed with this knowledge and a growing sense of self-confidence, I started meeting Autistic people in real life, posting about Autism online, and attending local meetups for neurodiverse people.

I found out there were thousands of Autistics just like me, who discovered their disability in adulthood after years of confused self-loathing. As children, these Autistic folks had been visibly awkward, but they were mocked for it instead of given help. Like me, they had developed coping strategies to blend in. Things like staring at a person's forehead to simulate eye contact, or memorizing conversational scripts based on exchanges they saw on TV.

Many of these stealthily Autistic people fell back on their intellect or other talents to gain acceptance. Others became incredibly passive, because if they toned down their personalities, they wouldn't have to risk being too "intense." Beneath the inoffensive, professional veneers they had developed, their lives were falling apart. Many of them suffered from self-harm, eating disorders, and alcoholism. They were trapped in abusive or unfulfilling relationships, with no clue how to feel seen and appreciated. Nearly all of them were depressed, haunted by a profound sense of emptiness. Their entire lives had been shaped by mistrust in themselves, hatred of their bodies, and fear of their desires.

I noticed that there were clear patterns in which kinds of Autistic people succumbed to this kind of fate. Autistic women, transgender people, and people of color often had their traits ignored when they were young, or have symptoms of distress interpreted as "manipulative" or "aggressive." So did Autistic people who grew up in poverty, without access to mental health resources. Gay and gender nonconforming men often didn't fit the masculine image of Autism well enough to be diagnosed. Older Autistics never had the opportunity to be assessed, because knowledge about the disability was so limited during their childhoods. These systematic exclusions had forced an entire massive, diverse population of disabled people to live in obscurity. This gave rise to what I am now calling *masked Autism*—a camouflaged version of the disorder that's still widely neglected by researchers, mental health providers, and Autism organizations that aren't led by Autistic people, such as the much-reviled Autism Speaks.

When I use the term *masked Autism*, I'm referring to any presentation of the disability that deviates from the standard image we see in most diagnostic tools and nearly all media portrayals of Autism. Since Autism is a pretty complex and multifaced disorder, that covers a lot of different traits, which can manifest in many different ways. I'm also talking about any Autistic person whose suffering wasn't taken seriously for reasons of class, race, gender, age, lack of access to health care, or the presence of other conditions.

Usually it's white boys with conventionally "masculine" interests and hobbies that are flagged as potentially Autistic when they are young. Even within that relatively privileged class, it's almost exclusively wealthy and upper-middle-class Autistic kids who get identified.[1] That group has always been the prototype for Autism when it's described by clinicians or depicted in media. All the diagnostic criteria for Autism are based on how it presents in this group. Every Autistic person is hurt by this narrow conception of the disorder, even the white, rich, cisgender boys who are most likely to be reflected by it. For far too long, we have been defined only by the "hassle" that white Autistic boys caused their well-off parents. Our complex inner lives, our own needs and sense of alienation, the ways that neurotypical people confused, confounded, and even abused us—all were ignored for decades because of this lens. We were defined only by what we seemed to lack, and only insofar that our disabilities presented a challenge to our caregivers, teachers, doctors, and other people who held power over our lives.

For years now, psychologists and psychiatrists have discussed the existence of "female Autism," a supposed subtype that can look a lot milder and socially appropriate than "male" Autism does.[2] People with so-called "female Autism" may be able to make eye contact, carry on a conversation, or hide their tics and sensory sensitivities. They might spend the first few decades of their lives with no idea they're Autistic at all, believing instead that they're just shy, or highly sensitive. In recent years, the public has slowly become familiar with the idea that women with Autism exist, and a few excellent books like Jenara Nerenberg's *Divergent Mind* and Rudy Simone's *Aspergirls* have worked to build awareness of this population. It's also helped that high-profile Autistic women like comedian Hannah Gadsby and writer Nicole Cliffe have come out publicly as Autistic.

There's a significant problem with the concept of "female Autism," though. It's a label that doesn't properly account for why some Autistics mask their Autistic qualities, or have their needs ignored for years. First, not all women with Autism have the "female Autism" subtype. Plenty of Autistic women visibly self-stimulate, struggle to socialize, and experience meltdowns and shutdowns. Autistic scientist and activist Temple Grandin is a great example of this. She speaks in something of a monotone, avoids eye contact, and even as a young child craved sensory stimulation and pressure. Though she's very visibly and typically Autistic by today's standards, Grandin was not diagnosed until adulthood.[3]

Autistic women aren't overlooked because their "symptoms" are milder. Even women with really classically Autistic behaviors may elude diagnoses for years, simply because they are women and their experiences are taken less seriously by professionals than a man's would be.[4] Additionally, not everyone who has their Autism ignored and downplayed is a female. Many men and nonbinary people have our Autism erased, too. To call the stealthy, more socially camouflaged form of Autism a "female" version of the disorder is to indicate that masking is a phenomenon of gender, or even of assigned sex at birth, rather than a much broader phenomenon of social exclusion. Women don't have "milder" Autism because of their biology; people who are marginalized have their Autism ignored because of their peripheral status in society.

When an Autistic person is not given resources or access to self-knowledge, and when they're told their stigmatized traits are just signs that they're a disruptive, overly sensitive, or annoying kid, they have no choice but to develop a neurotypical façade. Maintaining that neuro-typical mask feels deeply inauthentic and it's extremely exhausting to maintain.[5] It's also not necessarily a conscious choice. Masking is a state of exclusion forced onto us from the outside. A closeted gay person doesn't just decide one day to be closeted—they're essentially born into the closet, because heterosexuality is normative, and being gay is treated as a rare afterthought or an aberration. Similarly, Autistic people are born with the mask of neurotypicality pressed against our faces. All people are assumed to think, socialize, feel, express emotion, process sensory information, and communicate in more or less the same ways. We're all expected to play along with the rules of our home culture, and blend into it seamlessly. Those of us who need alternate tools for self-expression and self-understanding are denied them. Our first experience of ourselves as a person in the world, therefore, is one of being othered and confused. We only get the opportunity to take our masks off when we realize other ways of being exist.

I have found that my entire life and nearly every challenge I've faced can be understood through a masked Autistic lens. My eating disorder was a way to punish my body for its unusual, Autistic mannerisms, and a means of making it conform to conventional beauty standards, protecting me from negative attention. My social isolation was a way of rejecting other people before they could reject me. My workaholism was a sign of Autistic hyperfixation, as well as an acceptable excuse to withdraw from public places that caused me sensory overwhelm. I got into unhealthy, codependent relationships because I needed approval and didn't know how to get it, so I just molded myself into whatever my partner at the time was looking for.

After a few years of researching Autism and forming my understanding of masking as a social phenomenon, I began writing about it online. I found that thousands of people resonated and identified with what I had to say. It turned out being Autistic wasn't that rare at all (roughly 2 percent of people are diagnosed with it today, and many more have subclinical traits or cannot access diagnosis).[6] Many individuals in my professional and social circles privately came out to me as neurodiverse as well. I met Autistic people with full-time jobs in visual design, acting, musical theater, and sex education—not fields people associate with our logical, supposedly "robotic" minds. I got to know more Black, brown, and indigenous Autistics, who had long been dehumanized by the psychiatric community. I met Autistics who'd at first been diagnosed with things like Borderline Personality Disorder, Oppositional Defiant Disorder, or Narcissistic Personality Disorder. I also found scores of transgender and gender-nonconforming Autistic people like me, who had always felt "different" both because of their gender and their neurotype.

In each of these people's lives, being Autistic was a source of uniqueness and beauty. But the ableism around them had been a fount of incredible alienation and pain. Most had floundered for decades before discovering who they truly were. And nearly all of them were finding it very difficult to take their long-worn masks off. Even this fact made me feel more comfortable in my own skin, and less broken and alone. So many of us had been taught we had to hide ourselves. Yet the more we joined in community with one another, the less pressure to mask we felt.

By spending time with other Autistic people, I began to see that life didn't have to be all hidden anguish. When I was around other Autistics, I was more able to be blunt and direct. I could ask for accommodations, such as dimming the lights or opening a window to dilute the stench of somebody's perfume. The more other people around me relaxed, spoke passionately about their special interests, and rocked in place excitedly, the less shame I felt about who I was, and how my brain and body worked.

For years now I've been using my skills as a social psychologist to make sense of the scientific literature on Autism, and connecting with Autistic activists, researchers, coaches, and therapists in order to firm up my understanding of our shared neurotype. I've also worked on unmasking myself, getting in touch with the vulnerable, erratic, odd version of me I'd been socially conditioned to hide. I've gotten to know a lot of leading voices in the Autistic self-advocacy community and read up on the many resources that Autistic therapists, coaches, and activists have developed to help train themselves and others to lower their inhibitions and drop their masks.

Today I don't hide the fact that I am pained by loud noises and bright lights. I ask people directly for an explanation when their words or body language don't make sense. Traditional benchmarks of "adulthood," such as owning a car or having children, hold no appeal for me, and I've learned that is completely okay. I sleep with a stuffed animal every night, and a loud fan blowing to block out my neighborhood's ambient noise. When I'm excited, I flap my hands and squirm in place. On good days, I don't think any of these things make me childish, or cringey, or bad. I love myself as I am, and others can see and love the real me. Being more honest about who I am has made me a more effective teacher and writer. When my students are struggling, I'm able to connect with them about how difficult maintaining a normal life really can be. When I write in my own voice, from my own perspective, I connect with an audience far more deeply than when I try to seem like a generic, respectable professional. Before I started unmasking, I felt cursed, and almost dead inside. Existence seemed like one long slog of faked enthusiasm. Now, though life can still be difficult, I feel incredibly alive.

I want every Autistic person to feel the massive relief and sense of community I found by recognizing myself and beginning to unmask. I also believe that it is essential for the future of the Autistic self-advocacy community that we each work on living more authentically as ourselves and demand the accommodations we need. With this book, I hope to help other Autistic people understand themselves, join forces with fellow neurodiverse people, and gradually find the confidence to take their masks off.

Unmasking has the potential to radically improve an Autistic person's quality of life. Research has repeatedly shown that keeping our true selves locked away is emotionally and physically devastating.[7] Conforming to neurotypical standards can earn us tentative acceptance, but it comes at a heavy existential cost. Masking is an exhausting performance that contributes to physical exhaustion, psychological burnout, depression, anxiety,[8] and even suicide ideation.[9] Masking also obscures the fact that the world is massively inaccessible to us. If allistics (non-Autistics) never hear our needs voiced, and never see our struggle, they have no reason to adapt to include us. We must demand the treatment we deserve, and cease living to placate those who have overlooked us.

Refusing to perform neurotypicality is a revolutionary act of disability justice. It's also a radical act of self-love. But in order for Autistic people to take our masks off and show our real, authentically disabled selves to the world, we first have to feel safe enough to get reacquainted with who we really are. Developing self-trust and self-compassion is a whole journey unto itself.

This book is for any person who is neurodiverse (or suspects that they are neurodiverse) and wants to attain new levels of self-acceptance. Neurodiversity is a wide umbrella, including everyone from Autistics, to ADHDers, to people with Schizophrenia, brain injuries, or

Narcissistic Personality Disorder. Though the book's focus is masked Autistic people, I have found there is considerable overlap between Autistics and other neurodiverse groups. Many of us share mental health symptoms and traits and have overlapping or comorbid diagnoses. All of us have internalized mental illness stigma and felt the shame of deviating from what's considered "normal." Almost every person with a mental illness or disability has been crushed under the weight of neurotypical expectations, and has repeatedly tried and failed to earn acceptance by playing the rules of a game that was designed to harm us. And so, for nearly every neurodiverse person, the journey toward self-acceptance involves learning to unmask.

In the following chapters, I'll introduce you to a variety of Autistic people who flout the popular stereotypes. I'll also explain the history of how Autism has been defined, and how that's led us to the obscured and estranged place we're in today. Using the real-life stories of Autistic people, as well as a bevy of psychological research, I'll illustrate the many ways that masked Autism can present and explain why so many of us never realize we have a pervasive disability until relatively late in life. I'll discuss how painful a lifetime of masking can be, and point to data showing it takes a real toll on our mental, physical, and relational health.

Most important, this book will outline strategies a masked Autistic person can take to stop hiding their neurodiverse traits, and describe what a world more accepting of neurodiversity might look like. My hope is that one day, each of us can accept ourselves as the wonderfully weird, mold-breaking individuals we truly are, and live as ourselves, without fear of ostracism or violence. I've spoken to a variety of Autistic educators, therapists, coaches, and writers to help develop these resources, have tested them in my own life, and interviewed Autistic people who've used them to improve their own lives. These experiences provide concrete examples of what an unmasked (or less-masked) existence really looks like. When you stop judging yourself according to the neurotypical gaze, everything from your relationship norms and daily habits, to the way you dress yourself and design your home is free to change.

A life less trapped under the mask is possible for each of us. But building such a life can be extremely daunting. When we think about why we started masking in the first place, it tends to bring up a lot of old pain. One of the coaches and disability advocates whose work has helped to inform this book, Heather R. Morgan, stressed to me that before we examine our masks and learn to take them off, we must first recognize that the version of ourselves we've been hiding from the world is somebody we can trust.

"I think it can be risky for people to try to think about where their mask comes from and think about taking the mask off before they first know that there's somebody safe underneath of it," she says. "Even talking about unmasking if we don't have a safe place to land can be terrifying."

In my own life and in the lives of the Autistic people I interviewed for this book, I've seen proof positive that the process of unmasking is worth it. But if you're just starting out on this journey, and you're feeling adrift and confused about who you really are, you might not yet believe there's a worthwhile version of you waiting on the other side. You might still be haunted by negative media images of Autism or be worried that unmasking might make you less functional, too strange, or somehow impossible to love. You probably also recognize that there are real, material risks to letting your disability be visible, particularly if you occupy a marginalized position in society. You might associate authenticity with being unsafe for incredibly rational reasons, and not be sure how and when unmasking could be worth it for you. So, let's first take a moment to consider the positive sides of unmasking, and what a less inhibited life might look like for you.

Below is an exercise developed by Heather R. Morgan, which she administers to clients on their very first meeting together. It is designed to help masked people develop more trust in themselves and consider the existence of something beautiful on the other side of the mask.

Values-Based Integration Process	
Step 1: Find Your Why	

Instructions: Think of five moments in your life when you felt like you were FULLY ALIVE. Try to find moments from throughout your life (childhood, adolescence, adulthood; school, work, vacation, hobbies).

Some of the moments might leave you with a sense of awe and wonder—"*wow, if all of life was like that, life would be amazing!*"

Some of the moments might leave you feeling deeply recharged and ready to face the next challenge, or satisfied and fulfilled.

Write down each of these moments. Tell the story of each moment in as much detail as possible. Try to think specifically about *why* the moment stuck with you so dramatically.

Moment #1:	
Moment #2:	
Moment #3:	
Moment #4:	
Moment #5:	

It may take you some time to complete this exercise. You can spend days or even weeks reflecting on it, making sure you recall moments from a variety of settings and time periods. We'll return to these moments later in the book, but for now, you can just bask in how good it feels to recall whatever examples do come to mind.

As we discuss the systemic forces that lead so many of us to mask, and explore how masking harms Autistic people's lives, you may find it helpful to return to these memories from time to time, and draw strength from them. Let your memories serve as a reminder that you are not broken, and that the blueprint for building a worthwhile, authentic life already exists within you.

CHAPTER 1

What Is Autism, Really?

When Crystal was young, she exhibited many behaviors psychologists today would recognize as traditionally Autistic: she lined up toys in rows instead of playing pretend with them, chewed on her blanket while staring at the wall, and had trouble understanding in-jokes and teasing. But she didn't "look Autistic enough" to get easily diagnosed in the 1990s, when she was growing up.

"My mom actually thought I should get assessed," she says. "But my grandpa shut it down. He was all, no, no way, Crystal's such a good girl! There's nothing wrong with her. Don't even think about stuff like that."

Crystal's grandfather probably figured he was protecting her from getting stuck with a label that would bring a lifetime of abuse. He certainly isn't alone in that. Label avoidance (taking steps to evade diagnosis) is a very common consequence of disability and mental health stigma.[1] Publicly identifying as disabled does mean being viewed as less competent—and less human—by many people. As damaging and self-defeating as it can be to camouflage one's disability status, it is by no means a paranoid act. It's a rational reflection of the prejudices disabled people face. It's not unique to Autism, either; many people with mental illnesses[2] and hidden physical disabilities[3] elect to avoid the mark of shame a diagnosis might bring.

My dad hid his cerebral palsy and seizure disorder for his entire life. No one knew about his condition other than my grandmother, my mom, and eventually me. He never went to college because he would have needed to reveal his access needs to campus disability services. He only ever applied to jobs that didn't require him to write or type, lest his poor fine motor control be revealed. As a child, I typed up the flyers for his lawn mowing business, because he couldn't work the computer himself. I only found out about his condition as a teenager; he sobbingly confessed it to me, as if it were a terrible secret, after his marriage to my mother had already fallen apart. He told me that his mother had made him hide his condition because it wouldn't have been acceptable to be openly disabled in the tiny Appalachian town where he grew up. Shame and self-loathing followed him until the day that he died of diabetes (a condition he developed as an adult and also refused to treat).

I didn't find out I was Autistic until many years after his death, but he was the first person who demonstrated to me just how painful and self-destructive hiding your disability can be. He had erected an entire life around hiding who he was, and his defensive mechanisms had slowly killed him.

Label avoidance was common among the parents of potentially Autistic children during the 1990s, because the condition was so poorly understood and demonized.[4] Autistic people were assumed to be intellectually disabled, and intellectually disabled people were not valued or respected, so many families did their damnedest to keep the label off their kids' backs. Though Crystal's grandfather intended to protect her from bigotry, and from being infantilized, he also denied her important self-knowledge, educational resources, and a place in the Autistic community. Without consulting Crystal, her family determined it would be better for her to suffer and hide her neurodiversity than to have a name for her marginalized position in the world. The weight of this decision is one Crystal continues to deal with now, as an adult who was diagnosed in her late twenties.

"Now I know I'm Autistic, but I kinda found out about it too late," she says. "If I tell people, they don't want to believe me. I have my life together too much for them to realize how hard it all is. Nobody wants to hear now about how hard it's always been, always still is, frankly."

At this point, I have heard hundreds of Autistic people tell versions of Crystal's story. Some of the details change, but the narrative arc is always the same: A child exhibits early signs of difficulty, but their families and teachers balk when disability is raised. Parents or grandparents who themselves have Autism spectrum traits dismiss the child's complaints, claiming that everybody suffers from the social stress, sensory sensitivities, stomach issues, or cognitive fuzziness they themselves experience. Everyone in the child's life views disability not as an explanation of how a person functions (and what help they need in order to function), but a sign of damage. So they push the label away, and tell their child to stop making such a fuss. Believing they are helping their child "rise above" a limitation and be tough, they encourage the child not to be visibly odd, or to ever ask for assistance.

Though a masked Autistic child has no way of explaining why they find life so difficult, they suffer all the same. Peers detect there's something unnameably "off" about them, and exclude them despite their best attempts at friendliness. When the child makes themselves small and inobtrusive, they're granted some of the affection they desperately crave and never get enough of. So they do it more and more, quieting the voice inside themselves that says how they're being treated isn't fair. They work hard, demand little, and play by society's rules as closely as possible. They grow into an adult who is even more self-effacing, and even less capable of voicing how they feel. Then, after decades of forcing themselves into a restrictive neurotypical box, they have some kind of breakdown that finally makes all the turmoil bubbling beneath the surface impossible to ignore. It's only then that they discover they're Autistic.

In Crystal's case, the breaking point took the form of a months-long case of Autistic burnout. Autistic burnout is a state of chronic exhaustion where an Autistic person's skills begin to degrade, and their tolerance to stress is greatly reduced.[5] It hit Crystal like a Mack truck after she completed her senior thesis in college. College had taken her a few years longer than the rest of her friends, though she couldn't explain exactly why. She was always having to drop classes in order to hold her life together. A full course load just wasn't possible. When people asked about it, she lied and said she also worked a full-time job.

In her final year of college, Crystal was required to oversee set design for the theater department's biggest show of the year. Designing dozens of props, sourcing their materials, managing the building of them, and then keeping track of all the items in a big Google spreadsheet was simply too stressful for her to manage, especially while taking her final remaining classes. She pushed through, losing hair and losing weight, but once the project was completed, she collapsed.

"After I graduated, I was in bed at my mom's house for three months," she says. "Didn't apply to jobs. I barely showered, had all these McDonald's wrappers on the floor of my bedroom, and my family still insisted I was just being lazy."

Eventually, Crystal became so lethargic that she no longer wanted to watch TV or play with the family dog. That was concerning enough for her mother to suggest she go see a therapist. An Autism assessment came shortly thereafter.

"At first I couldn't believe it," Crystal says. "My family still doesn't believe it. They had every indication, my whole life, but they don't want to see it."

At last, Crystal had an explanation for why she couldn't get as much done as other people, and why basic-seeming tasks like running to the bank or sitting through a two-hour lecture left her too tired to think or speak. Regular life actually did require more willpower out of her; Autistic people frequently experience inertia in starting a task,[6] and challenges in breaking complex activities down into small steps that follow a logical sequence.[7] This can make everything from basic household chores to applying to jobs and filing taxes incredibly challenging, or even impossible without help.

In addition to all the baseline cognitive and sensory challenges that came with Autism for Crystal, she was also having to put a lot of energy into always seeming "normal." She constantly fought the urge to suck on her fingers, and when people spoke to her, she had to forcibly point her attention at their words and face. Reading a book took her twice as long as the average person. All she had the energy to do at the end of the day was sit in bed and eat french fries. Crystal's mother and grandfather were unsatisfied by this newfound explanation, though. They said that if she had really been hurting that bad all her life, they would have realized it.

"I wish I could make them understand," she says, "Autism isn't what you think."

Defining Autism

One of the reasons Autism often gets overlooked in women like Crystal is a fundamental misunderstanding that professionals and the public have about what Autism even is. Until fairly recently, most people believed Autism was rare, that only young boys had it, and that it was always easy to see. Think of Dustin Hoffman's portrayal in the film *Rain Man*: he's institutionalized as a child because he's profoundly disabled and too "difficult" to have at home, he never gives eye contact, wanders off dangerously when not closely watched, and has a preternatural talent for math that his nondisabled brother exploits for personal gain. This is how all of us were trained to view the disability: a horrible condition that renders you freakish and helpless, your life only as valuable as your savant-like skills are to other people.

By the mid-1990s, when Crystal was a kid, some people also had a vague awareness of what was then called Asperger's Disorder.

Asperger's was stereotyped as a "higher functioning" flavor of Autism found in really smart, nerdy, usually rude men who worked in fields like tech. In both forms, Autism was associated with being awkward and uncaring (and male) with a penchant for numbers. People had little to no understanding of Autism's causes, what it felt like to be an Autistic person, or that the disability shares features with other disorders like epilepsy, Social Anxiety Disorder, Attention-Deficit Hyperactive Disorder (ADHD), or Post-Traumatic Stress Disorder (PTSD).

Despite what people believe, Autism is not defined by rudeness, masculinity, or having any kind of mathematical skill. In the scientific literature, it's arguable whether the disability should even be defined by the presence of clear behavioral signs, such as trouble reading social cues or hesitating to initiate contact with other people.[8] Instead of looking to the external signals of Autism that others might pick up on, it's important that we instead focus on the neurobiological markers of the neurotype, and the internal experiences and challenges that Autistic people themselves report.

Autism is neurological. Autism is a developmental disability that runs in families[9] and appears to be largely genetically heritable.[10] However, it is also *multiply determined*, meaning it has no single cause: a whole host of different genes appear to be associated with Autism,[11] and every Autistic person's brain is unique and exhibits its own distinct patterns of connectivity.[12] Autism is a *developmental* disability because compared to neurotypical milestones, it comes with delays: many Autistic people continue to grow in their social and emotional skills for much later in life than allistics tend to.[13] (However, this may be due to the fact that Autistic people are forced to develop our own social and emotional coping skills from scratch, because the neurotypical methods taught to us don't suit how we process information— more on this later.) Autism is associated with specific and pervasive differences in the brain, which result in us diverging from neurotypical standards, in terms of how our brains filter and make sense of information.

Autistic people have differences in the development of their anterior cingulate cortex,[14] a part of the brain that helps regulate attention, decision making, impulse control, and emotional processing. Throughout our brains, Autistic people have delayed and reduced development of Von Economo neurons (or VENs), brain cells that help with rapid, intuitive processing of complex situations.[15] Similarly, Autistic brains differ from allistic brains in how excitable our neurons are.[16] To put it in very simple terms, our neurons activate easily, and don't discriminate as readily between a "nuisance variable" that our brains might wish to ignore (for example, a dripping faucet in another room) and a crucial piece of data that deserves a ton of our attention (for example, a loved one beginning to quietly cry in the other room). This means we can both be easily distracted by a small stimulus and miss a large meaningful one.

Autistic brains have unique connection patterns that deviate from what is normally observed in neurotypical people. When infants are born, their brains are typically hyperconnected; much of human development is a process of slowly pruning unhelpful connections and becoming more efficient at responding to one's environment, based on life experience and learning. In Autistic brains, however, researchers have found that some regions remain hyperconnected throughout the life span, whereas other regions may be underconnected (relatively speaking). It is difficult to sum up these connectivity patterns because, as neurobiologists at the Weizmann Institute of Science have found, every Autistic brain exhibits a different connectivity pattern. Our brain wiring appears to actually be more diverse than the wiring of neurotypical brains, which researchers believe have a consistent pruning pattern.[17] The researchers at the Weizmann Institute have theorized that this means Autistic brains respond to our environments differently; whereas neurotypical brains are believed to readily adapt to the sensory and social input they receive from the outside world, Autistic brain development and pruning appears to be "disrupted."[18]

Autistic people also exhibit less of what neuroscientists call *global-to-local interference*:[19] we are inclined to zero in on small details, even when those details don't jibe with the overall "big picture" that a non-Autistic person might see. For example, one series of studies found that Autistic people are far better than allistics at copying down a drawing of a distorted 3-D object that couldn't exist in real life.[20] Allistics got caught off guard by how impossible and illogical the overall image was, whereas Autistics could just focus on the individual lines and shapes that made up the image, and re-create the drawing from the bottom up. This high degree of attention to detail also applies to how we navigate social situations: we focus on the small features of a person's face rather than taking in their likeness or emotional expression as a whole, for instance.[21] This helps explain why many Autistic people have *prosopagnosia* (the inability to recognize faces),[22] and experience difficulty reading emotions on neurotypicals' faces.

Together, all of this means that Autistic people tend to have the following qualities:

- We are hyperreactive to even small stimuli in our environment
- We have trouble distinguishing between information or sensory data that should be ignored versus data that should be carefully considered
- We are highly focused on details rather than "big picture" concepts
- We're deeply and deliberatively analytical
- Our decision-making process is methodical rather than efficient; we don't rely on mental shortcuts or "gut feelings"
- Processing a situation takes us more time and energy than it does for a neurotypical person

Now that I've explained some of the neurological markers correlated with Autism, I think it's important to clarify a finer point: the fact that a disability has some biological markers does not mean it is more "real" or legitimate than a disability that you can only observe in a person's behavior. And Autism is still diagnosed based on behavior and reported challenges the Autistic person is facing, not on a brain scan. The fact that Autism has neurological features doesn't mean it is a more sympathetic disability than, say, an eating disorder or substance addiction. It also doesn't mean Autistics are doomed to always function in a particular way, or to always struggle.

While understanding the biology of human difference is helpful in a lot of ways, there are real risks to reducing a disability to its physical "causes." It can lead people to believe that our biology is our destiny, and that we are lesser to neurotypicals in some unchangeable way. In fact, some research suggests that when people understand disabilities such as depression and ADHD as being purely biological, they actually show more stigma toward people with those conditions, not less.[23] The idea that a disabled group *can't help being the way they are* is dehumanizing and restrictive, even though some also find it liberating and validating.

When society first starts flirting with accepting a marginalized group, that acceptance is often wrapped up in a *born this way* type narrative. For example, in the early 2000s, many straight allies claimed to support gay people because being gay wasn't a choice, and we couldn't help being the way that we are. There was a lot of pop science writing at that time exploring the search for the "gay gene,"[24] and suggesting that certain hormone exposures in the womb might predispose a fetus to being gay. Today we don't have conversations about the biological causes of gayness very much anymore. In the United States at least, being gay has started becoming accepted enough that queer people don't have to justify our existence by saying we can't help but be this way. If someone were to choose to be gay, that wouldn't be a problem, because being gay is good. Similarly, Autistic people deserve acceptance, not because we can't help but have the brains we have, but because being Autistic is good.

Autism is associated with a deliberative processing style. When making sense of the world, Autistic people usually defer to logic and reason rather than emotion or intuition. We dive deep into all the pros and cons, sometimes excessively so, not knowing where to draw the line between an important variable and an unimportant one. We tend not to get habituated to familiar situations or stimuli as readily as other people, so we often think through a situation as if it's completely new to us, even if it isn't.[25] All of this requires a lot of energy, focus, and time, so we get exhausted and overloaded quite easily. However, it also makes us less prone to errors. Experimental research shows that Autistic people are far less susceptible to the biases allistic people commonly fall prey to.[26] For example, consider this relatively simple problem:

A bat and a ball together cost $1.10. The bat costs $1.00 more than the ball. How much does the ball cost?

In experimental studies, over 80 percent of non-Autistic people get this question wrong. They parse the question quickly, go with their gut, and answer that the ball must cost ten cents.[27] The correct answer is that the ball costs five cents, and the bat costs a dollar more, $1.05, which together adds up to $1.10. It takes an extra moment of careful processing to skip the "obvious" (and wrong) answer and provide the correct one. For most allistic people, the default way of thinking is to go with what's obvious. But since Autistic people do not process information intuitively, we don't see "obvious" answers to things, and have to carefully break the question down instead. This results in us being far more likely to get the answer right.

This slow, deliberative style of processing comes with its fair share of downsides. We can't always pick up on irony or "obvious" implied meanings people haven't said explicitly. Allistic people often accuse us of overthinking things, or being too slow and hesitant to come up with a response. We also get overwhelmed when presented with mountains of data, which neurotypical people find much easier to just ignore.

Autistic people process the world from the bottom up. If you want to understand Autism as a disability and a source of human difference at a glance, it's best summed up this way: we process in a careful, systematic, bottom-up way. Allistic folks, in contrast, make sense of the world in a very top-down fashion. They'll enter a new environment, such as an unfamiliar restaurant, take a quick look around, and jump to reasonable conclusions about how to order, where to sit, what kind of service to expect, and even how loudly they should talk. Their brains will immediately begin to filter through sounds, lights, and other stimuli, and adjust accordingly. They might notice a clanging pinball machine in the corner for a moment, for instance, but soon habituate to it, and become able to ignore it. When the waiter approaches, they probably can chat without much difficulty, even if something unexpected gets said or the item they planned to order is sold out. They don't rely on memorized conversational scripts, and they don't have to carefully parse every single piece of data they encounter to make sense of it. They can wing it.

Autistic people, on the flip side, don't rely on knee-jerk assumptions or quick mental shortcuts to make our decisions. We process each element of our environment separately, and intentionally, taking very little for granted. If we've never been in a particular restaurant before, we may be slow to make sense of its layout or figure out how ordering works. We'll need really clear-cut indications of whether it's the kind of place where you sit down and get table service, or if you're supposed to go to a counter to ask for what you like. (Many of us try to camouflage this fact by doing extensive research on a restaurant before setting foot inside.) Every single light, laugh, and smell in the place is taken in individually by our sensory system, rather than blended into a cohesive whole. To cope with unpredictability, we analyze our experiences for patterns, and memorize rule sets: *if the waiter says X, I reply with Y.* When something unexpected happens, we have to carefully sort out how to respond. Too much change may cause us to become really exhausted, or to freak out.

Autism touches every part of the Autistic person's life. Of course, many non-Autistic people might resonate with some of the feelings and sensations I just described. There's a difference between being *allistic* (which simply means non-Autistic) and being fully *neurotypical* (which means lacking any mental illness or cognitive disability). An allistic person with a social anxiety disorder may also feel overwhelmed in busy bars and restaurants, just as Autistic people do. Someone with post-traumatic stress disorder may similarly be rattled by a noisy

pinball machine. The difference between Autism and these other disorders, however, is that Autism is a cognitive and sensory difference
that affects every area of life. You wouldn't expect a socially anxious
person to get overwhelmed by the sound of a clanking radiator when
they're alone at home, for example (unless they're also Autistic or have
a sensory processing disorder).

Because the neural and cognitive features of Autism are so pervasive, it affects almost every aspect of a person's body and brain. It's related to coordination and muscle tone, the ability to read emotions on
people's faces, communication skills, reaction time, and even how a
person recognizes feelings of pain or hunger.[28] When I look at a person's face, I don't simply see "happiness" or "sadness" radiating off
them, for example; I see minute changes in their eyes, forehead, mouth,
breathing, and posture, which I then have to effortfully piece together
to make an informed guess about how they feel. Often, it's too much
discordant data to make sense of. When I don't have the energy to
carefully process others' emotional expressions, people are inscrutable
to me and arouse a lot of anxiety.

Autism can influence how intensely we focus on an activity, and
how we perceive textures, tastes, and sounds.[29] Autism can predispose
a person to having fanatical interests (often referred to as *special interests*)[30] and to following rules very rigidly. Many of us have trouble
identifying sarcasm or reading nonverbal signals. Disruptions to our
routines or expectations can make us panic. Learning new skills may
take us far longer than other people.

Autism is behavioral. Autism is associated with repetitive self-
stimulatory behavior ("stimming"),[31] which can be something as benign as hand-flapping, or as severe as chewing one's fingers until they
bleed. Stimming is an important means of self-regulation. It helps
soothe us when we're anxious or overloaded with stress, and it helps
us express joy and enthusiasm. There are a variety of ways to stim, and
stimming can make use of any of the five senses. Some of us stim
using *echolalia*, the repeating of words, sounds, or phrases that feel
good vibrating in our throats. Others stim by engaging the body's

proprioceptive system (the neural system that tracks the body's physical movement) by jumping up and down or swaying in place. Sucking on candy, smelling scented candles, staring at lava lamps, listening to recordings of rain and thunder—all of these activities can be stims. All humans stim to an extent (if they didn't, fidget spinners wouldn't have become so popular several years ago), but Autistic people stim more frequently, more repetitively, and more intensely than neuro-typicals do.

Repetitiveness is a key feature of Autistic behavior, according to the *Diagnostic and Statistical Manual of Mental Disorders* (the *DSM*). And it is true that many of us crave the stability that repetition provides. Because we find the external social world so unpredictable, most of us prefer consistent routines. We often eat the same meals over and over again, or only enjoy a limited range of foods (sometimes called *samefoods* in the community). We hyperfixate on activities that we enjoy and can get so engrossed in them that we forget to eat or take a break to stretch our legs. We echo phrases from movies and TV because they help us emulate "normal" social behavior, or because we lack our own words for how we are feeling, or simply because the sounds feel pleasant to have vibrating in our vocal cords. Even having special interests can be viewed as a repetitive behavior. Many of us watch the same movies over and over or read and compile facts about our favorite subjects far beyond the point that an allistic person would find entertaining.

For many masked Autistic people, however, repetitive behavior is something that needs to remain hidden. If you chew your fingers a lot or keep humming the same three-note tune to yourself, people will notice and mock you for it. If you come across as *too* obsessed with a weird subject (say, mortuary science), people will be put off by your enthusiasm and keep their distance. Most of us have to figure out ways to conceal our stimming and special interests. We might maintain a secret blog about our interests, for example, or find socially acceptable ways to get our energy out, such as long-distance running or fidgeting with our phones.

Autistic people are at risk. Timotheus Gordon Jr. is an Autistic researcher, advocate, and the founder of Autistics Against Curing Autism Chicago. He tells me that for him, choosing to stim (or how to stim) is highly dependent on which neighborhood he's in, and how people are likely to react.

"Walking into certain neighborhoods in Chicago or in the Chicagoland area, I can't wear my headphones to enjoy music," he says, "otherwise I'll get robbed potentially. Or if I walk around and fidget with toys, police or certain people in the neighborhood will think I'm strange or doing something illegal and I might get arrested, killed, or beat up."

Timotheus says that in some circumstances, he masks his need to stim by choosing a more socially acceptable outlet, such as bouncing a basketball. As a Black Autistic person, he is frequently having to take the temperature of his surroundings, gauging how others will react to his actions, and modulating himself accordingly. The risks of being himself are simply too great to take for granted.

Autistic people are at a high risk of violence, as well as negative mental health outcomes. Since we can't openly stim or engage in other repetitive behaviors, some masked Autistic people reach for flawed coping strategies to help manage stress. We're at an elevated risk of eating disorders,[32] alcoholism and drug addiction,[33] and insecure attachments to others.[34] We tend to maintain shallow relationships, out of fear that people would hate getting to know our "real selves." We may withdraw from other people, leading to negative emotional and psychological outcomes. And the more isolated we are, the less practice we get socializing, leading to a feedback loop of social disempowerment and shame.

Autism is also highly correlated with physical symptoms such as gastrointestinal issues,[35] connective tissue disorders,[36] and seizures[37] largely for genetic reasons. It co-occurs with other disabilities such as Attention Deficit Hyperactive Disorder (ADHD)[38] and dyslexia at a high rate.[39] Many Autistic people have trauma histories and post-traumatic stress symptoms, and as I've already mentioned, a lifetime of masking puts us at a high risk of conditions like depression and anxiety.[40] These are some of the most common conditions that co-occur alongside Autism, but later in the book we'll discuss additional disorders that overlap (or are mistaken for) Autism.

Autism is a neurodivergence. Autism is a type of functioning (or a *neurotype*) that differs from what psychology defines as normative or neurotypical (NT). Autism is a particularly diverse and varied form of neurodivergence; there are just so many ways in which we are punished for deviating from the norm. Every case of Autism is a bit different, and traits can present in seemingly contradictory ways. Some Autistic people can't speak; others are incredibly hyperverbal from a young age, with huge vocabularies. Some Autistics can read people's emotions so easily that it's overwhelming; others empathize with animals or objects, but not people; some of us have zero emotional empathy.[41] But all of us are full-formed humans with a capacity to care for others and behave ethically. Some Autistic people have no "special interests"; others are fanatical about dozens of subjects. Some of us have skills we are adept at; others need help in every facet of our existence. What unites us, generally speaking, is a bottom-up processing style that impacts every aspect of our lives and how we move through the world, and the myriad practical and social challenges that come with being different.

Since mainstream standards for behavior are so narrow, there are a variety of ways in which a person can diverge—and be punished for diverging. Having frequent panic attacks is a neurodivergence, as is exhibiting signs of an eating disorder. If you struggle in your close relationships because of attachment trauma or an inescapable fear of rejection, you're neurodivergent too (you might also get stuck with a particularly stigmatizing label, such as Borderline Personality Disorder).

Almost anyone can be viewed as defective or abnormal under our current medicalized model of mental illness—at least during particularly trying periods of their lives when they are depressed or their coping breaks down. In this way, neurotypicality is more of an oppressive cultural standard than it actually is a privileged identity a person has. Essentially no one lives up to neurotypical standards all of the time, and the rigidity of those standards harms everyone.[42] Much as hetero-normativity harms straight and queer folks alike, neurotypicality hurts people no matter their mental health status.

Autism is just one source of *neurodiversity* in our world. The term *neurodiverse* refers to the wide spectrum of individuals whose thoughts, emotions, or behaviors have been stigmatized as unhealthy, abnormal, or dangerous. The term was coined in 1999 by sociologist Judy Singer. In her honor's thesis, Singer wrote about the difficulty of making sense of her daughter's disabilities, which closely resembled traits her own mother exhibited when Singer was growing up. At the point that Singer was writing, Autism was poorly understood, and adults with Autistic traits, such as Singer's mother (and Singer herself) rarely re-ceived diagnoses. Singer's daughter seemed to inhabit a space some-where between Autism, ADHD, and a variety of other disabilities. All three women were difficult to neatly categorize, which only obscured just how marginalized and socially adrift they all were. Just because their challenges couldn't be easily named didn't mean they didn't exist.

"My life as a parent was a battleground for various belief systems," she writes,[43] "all of which had one thing in common: an inability to come to terms with human variability."

Singer and her family were disabled in a way that no one knew how to name, so she created a name for them: they were *neurodiverse*, and they suffered because the world demanded they be *neurotypical*. These terms would be popularized by journalist Harvey Blume and widely adopted by disability advocates a few years later. The label *neuro-diverse* includes everyone from people with ADHD, to Down Syn-drome, to Obsessive-Compulsive Disorder, to Borderline Personality Disorder. It also includes people with brain injuries or strokes, people who have been labeled "low intelligence," and people who lack any formal diagnosis, but have been pathologized as "crazy" or "incompe-tent" throughout their lives. As Singer rightly observed, neurodiversity isn't actually about having a specific, catalogued "defect" that the psychiatric establishment has an explanation for. It's about being different in a way others struggle to understand or refuse to accept.

Autism is diverse. Though the neurological and mental features of Autism cut across a wide swathe of people, the way it presents is always a bit different. In fact, Autistic traits can manifest in downright paradoxical ways. At times, I can be so intensely focused on a task (such as reading or writing) that the rest of the world entirely drops away. When I'm hyperfixating, I fail to notice things like someone speaking to me or smoke filling the room because I forgot to turn the oven off. At other times, I'm an anxious and distractible wreck, unable to make my way through a single sentence of a book because my pet chinchilla is hopping around in his cage and making the bars rattle. These two very disparate responses have the same root cause: the overexcitability of Autistic people's neurons and the inconsistent way that we filter stimuli (at least compared to allistics). We tend to be both easily disturbed by sound in our environment, and unable to tell when a noise actually merits our attention, at the same time.[44] I often brute-force my way into paying attention to something by shutting the rest of the world out. I think it's also likely that lifelong masking has rendered me hypervigilant, almost as a trauma response. My sensory system is used to scanning the environment, to determine whether I'm alone and thus "safe" enough to be myself. Trauma survivors often become hypervigilant, which tends to come with intense sensory issues.[45] Some researchers have also theorized that sensory issues in Autistics are, at least in part, caused by the anxiety and hypervigilance we experience from living in a world that doesn't accommodate us, and often treats us with hostility.[46]

Most people have heard that Autism is a spectrum, and it's really true: each of us has a unique constellation of traits and features, all at various degrees of intensity. Some people are also subclinically Autistic, meaning they might not qualify for an official diagnosis, in the eyes of psychiatrists, but share enough struggles and experiences with us that they belong in the community. Relatives of diagnosed Autistic people, for example, frequently are found to exhibit subclinical traits.[47]

Of course, what's considered to be "subclinical" is often more a function of a person's ability to hold down a job and conform to societal rules than it is a reflection of how much they are suffering.

"Everybody is a little bit Autistic," is a common refrain that masked Autistic people hear when we come out to others. This remark can feel a bit grating to hear, because it feels like our experiences are being downplayed. It's similar to when bisexual people get told that "everybody is a little bit bi." When most people make remarks like these, they're implying that because our difference is so universal, we can't actually be oppressed for it, and should just shut up about it. However, I do think that when allistic people declare that everyone is a little Autistic, it means they are close to making an important breakthrough about how mental disorders are defined: why do we declare some people broken, and others perfectly normal, when they exhibit the exact same traits? Where do we draw the line, and why do we even bother doing so? If an Autistic person benefits from more flexibility at work, and more social patience, why not extend those same benefits to everybody? Autistic people are a normal part of humanity, and we have qualities that can be observed in any other non-Autistic human. So yes, everyone is a little bit Autistic. That's all the more reason to broaden our definition of what is deserving of dignity and acceptance.

Autism can appear in any person, regardless of their age, class, gender, race, or other disability status. Despite the incredible diversity of Autism and Autistic people, the average person (and even many mental health professionals) has a singular image of Autism in their minds. You might sometimes hear this called "typically presenting" Autism, though that's really a misnomer. It's more like *stereotypical* Autism.

"Typical" Autism

"Typical" Autism is visible from an early age, and usually results in a diagnosis by the time a child is in early elementary school. Typical Autistics don't communicate the way neurotypical society wants them to; they might be nonverbal or slow to develop speech, and they avoid gazing at other people or approaching them. They engage in repetitive behaviors that are recognizable: they rock in place, slap themselves in the head, or yell and chirp. Their sensory pain and social overwhelm is near-constant, and they can't hide how profoundly they're suffering. Their parents have trouble managing their meltdowns and sensory overloads, seeing these responses as "behavioral issues," or "noncompliance." They may complain Autism has "stolen" their once well-behaved baby from them. Typical Autistics are probably boys, and they're probably white, and they are likely to come from wealthy or upper-middle-class families who can access diagnosis and therapeutic support (and who tend to have pretty restrictive norms of what constitutes "appropriate" public behavior).

In reality, typical Autistics aren't all that typical. The vast majority of Autistic people who have been diagnosed flout this incredibly rigid set of criteria in one way or another.[48] That's despite the fact all existing diagnostic tools for Autism were developed with wealthy, white, gender-conforming boys in mind. When we consider the evidence that Autism is underdiagnosed in girls, Black, indigenous, Asian, and Latinx people,[49] and those in poverty,[50] among other groups, we can see that "typical" Autism is probably even less typical than official figures would have us believe.

The line between "typical" Autism and "atypical" Autism is quite permeable, and often has more to do with a person's position in society than it does the supposed severity of their Autistic traits. Crystal had all the classic indicators of Autism: repetitive play, lack of social engagement, self-stimulatory behavior, difficulty staying on task at school. But because Crystal didn't look like the "typical" Autistic person, she didn't register as disabled to most of the world. For all the distress she was in, teachers and school counselors never again raised it as a possibility.

"Report cards called me a joy to have in class, and *sensitive*," she says. "Which was a sneaky way of saying they thought I cried too much and got too hurt when kids were mean to me. Spacing out in math class wasn't like, this alarming sign I was retreating into a shutdown. I was just a daydreamy girl who cried sometimes, which for a lot of my male teachers was probably their feminine ideal, when you think about it."

An *Autistic shutdown* happens when an Autistic person gets so overstimulated and stressed, they can no longer process their surroundings.[51] It's the quieter, more interior counterpart to an Autistic *meltdown*, which tends to involve more crying, self-harm, or outward aggression. Shutdowns are essentially a way of dissociating from one's surroundings. It can look like falling asleep very suddenly, becoming unresponsive, or just kind of zoning out (which is how it presented in Crystal's case). Crystal suspects that had she been an Autistic boy, her shutdowns would have been viewed differently. Boys are supposed to have agency and confidence, and engage actively with the world. Being nonresponsive and depressed might have inspired early intervention, rather than morphing into an unspeakable family secret. Instead, Crystal's parents told her to stop being "so weird" and to sit up and "look alive." When confusion and frustration made her want to break down and cry, she was similarly told to tamp those urges down.

"Getting smaller and asking for nothing was how I kept people from calling me too sensitive so often," she says. "That and assuming that if I was bad at something, it's because I was never, ever gonna be good at it. Better to not ask."

Now that she knows she's Autistic, Crystal is trying to unlearn these deep-seated beliefs about herself. She wants to become someone who doesn't apologize for crying, and doesn't always cope with stress by locking herself away from the world. She wants to be able to build a life around the fact that a twenty- or thirty-hour workweek is the most she can manage. And she wants to relearn math with a nonjudgmental tutor, who'll explain things to her in a direct, patient way, without any implied meanings or latent sexism.

"Can I look back one day and say to myself, all the things I hate about myself are actually my greatest strengths?" She ponders. "I don't know. Someone should have always been telling me that. But you try to accept what happened. I can't really yet. I'm too pissed."

Like many people who have only recently figured out they're Autistic, Crystal is still reeling about her newfound identity, and can't seem to stop thinking about how unfairly she was treated in the past. There's an entire class of Autistic people who are excluded and alienated in these ways, and we'll get to meet many more of them in the next few chapters. But first, we need to dive into exactly why the image of typical Autism is what it is.

Why Is Autism Synonymous with White Boys Who Love Trains?

The Autistic people who wind up needing to mask the most are usually those who are undiagnosed due to things like gender, race, or socioeconomic status. These same populations of people also tend to be raised to be more agreeable and pleasant than their white male peers. For example, developmental psychology research has repeatedly noted that even small acts of play-aggression in girls are severely discouraged and punished by their teachers and parents as "inappropriate." A girl might be admonished for slamming a couple of toys into one another, for example. Meanwhile, most boys are allowed to be rough and sometimes violent in their play.[52] Because girls are held to a much more restrictive social standard than boys are, they learn to hide any troublesome, "violent," or disruptive Autism features much earlier. Similar dynamics are at play for Autistic people of color and trans Autistic people of a variety of identities, as well as other maskers.[53]

For a long time, Autism researchers believed the condition was truly less severe and less common in people of color and girls. Today, some still truly believe "female Autism" is less severe, though most professionals recognize that members of these marginalized groups are simply not given as much social latitude to be strange or disruptive, and that the same qualities are perceived differently in a boy than in a girl.[54] However, the legacy of erasing Autistic girls, trans and gender-nonconforming Autistics, and other marginalized populations lingers.

The idea that Autism is a "boy's" disorder goes all the way back to when the condition was first described at the turn of the twentieth century. Hans Asperger and other early Autism researchers did study girls on the spectrum, but generally left them out of their published research reports.[55] Asperger in particular avoided writing about Autistic girls because he wanted to present certain intelligent, "high-functioning" Autistic people as "valuable" to the Nazis who had taken over Austria and were beginning to exterminate disabled people en masse. As Steve Silberman describes in his excellent book *Neuro-Tribes*, Hans Asperger wanted to spare the "high functioning" Autistic boys he'd encountered from being sent to Nazi death camps. Silberman described this fact somewhat sympathetically; Asperger was a scientist who had no choice but to collude with the fascist regime and save what few children he could. However, more recently unearthed documents make it clear that Asperger was far more complicit in Nazi exterminations of disabled children than had been previously believed.[56] Though Asperger held intelligent, "little professor" type Autistics close to his heart, he knowingly sent more visibly debilitated Autistics to extermination centers.

Informed by eugenicist ideals that only granted rights to those who were "valuable" to society, Asperger focused on describing Autism as a disorder for intelligent, yet troubled boys, usually ones from wealthy families. Girls with disabilities were seen as more disposable, so they were left out of the conversation.[57] Black and brown Autistics weren't described at all by Asperger or most of his contemporaries, even those who were doing research in more racially diverse countries such as the United States. The existence of LGBTQ and gender non-conforming Autistics was similarly ignored. In fact, the developer of the first therapeutic "treatment" for Autism, Applied Behavioral Analysis therapy, was Ole Ivar Lovaas, who also invented anti-gay conversion therapy.[58] That legacy still haunts the lives of many LGBTQ Autistics, who often feel out of place both in mainstream queer spaces and in Autism groups.[59]

Since early published research in both English and German only described Autistic boys, some psychiatrists from that era concluded the condition was caused by an "extremely male brain."[60] Autistic people were supposedly too analytical, too rational, and too individualistic to function in society on their own. This view influenced how all the diagnostic guidelines were written, and created a feedback loop that endured for decades: the Autistics who got diagnosed were primarily wealthy white boys, and those boys continued to set the standard of what Autism was and how it was understood in the studies that followed.[61] The few white girls who were diagnosed had to be very obviously "masculine" in how their Autism presented. Nonwhite Autistics were instead identified as defiant, antisocial, or schizophrenic—all disorders that made it easier to incarcerate them, or forcibly place them in institutions.[62]

A century after these trends first began, massive gender- and race-based disparities in Autism diagnoses still exist. For decades, Autistic boys have outnumbered girls at a ratio of 4 to 1.[63] Girls like Crystal are still routinely passed over and denied assessments, because they are well-behaved and too pleasant to "really" be Autistic. Autistic trans people and people of color are similarly excluded.[64] When any of us do discover our identities and come out, we risk being told we "don't look Autistic."

In media, nearly every Autistic character is a white man with a monotone voice, rude demeanor, and a penchant for science. Think of the irascible genius Rick from *Rick and Morty*,[65] the hypercompetent yet cold Shaun Murphy from ABC's *The Good Doctor*, or the nerdy and condescending Sheldon Cooper from *The Big Bang Theory*. In this cultural landscape, there's little room for Autistics who are sensitive, emotionally expressive, artistic, or uninterested in academic success. Autism is so broadly associated with assholery that many of us initially hate associating with the term, and try to overcompensate by being excessively easygoing and nonconfrontational. It takes many years of research and meeting real-life counter-examples for most of us to recognize Autism isn't the cold, robotic condition we've been told it is.

Being exposed to these misconceptions and shallow stereotypes can have a profound impact on how Autistic people see ourselves, and which qualities we aim to mask.

In the exercise below, I'd like you to ponder what messages about Autism you might've absorbed as a child, and how that may have shaped your self-perceptions and your mask. For reasons we'll get into more thoroughly in the next few chapters, an Autistic person's mask tends to be informed by the Autistic qualities they have been trained to hate or fear the most.

Autism Stereotypes:
How Have They Affected You?

1. Think of some images of Autism that you saw on TV or in movies. If you can, name a few Autistic characters or figures you saw during this time.

2. Pick a few Autistic characters (or characters implied to be Autistic) and describe them in three to five words. For example, I might describe Dustin Hoffman's Rain Man as distant, a genius savant, and helpless.
   Character:_____ Traits: _____
   Character:_____ Traits: _____
   Character:_____ Traits: _____

3. Complete the sentence: Before I knew better, I assumed all Autistic people were _____, _____, and _____.

4. In what ways are you different from these images of Autism?

5. Has anyone ever told you that you "don't look Autistic" or that you "can't be Autistic"? What do you think they meant by that? How did hearing that feel?

These days, varied portrayals of Autistic people do exist. Abed Nadir on the sitcom *Community* is a Palestinian Muslim man with a sharp wit and a penchant for movies, as well as the more clichéd chilly demeanor and difficulty smiling. In the popular multiplayer game *Overwatch*, Symmetra is a confident Autistic Indian woman who blasts her opponents with turrets she's invented. Beth Harmon of the Netflix series *The Queen's Gambit* is a beautiful, substance-addicted chess player, and is heavily implied to be Autistic. I only started seeing characters like these when I was in my late twenties, after I already knew I was Autistic, had met a variety of Autistic people in real life, and began seeking representation that went beyond the tortured white genius image. Diversifying and deepening my knowledge of what Autism could be was absolutely essential to understanding myself and slowly beginning to build self-love and acceptance. For many of the masked Autistic people I interviewed for this book, meeting a variety of mold-breaking, "atypical" Autistics of many different backgrounds was similarly important.

Suspect You're Autistic?

Masked Autistic people are basically everywhere, though by our very nature we're socially invisible. You can find us in any number of fields people might not associate with stereotypically Autistic behavior, including sales, the service industry, and the arts. Because so many of us mask through inhibition and withdrawal, we might not stand out as socially awkward, at least not in a way anyone can pinpoint. Though many of us experience sensory issues, anxiety, meltdowns, and debilitating mental health symptoms, we push as much of that misery into the private realm as possible. Our elaborate veils of coping mechanisms and camouflaging can create the illusion we don't need help. Often this comes at the expense of giving up on the areas of life where we might need assistance. We may eschew relationships, drop out of grueling academic programs, avoid working in fields that require networking and socializing, or completely disengage from activities that involve using our bodies, because we feel so detached and uncoordinated in them. Most of us are haunted by the sense there's something "wrong" or "missing" in our lives—that we're sacrificing far more of ourselves than other people in order to get by and receiving far less in return.

Due to the fact that Autism is so severely underdiagnosed, it's hard to estimate just how prevalent the neurotype really is. We do know that as public awareness of Autism has increased, and as diagnosis procedures have gotten a tiny bit less biased, the diagnosis rate has continually gone up. As of 2020, one in 54 children is diagnosed as Autistic, up from one in 68 just four years ago. In the 1990s only one in every 2,500 children was diagnosed.[66] This upward trend shows no sign of stopping, as all evidence suggests the condition is still profoundly underrecognized in women, trans people, Black and brown people, people in poverty, and those without access to screening and therapy. In the United States, as many as 50 percent of all people who need mental health support lack access to it,[67] so we are talking about a truly massive underdiagnosis rate.

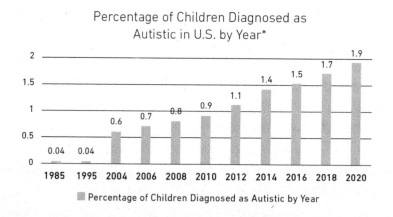

Percentage of Children Diagnosed as Autistic in U.S. by Year*

Source: Centers for Disease Control and Prevention (CDC)

From all this data, we can assume that at least half of all Autistic people in the United States currently fail to get diagnosed. That's a conservative estimate, based on the assumption that every Autistic person with access to therapy gets an accurate diagnosis, a fact we know not to be true. It's also worth bearing in mind that Autism runs in families, and that for every diagnosed Autistic child reflected in that chart, there's probably several other relatives who exhibited Autism spectrum traits. In my own family, almost everyone has some Autistic traits and can be considered a part of the Autism community, even if some might not qualify based on an official assessment or might not be interested in identifying as disabled.[68]

If you're reading this book, you probably suspect that you or someone you know is a masked Autistic, or otherwise neurodiverse. I have been writing about my own journey of Autistic self-discovery for many years now, and every single time I post online about it, I'm inundated with messages from people who are questioning whether they're on the spectrum, and want my advice on how to find out. Usually, their first question is how to get tested for Autism Spectrum Disorder. My initial response to that is to present them with three questions:

1. Do you have health insurance that covers Autism assessments?
2. Can you find an Autism assessment specialist in your area who has a proven track record of working successfully with Autistic adults?
3. What do you hope to get out of a formal diagnosis?

The first and second questions can prove quite dispiriting to answer. In the United States, many health insurance plans do not cover Autism assessment in adults.[69] A limited number of specialists are qualified to assess and diagnose Autism (your average psychologist can't do it), and the diagnostic process typically involves multiple tests, screening surveys, and even interviews with the Autistic person's family and friends. Without insurance coverage, this process can cost anywhere from $1,200[70] to $5,000.[71]

Even when a person can afford to be assessed, identifying a specialist who knows how to diagnose Autistic adults can be prohibitively difficult. My friend Seb (who's in their mid-twenties) sought out an assessment in the UK and was subjected to tests clearly designed for small kids. A therapist asked Seb to arrange various toys on a table and make up stories about them (this is part of a common diagnostic tool called the Autism Diagnostic Observation Schedule, or the ADOS, and it was developed for use in children).[72] A questionnaire was given to Seb's mother to fill out, and Seb wasn't permitted to look at what she'd said. They were completely disempowered by the whole process. Some people whom I interviewed for this book reported being turned away by multiple assessors, for things as simple as being a woman, dressing well, or having voices that weren't completely monotonous. Sometimes assessors decide to give adults labels they view as less stigmatizing, such as nonverbal learning disorder, rather than identifying them as Autistic explicitly.

"I had to see two specialists," Crystal tells me. "The first one said basically the same thing my grandpa used to say: girls usually aren't Autistic. You're doing fine in life. Don't worry about it."

To this day, a majority of Autism assessment tools are based on the decades-old ones developed for white male children from wealthy and middle-class families.[73] With years of clinical experience, some experts learn to recognize Autism in those who mask. They may know, for example, that masked Autistics can make eye contact, though many of us stare too strongly by neurotypical standards, or for too long. They might understand that Autistic women and people of color have to appear friendly as a means of survival, so their tone of voice might not be totally flat. Perhaps they're even aware of Autism's link with substance addictions and eating disorders, particularly among people who have to fake neurotypicality all day long at their jobs. However, these facts are not a core part of how assessors are trained, and many spend their entire careers reinforcing old sexist, white supremacist notions of how the disability looks.

This brings me to my third question: what do you hope to get out of being formally diagnosed? It can come with serious social and legal benefits under the Americans with Disabilities Act (and laws in other countries like it), and other antidiscrimination statutes worldwide. You might hope that people will take your problems more seriously when a psychiatrist has validated them. A formal diagnosis means you can receive disability accommodations at school or work, and you can pursue a legal case if an employer or landlord shows documentable signs of bias against you. In some places a diagnosis can qualify you for a medical marijuana card, or a therapy animal. Family members who have told you that you're whiny and lazy may finally get off your case when they realize you have a developmental disorder. A therapist or medical care provider may tailor their treatment of you to your neurotype. These are the kinds of outcomes many neurodivergent people hope for when they pursue formal recognition.

Unfortunately, a diagnosis is not a guarantee you will receive any of these benefits. Proving in a court of law that you've been discriminated against as an Autistic person requires extensive documentation[74] and is prohibitively expensive to pursue for most disabled people. Even though a diagnosed disability entitles you to accommodations on paper, many employers and educators refuse to provide them, or mistreat the employees and students who request them (for more on the limitations of the ADA and its inconsistent enforcement, see Chapter 8). And as much as I'd like to promise that being recognized formally as an Autistic will get judgmental friends and family off your back, I've heard too many counter-examples to claim that's really the case. Your family members may find your disability even more threatening once it's validated by a doctor, or they might use your diagnosis to undermine your judgment or infantilize you. This isn't intended to dissuade you from seeking a diagnosis; I just don't want anyone to have the impression that a piece of paper signed by a psychiatrist magically unlocks a suite of resources and social respect.

Additionally, an Autism diagnosis does not grant you access to any particular therapy or medication, because there are no evidence-based treatments for Autism in adults. Most therapists are not trained to work with Autistic adults, and many of them harbor very shallow, outdated understandings of what the neurotype is. Even those who do specialize in Autism are usually trained primarily in working with Autistic kids, "helping" them to behave in a more agreeable, passive fashion. Here in Chicago, I'm aware of just one therapist who is competent in treating Autistic adults who mask, and the only reason I know they're competent is that other Autistic people have vouched for them to me. I do know several mental health providers in other cities who have confessed to me privately that they are Autistic, and love working with fellow Autistic patients. However, each of them has told me they cannot openly identify as Autistic professionally. There's too great a risk that their colleagues would view them as incompetent or unprofessional if they were open about their neurodivergence.

Of course, even the idea of pursuing a treatment "for" Autism is predicated on the idea we are broken or sick. This is an idea the neurodiversity movement completely rejects. There is no medication for Autism, no cure for it, and no way of changing one's neurotype. As a community, most Autistics oppose attempts to "fix" us. There are some modifications that can be made to existing therapeutic methods, to make them a better fit for Autistic adults, but unless a provider takes the time to self-educate, they may be unaware such modified treatments exist. For the most part, learning you're Autistic is a journey of self-acceptance, community building, and growing self-advocacy, and you might not need or want a diagnosis to go down that path.

For all the reasons outlined above, I firmly support Autistic self-determination. I prefer the terms *self-determination* or *self-realization* to *self-diagnosis,* because I believe it's more sensible to view Autistic identity through a social lens than a strictly medical one.[75] Diagnosis is a gatekeeping process, and it slams its heavy bars in the face of anyone who is too poor, too busy, too Black, too feminine, too queer, and too gender nonconforming, among others. The Autistics who lack access to fair diagnoses need solidarity and justice the most desperately out of all of us, and we can't just shut them out.

Though people like Crystal often regret having not been assessed for Autism at a young age, Autistic children who *are* diagnosed when they are young experience both greater access to resources, and more intense, institutionalized stigma. Being identified formally as disabled is very much a double-edged sword; a diagnosis can even be used against you in divorce proceedings or child custody cases, or to force a legal adult under a financial conservatorship. This doesn't mean I would recommend against pursuing diagnosis in all cases. I know masked Autistic parents who are very glad their Autistic children got assessed and diagnosed when they were young. For many Autistic parents, it's the diagnosis of their children that kicks off their own exploration of an Autistic identity. Having a recognized diagnosis of Autism in the family can also ensure that professionals take your suspicion you're Autistic more seriously (that certainly has been true in my case).

The parents I know who have had a positive experience with assessment entered the diagnostic process recognizing they would need to fight many battles to have their child's agency and humanity respected. This is true of the adults who have successfully pursued formal diagnosis for themselves as well. Unfortunately, Autistic people are frequently put in the position of having to educate our own health care providers. Autistic children in particular need strong advocates in their corner, fighting to make sure their boundaries are respected and that any treatment they are given is actually in their best interest. If you wish to get diagnosed, or wish for your child to be, you should go into the process with accurate expectations, armed with as much information as possible, and ready to fight or switch providers multiple times if needed.

If you don't wish to brave the long, arduous, and often expensive process of being assessed, you do not have to. Medical documentation does not make your experience any more real. Self-realized Autistics are not lesser members of the community. In most Autistic self-advocacy spaces I frequent, I have no idea who is diagnosed and who is not, because it truly does not matter.

I believe that Autistic people have the right to define who we are, and that self-definition is a means of reclaiming our power from the medical establishment that has long sought to corral and control us. Our deviance from the norm doesn't have to be the core part of how we understand ourselves. We can push for social norms to be widened, until we reach the point that Autism is viewed as a neutral fact about a person's being, on par with needing glasses or having freckles. As we make major gains in public awareness and advocacy, we will begin to occupy a less disabled position in society. But we'll still all be Autistic. Accordingly, we shouldn't let the view of Autism as an impediment shape how we see ourselves or determine who belongs among us.

A Few Notes on Terminology

Throughout this book, I capitalize "Autistic" for the same reason members of the Deaf community capitalize "Deaf"—to indicate it is a part of my identity I am proud of, and to signal Autistics have our own culture, history, and community. Since Eugen Bleuler first coined the word in the early 1900s, Autism has largely been used in negative and dehumanizing ways, and to this day many parents and educators are still deeply frightened by it. By capitalizing Autism, I signal that it's actually an important, meaningful aspect of who we are, one we don't need to shy away from.

Throughout, I will also refer to Autism as a disability. *Disability* is not a bad word, because being disabled is not a shameful thing. We are not "differently abled"—we are disabled, robbed of empowerment and agency in a world that is not built for us. "Differently abled," "handicapable," and similar euphemisms were created in the 1980s by the abled parents of disabled children, who wished to minimize their children's marginalized status. These terms were popularized further by politicians[76] who similarly felt uncomfortable acknowledging disabled people's actual experiences of oppression.[77] These words obscure reality and reflect a discomfort many people have with disabled bodies and brains. A person who is completely blind is not "differently sighted"— they lack an ability that other people have, in a world that was designed by and for people who can see. The world actively *dis-ables* people by failing to provide accommodations they need. Naming the reality of disability shows respect for disabled people and awareness of how we are oppressed. "Differently abled" attempts to erase that behind a cutesy euphemism, and many of us find the term offensive.

In a similar vein, I almost always will use "Autistic" and not "person with Autism." Many non-disabled parents of Autistic kids prefer what's called "person first" language rather than "disability first" or "identity first" language.[78] Disability service organizations that are not run by disabled people tend to advocate for person first language as well. I also know many clinicians and social workers who tell me that when they were in school, they were taught to always separate a person's disability from their identity in this way.

When people use person-first language, they often say it's because they don't want disabled people to be defined by their disability. However, phrases like "person with Autism" distance a person's disabled status from their humanity in a way that can be quite harmful. Autism is not a thing that is added on to a person—it's integral to their life and cannot be removed from who they are. We don't call Asian people "people with Asianness" and we don't call gay folks "people with homosexuality" because we recognize it is respectful to view these identities as parts of their personhood. Language such as "identifies as Autistic" can also come across as dubious. If I really respect a trans woman's gender, for example, I wouldn't say "this person identifies as a woman." I'd simply say, "she's a woman" and leave it at that.

The vast majority of Autism self-advocates prefer identity-first language and dislike euphemisms like "special" and "differently abled," for all the reasons I've outlined here. They also discourage describing a person as "high" or "low" functioning, preferring instead things like "high support needs." Here's a table summarizing some of the most common terminology preferences expressed by the community:

Autism Terminology: Common Dos and Don'ts	
Use This	**Avoid This**
Autistic person Autist Autistic On the Autism spectrum	Person with Autism
Is Autistic	Identifies as having autism
Is disabled Has a disability	"Special needs" "Differently abled" "Handi-capable"
Neurotypical (NT) Allistic Non-Autistic	Normal
Has high support needs Has low support needs	Low functioning High functioning
Masked Autism	Female Autism Asperger's High-functioning Autism
Nonverbal Loses speech	Mute Dumb
Intellectually disabled Developmentally disabled	R*tarded Stupid "Special"
Direct language about what a person can or can't do, and what kind of support they need	Euphemisms, language that minimizes challenges, language that belittles or condescends

Autistics are a diverse group, though, and we don't all have to agree on which terms we like and dislike having used for ourselves. If you are Autistic, you get to decide what language works best for you. Some people prefer to say they are "on the spectrum," for example, rather than strictly Autistic. Others identify as having Asperger's, though that disorder label no longer exists, and was rooted in Hans Asperger's eugenicist research.[79] I recognize that people who had that term forced on them in the past may feel an attachment to it, or a desire to reclaim it. The word *bisexual* was once a mental illness label,[80] but we don't tell bisexual people they can't use it because of its offensive history. When someone like folklorist Anand Prahlad writes a book like *The Secret Life of a Black Aspie*, it's clear his use of the term "Aspergers" is not intended to reinforce old, white supremacist notions of what the disability is. I find it's far more important to question the belief that supposedly "higher functioning" Autistic lives matter more than others than it is to scrub all people's language of outdated or problematic terms. Additionally, it is vital that the disability self-advocacy community remain accessible to all people of all ability levels. That requires we extend grace and understanding to people who don't communicate exactly the way we might like them to.

Though most of the community discourages the use of such terms, some Autistic people do identify as "low functioning" or "severely Autistic." Functioning labels oversimplify the Autistic experience, and they do serve to imply that we should be defined by how productive and independent we are. That's a big problem. At the same time, function labels can occasionally be used to highlight the fact that those of us who can talk, dress ourselves, or hide our meltdowns have social privileges other Autistic people do not have. I don't function "highly" in every single realm of my life, but I am able to get by more easily than many other Autistics. My acceptance in society is conditional on my behaving respectably and being productive. That's really a deeply ableist reality, but I shouldn't pretend it isn't true. Though having to mask as a desirable, respectable person can be very soul-crushing, it does protect me from physical violence, institutionalization, poverty, and loneliness. I can understand why my friend Angel believes it's worth pointing out that his life as a nonspeaking person with intellectual disabilities is really different from mine. Angel says he is low functioning, and says that he has severe Autism; though some in our community find that offensive, I stand by his right to name his own experience.

I love that every Autistic person has their own unique relationship to these labels, and their own thoughts. Our disagreements show that the Autistic community is diverse, filled with people who form their own opinions and speak their minds. We're not a monolithic group, and our individual journeys shape how we express our identities to the world. I've done my best in this book to honor the terminology each individual Autistic person uses for themselves. This means that sometimes I'll call someone a "person with Autism" or a "low-functioning" person, even though self-advocacy groups have good reasons to discourage allistics from using such words thoughtlessly. If someone self-identifies as an Aspie or as having Asperger's, I'll accurately reflect that as well. I hope that even if you have specific stances on which terms you like and dislike, you can respect my interview subjects' agency to name themselves, as I have strived to do.

CHAPTER 2

Who Are the Masked Autistics?

Bobbi, an Autistic nonbinary person in their mid-thirties, says, "I wasn't raised or 'socialized' as an Autistic girl. I was raised as a weird kid, and a gender failure."

Bobbi says that as a child, they were interested in sports, local plants and mushrooms, and pro wrestling. They were considered "tomboyish," and were socially ostracized from their peers because they were awkward and rude, and refused to behave in "ladylike" ways. Even when Bobbi tried to conform to gender norms, they failed spectacularly. They lacked the fine motor control to do makeup or write in pretty cursive letters. When girls subtly bullied them in the lunchroom for their short, self-chopped haircut, Bobbi couldn't understand what was happening. They assumed that when girls yelled, "Hey Bobbi, nice haircut," they were being sincere.

No one flagged Bobbi as potentially Autistic, and they certainly didn't recognize Bobbi as potentially transgender, either.

"I was just in this category of 'weird annoying kid' off to the side," they tell me.

In both respects, it was easy for adults to write off Bobbi's struggles as a mere annoyance, rather than a sign Bobbi was marginalized both in terms of gender and disability status. Masked Autism and being a closeted gender minority often go hand in hand, and the experiences share a lot of features. The baffled families of transgender people and adult Autistics alike tend to claim there "were no signs" of these identities when the person was young.[1] In actuality, there were often many signs, which the child's family either did not know to look for, or didn't wish to see.[2] Signs of nonconformity were likely met with admonishment, "helpful" condescending corrections ("you look so unhappy, please smile!"), or by freezing the child out until they conformed. Bobbi was sarcastically complimented quite often, not just for their hair, but for how they carried themselves, spoke, thought, and for the comfortable, practical ways that they dressed. As they grew older, they began to figure out what was expected of them, and shifted their gender presentation to be more feminine so they could be seen as fully human.

No one in young Bobbi's life could see them as they truly were. When your belief system teaches that disability and gender variance are embarrassing and disgusting, it's hard to look at your child and recognize those traits. It certainly didn't help that in movies and television programs in the 1980s and 1990s, Autistic people were all silent, passive nonentities, and transgender people were perverted serial killers or trashy daytime TV curiosities.

These days, Bobbi surrounds themselves with fellow Autistic and transgender people. They first discovered their disability after their eldest son was assessed in elementary school, and in the couple of years since then they've tried to build relationships that help them feel normal and seen for the first time. They described their friend group to me as a land of misfit toys. They're all people who'd been shut out of mainstream society, most of them in multiple ways. Even the public conversation about Autism ignores their existence much of the time.

"We have to make society over again from the ground up," they say. "Our own little neuro-queer microsocieties. Because no one else will think to include us."

In this chapter, I'd like to introduce you to the groups of people who most commonly become masked Autistics. These are the people who have been systematically denied access to diagnosis for decades, and are frequently still ignored in public and psychiatric conversations about neurodivergence. They're Autistic women like Crystal, Autistic trans people like Bobbi, and Black genderqueer people like Anand Prahlad. Some had their neurodivergence erased because they grew up in poverty, or because they had physical ailments that obscured their Autistic traits. Some are assumed to be too "high functioning" to need accommodations, but actually suffer deeply from a lack of accessibility and support. Others are pretty clearly debilitated by disability but were misdiagnosed as Borderline or Narcissistic instead of Autistic. In their stories, you'll see just how multifaceted the Autistic community is, and how painfully limiting stereotypes about the disability really are to each of us. You may also see yourself reflected in these stories or recognize someone you know. The more Autism is understood and embraced in its full, rich diversity, the less need there will be for these multiply marginalized Autistic people to keep themselves hidden behind a mask of quiet conformity.

Autistic Women and Gender Minorities

Most of the writing and research about gender-based disparities in Autism focuses on the fact that girls are woefully underdiagnosed. Researchers, therapists, and even some Autistic self-advocates talk about "female Autism,"[3] pointing to the fact that among girls, Autistic qualities do seem less severe or obvious on average.

When Autistic girls engage in self-stimulatory behavior, it tends to be less physically damaging: less arm biting, more hair twirling or opening and closing a book quietly many times.[4] When Autistic girls are shy and withdrawn, people are less concerned by it than they would be if a boy exhibited the same reticence. On the flip side, when Autistic girls have meltdowns, it tends to get written off as an emotional outburst. When they *do* act out or behave aggressively, they're more likely to be punished severely for not being ladylike, resulting in them learning to censor their aggression at an earlier age than most boys do.[5] Adults speak to young girls using more emotion-related words than they do when speaking to boys,[6] which means Autistic girls often get a leg up in social and relational skills. Much of the play that girls stereotypically engage in (and are encouraged to engage in) involves mimicking adult social interactions, such as playing house or pretending to run a store.[7] As a result many Autistic girls learn how to fake their way through routine conversations at a younger age than boys do.

For these and a variety of other reasons, Autistic girls are assessed and diagnosed at older ages.[8] Many are diagnosed as adults, or are never diagnosed at all. Like Crystal, many Autistic women develop an inoffensive, quiet personality as a crutch to counterbalance their social disadvantages. Unfortunately, adopting a docile persona makes it even harder for their suffering to be seen as a real problem.

Below is a table summarizing some of the most well-known "female Autism" traits. It's adapted from a list originally published on the now-defunct site Help4Asperger's, which was maintained by the author of the book *Aspergirls*, Rudy Simone.[9] This is by no means an exhaustive list, and shouldn't be taken as a diagnostic tool. As I've already mentioned, the idea that all women have "female Autism" is a reductive one. Still, clinicians often fall back on tables like these to determine if an adult woman might potentially be an undiagnosed Autistic, so it's something to be cognizant of. If someone is aware that a phenomenon such as "female Autism" exists, they're often taught it looks something like this:

Traits Commonly Associated with "Female Autism"[10]

Emotional

- Strikes others as emotionally immature and sensitive.
- Prone to outbursts or crying jags, sometimes over seemingly small things.
- Has trouble recognizing or naming one's feelings.
- Ignores or suppresses emotions until they "bubble up" and explode.
- May become disturbed or overwhelmed when others are upset, but uncertain how to respond or support them.
- Goes "blank" and seems to shut down after prolonged socializing or when overstimulated.

Psychological

- Reports a high degree of anxiety, especially social anxiety.
- Is perceived by others as moody and prone to bouts of depression.
- May have been diagnosed with mood disorders such as Bipolar Disorder, or personality disorders such as Borderline or Narcissistic Personality Disorder, before Autism was discovered.
- Fears rejection intensely and tries to manage how other people feel to avoid it.
- Has an unstable sense of self, perhaps highly dependent on the opinions of others.

Behavioral

- Uses control to manage stress: follows intense self-imposed rules, despite having an otherwise unconventional personality.
- Is usually happiest at home or in a familiar, predictable environment.
- Seems youthful for their age, in looks, dress, behavior, or interests.
- Prone to excessive exercise, calorie restriction, or other eating disordered behaviors.
- Neglects physical health until it becomes impossible to ignore.
- Self-soothes by constantly fidgeting, listening to repetitive music, twirling hair, picking at skin or cuticles, etc.

Social

- Is a social chameleon; adopts the mannerisms and interests of the groups they're in.
- May be highly self-educated but will have struggled with social aspects of college or their career.
- Can be very shy or mute, yet can become very outspoken when discussing a subject they are passionate about.
- Struggles to know when to speak when in large groups or at parties.
- Does not initiate conversations but can appear outgoing and comfortable when approached.
- Can socialize, but primarily in shallow, superficial ways that may seem like a performance. Struggles to form deeper friendships.
- Has trouble disappointing or disagreeing with someone during a real-time conversation.

In this list of traits, I do recognize elements of myself and many adult-diagnosed Autistics I know of all genders. There's a particular way the neurotype tends to present among people who only discovered the identity late in life. We tend to be emotionally withdrawn yet friendly and socially adaptive. We're social chameleons, and masters at making people like us, but we never let much of our real selves show. We erect rigid rules around our lives to manage stress and make an unpredictable social world feel a little less scary: *make eye contact for this many seconds, eat this easy-to-prepare meal at this time of day, never talk about yourself for too long.* Try as we might to be agreeable, people still comment on how "oversensitive" or "immature" we are, or imply we're hard to read. When we struggle, people talk down to us, or try to socially "mother" us into more normative behavior.

Lists like these are still pretty popular among therapists[11] and in online spaces for Autistic people and our families.[12] Sometimes therapists who are seeking to educate themselves on "female Autism" will encounter this list online and let it inform their views, or pass it along to their patients. It offers a very broad, very gendered list of traits that reflect a lot of cultural biases and assumptions. What does it mean, for example, to "seem youthful"? Would a large, hairy man who loves collecting Funkopop toys but also enjoys MMA fighting be considered youthful? Or would that label instead apply to a petite woman who wears dresses and speaks in a high-pitched voice about her love of horses? All too often, the difference between who gets perceived as an innocent, shy Autistic and who gets viewed as creepy, awkward, and obviously disabled is more a function of things like race, gender, and body size than it is any innate difference in personality or behavior. There is no objective definition of what makes someone moody or a social chameleon, either. It's easier to socially camouflage if you're the kind of person society doesn't view with much suspicion in the first place.

This cluster of traits is commonly called "female Autism," but that label ignores the fact that a large percentage of Autistic people are transgender and gender nonconforming.[13] I'm transgender and Autistic, and find that my experiences don't fully slide into either the "female" or "male" Autism narratives. I've always had some male Autistic traits, like a tendency to be didactic and speak in a confident monotone, yet I was also a "sensitive," "immature" kid who played imaginary games with toys into my teens. Calling any of these qualities signs of "male Autism" versus "female Autism" is as gender reductive as saying there's an innately "masculine" or "feminine" personality type.

Like Bobbi, I was raised and socialized as a bit of an odd freak more than I was a "boy" or a "girl." Neither girls nor boys related to me as one of their own, and I didn't identify with them, either. I felt more like a mystical fairy creature dropped into the wrong reality than I felt like a "female," or even a human being. I played Legend of Zelda: Ocarina of Time and recognized myself for the first time in the game's wordless, androgynous protagonist Link. He didn't speak, and didn't belong in the community of childlike elves he'd been raised in. His difference was what marked him as special and destined to save the world. Link was brave, strong, and softly pretty, all at the same time. He was clueless and ineffectual in most social situations, but that didn't keep him from doing important things or from being met with gratitude and affection everywhere he went. I loved absolutely everything about Link, and modeled my own style after him for many years. I wore tunic-style dresses and kept my hair long and blond, which read as "feminine" enough to other people that they rewarded me for correctly playing the role of an attractive girl. But in actuality, it was a sneaky way to cosplay as my favorite male video game character every day without consequence. On family camping trips that were uncomfortably bug-ridden, hot, and socially overwhelming, I wandered the woods, pretending I was Link on an adventure across Hyrule. I desperately needed a model of how to be comfortable in my own skin, and Link was there when nothing else was available.

This is actually a really common Autistic experience. Perhaps because so many of us are alienated from mainstream neurotypical life, we come to identify with fantasy creatures,[14] aliens, robots,[15] or animals instead of the people around us.[16] Our hyperliteral, analytic minds recognize that the rules of the gender binary are arbitrary and entirely made up,[17] so making up our own gender identities and rules of presentation seems like fair game. Identifying outside of the binary (and outside of humanity) also helps many of us put a name to how detached we feel from society, and from our bodies. *Of course it's hard for me to carry myself in a "ladylike" way, I'm a robot in a human suit!* There's a term for Autistic trans people who see their neurotype and gender identity as inextricably linked: *autigender.*[18]

I asked Bobbi if they see their Autism and transness as being associated, and they tell me, "Absolutely, yes, you can't have one part of me without having the other. My Autism is trans and my transness is Autistic. Bras were uncomfortable for gender reasons and because I can't deal with tight clothes. I did soccer and flag football to be 'one of the guys,' and because when I was running around, nobody could talk to me or ask me questions that were social traps. It's all wrapped up together."

I feel the exact same way as Bobbi. I love that my Autism and my transness are linked. On good days, I love being Autistic and see it as a natural, neutral part of my identity, so it never has struck me as a problem that it's shaped my gender. I'm not a "normal" person, have never been able to be one, so identifying outside of the gender binary as well as mainstream humanity feels like home.

Sadly, many "gender critical" parents and mental health professionals don't see it that way. Transphobic people often take the strong association between gender variance and Autism as a sign that we aren't "really" trans, we're "just" Autistic and confused.[19] They presume Autistic people are un-self-aware and easily manipulated, and therefore shouldn't be allowed to make decisions about our identities or what we do with our bodies.[20] When Harry Potter author J. K. Rowling published the piece "TERF (trans exclusionary radical feminist) Wars" on her blog in the summer of 2020, she specifically mentioned her fear that many transgender men are actually Autistic girls who weren't conventionally feminine, and have been influenced by transactivists on the internet into identifying out of womanhood.[21] In presenting herself as defending disabled "girls," she argued for restricting young trans Autistic people's ability to self-identify, and access necessary services and health care.

Rowling's perspective (which she shares with many gender critical folks) is deeply dehumanizing to both the trans and Autistic communities. We're fully fledged, complex people, who are entitled to the same body autonomy and self-determination as anyone else. And it's meaningless to question whether a trans Autistic person would have "still" been trans had they not been born neurodiverse, because Autism is such a core part of who we are. Without our disability (or our gender identity) we'd be entirely different people. There is no separating these aspects of ourselves from our personhood or personality. They're both core parts.

Laura Kate Dale is a transgender woman, video game critic, and author who has written extensively about how her neurotype and gender have run parallel throughout her life. In her memoir, *Uncomfortable Labels: My Life as a Gay Autistic Trans Woman*, she writes that though she was viewed as a boy when she was growing up, she didn't have the traditional "cis boy with Autism" experience.[22] She had many recognizably Autistic traits, such as an aversion to bright colors and strong flavors, and a detachment from physical reality that made it impossible to figure out what clothes to wear for any given day's weather. Yet when she was evaluated for a variety of disabilities as a kid, counselors didn't consider Autism. Society had deemed her a "boy," and "boys" with Autism weren't supposed to be so docile and sweet. She had many of the features of "female Autism," though the world did not yet recognize her as a female.

Laura writes, "You see, there are stereotypes about children assigned male at birth, and very few of them applied to me growing up. There's an expectation of brashness, over excitability, loudness and emotional closure. . . . I was a quiet, reserved child who was sweet and did what they were told and was always in the right place, at the right time, doing what was expected."[23]

Laura's interests were often very feminine, rather than boyish. Like Crystal, she didn't disturb class with meltdowns or hurt anybody's feelings by being blunt or rude. Since her internal suffering didn't pose any problems to her classmates or teachers, it flew under the radar, unremarked upon—which is exactly what happens to many cisgender Autistic girls. Even some of her Autistic traits got chalked up to her being a weird or effeminate kid, rather than a disabled one.

Laura's and Bobbi's experiences are perfect examples of why the term "female Autism" is misleading; it presents the root of masking as being a person's assigned sex at birth, or their identity, when really it's social expectations that lead to a person's disability getting ignored. Masking is a social experience, not a biological one. "Female Autism" isn't actually a subtype of the disorder; it's a way that people cope with their neurodiversity not being taken seriously. Often, it is women who are in that position. But many other marginalized groups go through it, too, and those trends have not been as widely recognized. Black and brown Autistics in particular are underdiagnosed at high rates, just as women are, because racism has similarly distorted how the disorder gets perceived and assessed. They also pay a huge price for being non-conforming and noncompliant, and are thus expected to mask as a means of survival.

Black and Brown Autistics

Racism has permeated psychology and psychiatry from its genesis. Early clinicians came from white, European backgrounds, and used their culture's social norms as the basis for what being healthy looked like.[24] It was a very narrow and oppressive definition, which assumed that being genteel, well dressed, well-read, and white were the marks of humanity, and that anyone who deviated from that standard was not a person, but an animal in need of being tamed.[25]

The modern concept of mental illness as a medical condition first formed during the Victorian period in England, a time and place where restraint and dignity was equated with sanity.[26] Even poor English people who couldn't maintain the polished appearance and icy etiquette of the wealthy were considered to be somewhat savage and sick. Cultures that were more emotionally expressive or less filtered were pathologized as irrational, oversexualized, and aggressive. The mental health needs of white, wealthy people (and the hassle rich mentally ill people presented to their high-status families) were the primary concern of early psychiatrists. Everyone else was, at best, an afterthought, and at worse an undesirable to be purged.

This history shaped how professionals saw and defined Autism from the very start, and its legacy is still with us today. Autistic people of color frequently end up having their Autism ignored due to racism and bigotry.[27] They're less likely to get referrals to Autism specialists.[28] They have an incredibly hard time finding culturally competent health care.[29] Only about 4 percent of all mental health providers in the United States are Black,[30] though Black people make up 13.4 percent of the country's overall population. When Black and brown Autistic people see white therapists, normal expressions of emotions like anger may be misperceived as excessive or "threatening," and misdiagnoses are very common.[31] That's if they get identified as having a mental health condition at all. Black Autistics are frequently obligated to mask their traits and any negative mental health symptoms because (like girls and gender minorities) society demands they be more obedient and agreeable than white boys are.

Comedian Chris Rock recently came out about being on the Autism spectrum; specifically, he was diagnosed with Nonverbal Learning Disorder. In an interview with *The Hollywood Reporter*, he describes how clear-cut indicators (such as an inability to pick up on social cues and a tendency to take all statements hyperliterally) were ignored until his mid-fifties. Because he was an outgoing, Black comedian, Autism seemed unthinkable as an explanation for the social and emotional challenges he was facing.[32] Rock says he downplayed his own mental health needs, too, because he'd internalized the idea only white people go to therapy.

This is a systemic and far-reaching problem. White Autistics are 19 percent more likely to be diagnosed than Black Autistics are, and 65 percent more likely to be diagnosed than Latinx Autistics.[33] Black and Latinx Autistic people also get their diagnoses at older ages, reflecting their delayed access to services.[34] Indigenous Autistics are underdiagnosed and delayed in their diagnoses at even more extreme rates.[35]

These long-standing racial and cultural gaps persist for a variety of reasons. The lower a family's socioeconomic status, the less likely they are to have access to health care of any kind, but particularly Autism testing, which is seldom covered by insurance and can cost thousands of dollars. Additionally, racism influences how teachers and specialists perceive and screen for Autistic traits in Black and brown kids. When a white kid doesn't listen to instructions and hurls blocks across the room, he might be gently chastised, or soothed. When a Black or brown kid does the exact same thing, he's "corrected" far more aggressively. He might even be treated as a future criminal in the making.[36]

The writer Catina Burkett is a Black Autistic woman, and she is acutely aware of how people's perceptions of her disability are mediated by *misogynoir*, the systemic oppression of Black women.[37]

"Many people with autism can also appear obstinate or are slow to react in new situations," Catina writes. "When I am inflexible, I am sometimes called unfriendly, insubordinate, lazy, aggressive or uncontrollable."

I've known quite a few white Autistic men who are, as Catina puts it, obstinate at work. If the white guy in question has an advanced degree or a desirable skill set, such as the ability to code, being a bit difficult to deal with doesn't necessarily get in his way. In fact, for some Autistic men in tech, being a bit arrogant or cold can work to their advantage. Their aloofness signals they must be a tortured genius, a Sherlock in an office of Watsons. Yet when a Black Autistic woman is even slightly flat in her emotional expressions, she has to worry people will call her "angry" or "unprofessional."

"One white female supervisor complained that I should learn to change my demeanor with different people," writes Catina. "[She] grew bitter and the work environment became hostile. Eventually, I had to quit."

Catina's boss was, in essence, asking her to *code switch*, and put on different linguistic and social presentations for different situations. Many Black Americans are conversant in code switching, having to shift between African-American English (or AAE)[38] and Standard English as they move between communities, and modulating their appearance, mannerisms, and volume to avoid being negatively stereotyped.[39] Code switching is similar to Autism masking in the sense that it's an effortful process of signaling you "belong" in a space, and of knowing when to hide the sides of yourself that the majority will be oppressive toward. Code switching is a cognitively demanding activity that can hinder a person's performance on challenging or demanding tasks,[40] and it is associated with psychological stress and feeling inauthentic and socially isolated.[41] A report in *Harvard Business Review* found that many Black code switchers described it as a state of hypervigilance, and that they needed to constantly police their actions and speech in order to minimize white discomfort or hostility.[42]

Black Autistic people can have a variety of complicated relationships to masking and code switching. Pretending to be neurotypical by one culture's rules is wearying enough. Having to do it in a variety of different ways, using different dialects and mannerisms depending on the setting, is an entirely different level of social performance. Autistic researcher and organizer Timotheus Gordon Jr. told me that learning to code switch in his speaking style actually led to him becoming more socially ostracized as an Autistic child, not less.

"Because I'm African American, I have a different English to speak," he says, "which is African-American English. So I was placed into speech therapy, in my opinion, to sound like a person who speaks the standard American English."

In speech therapy, Timotheus was trained to communicate more like a white, middle-class person would; in essence, he was being told to mask his culture. But since he went to a majority Black school, this didn't help him fit in, it marked him as different.

"I went to school with mostly African Americans, or folks of African descent. It backfired because I was mocked for speaking differently, or speaking like I'm from England."

Over time, Timotheus had to learn to mask his speaking style in order to fit in with his peers, but also to shift back into so-called standard American English when interacting with white people and institutions. Psychological research shows that code switching requires a ton of cognitive resources even for neurotypical people.[43] One masked Autistic woman I spoke to, Mariah, told me that for many years she thought code switching exhausted her. Eventually, though, she discovered that it was the masking as neurotypical that was wearing her out. For some Black Autistics like Catina, it can be prohibitively hard to manage both tasks. Since she couldn't will herself to transform into a cheery, enthusiastic personality at will, her boss viewed her as hard to work with.

For Autistic people of color, being seen as hostile or difficult can become downright dangerous. When Black and brown Autistics fail to comply with medical instructions or the directions of therapists, they're frequently institutionalized and stripped of legal autonomy.[44] They also have to worry about incarceration or death at the hands of police. In 2017, Chicago police sergeant Khalil Muhammad shot an unarmed, Black Autistic teenager named Ricardo Hayes. Muhammad claimed he felt threatened by Hayes, but an investigation revealed Hayes had been harmlessly jogging along the side of his street, and didn't show any aggression toward Muhammad.[45] Five days after the murder of George Floyd, an Israeli police officer in Jerusalem City shot and killed Eyad Hallaq, an Autistic Palestinian man who was profoundly intellectually disabled and unable to speak or comprehend instructions.[46] In April 2021, a Chicago police officer shot and killed thirteen-year-old Adam Toledo, who had his hands in the air. Adam was in special education and neurodivergent.[47] Approximately 50 percent of people who are killed by police have disabilities,[48] and Black and brown Autistics are at an especially elevated risk.[49] Being identified as Autistic can be socially and emotionally perilous for women and gender minorities, regardless of race; for Black and brown Autistics, being visibly disabled can be deadly.

In *The Secret Life of a Black Aspie*, folklorist Anand Prahlad illustrates in lush detail how it felt to mask his Autism and present a neurotypical, nonthreatening façade to the world:

"I learned to grow masks for school. I had to be careful there. Covering up was like an instinct, though. Like a brown walking stick turning green when it sits on a leaf. Watch . . . Watch hands. Watch lips. Watch eyebrows."[50]

Anand grew up on a plantation in the 1950s, just two generations from the end of slavery. Living in a rural area with his family (many of whom had Autistic traits), Anand found comfort in nature. Upon entering the school system, though, he had to mask up. In addition to being Black and Autistic, Anand is also genderqueer, so as soon as he was thrust into public school, he had to begin hiding his neurodivergence as well as his soft, feminine side.

Throughout the book, Anand describes how various social settings demanded different versions of him. There was the all-Black elementary school where he was seen as odd, and not sufficiently masculine, but mostly left alone; there was the integrated high school where white people placed a great deal of pressure on him to be a respectable vanguard for racial justice. As an adult, Anand became a professor. In the academy, he was required to hide all emotional vulnerability, censor all casual language and slang, and obscure anything else white colleagues would deem "unprofessional." Autistic people are usually pretty candid, and Black American culture tends to also value direct "real talk" about interpersonal issues.[51] But in majority-white, abled institutions, openly saying what you mean or complaining about anything scares people. Anand had to adapt to hide the parts of himself that were open, vulnerable, and real.[52]

Throughout his memoir, Anand describes how erecting false selves was necessary, but also made it impossible to genuinely connect with others. It's an experience I know that many masked Autistics can relate to. We have to keep other people at arm's length, because letting them see our hyperfixations, meltdowns, obsessions, and outbursts could mean losing their respect. But locking ourselves away means we can't ever be fully loved.

"I would never have survived following neurotypical rules," Anand writes. "But my rules weren't necessarily the best ones to follow in a relationship. For example, my rules said disconnect the minute I'm overwhelmed. Stop listening . . . Keep my secrets."

Anand went through several breakups and multiple divorces before finally getting diagnosed as Autistic. Instead of sharing his feelings with his partners, he'd run away, either physically or into the recesses of his mind. When his third wife suggested this might be caused by a disability, Anand finally was put on a path toward self-acceptance.

Masking is a sensible survival strategy when you have no other tools at your disposal. But the more you deviate from what society values, the more elaborate your masking must be. Hiding your Autism, your cultural Blackness, *and* your queerness or womanhood can be too much. Sometimes the only viable alternative is to shut down and become deeply inhibited. You can't offend anyone if you simply melt into the wallpaper.

Catina Burkett and Anand Prahlad both describe adopting this strategy, becoming quiet and repressed, keeping their heads down to avoid evoking white people's fear of confident Black personhood. Other Black Autistics get by in life the way Chris Rock has, working to come across as cheery, funny, and immensely likable. Just as many Autistic women and trans people adapt by becoming nonthreatening and small, Black Autistics frequently have to self-preserve by plastering on a smile.

Highly Verbal and Outgoing Autistics

In 1911, the psychiatrist Eugene Bleuler coined the term *autism*.[53] It literally means "isolated self." This is in contrast to the term for non-Autistic, *allistic*, which means other-self or connected-self.[54] Countless depictions of Autism on TV and in film focus on how alienated and in our own heads we supposedly are. Think of the Autistic boy in the series finale of *St. Elsewhere*, who is famously revealed to have dreamed up the entire show and all its characters while sitting off by himself, staring into a snow globe.[55] A more contemporary example is the titular character in Sia's widely panned[56] film *Music*, a nonverbal Autistic girl who barely seems to notice when her own grandmother dies right in front of her. In the film, Music can't speak, and can barely use the augmented communication device she's been given, and only connects with other characters through elaborately choreographed dream sequences.[57] She's an isolated, antisocial self, locked away in a world of her own making.

Though a majority of diagnosed Autistics report having introverted personality traits,[58] some of us are actually quite extroverted and out-going.[59] Experimental research suggests that some of the social skills deficits associated with Autism (for example, difficulty recognizing faces) are reduced among Autistics who are extroverted.[60] If you seek out a lot of social contact, you'll get more practice interacting with people, so it makes sense that extroverted Autistics gradually learn to more easily blend in. Extroverted Autistics also tend to have larger, more expressive emotions than their introverted peers, which can make them easier for neurotypicals to relate to.

Autistics can have intense and bright personalities just as easily as we can seem icy and withdrawn. Many can make strong eye contact, listen actively, and jump in excitedly when someone brings up a topic that interests us. Outgoing Autistics may fumble with social niceties, interrupt too often, seem "too enthusiastic," or even be accused of histrionics, but a high degree of interest in connecting with others does generally benefit them psychologically and socially.[61]

Unfortunately, because Autism is so singularly portrayed as a disorder that makes you cold and robotic, outgoing Autistics are seldom correctly identified and diagnosed as kids. Teachers and parents think of them as chatty social butterflies, or disruptive class clowns. People may even come to view their large emotional displays and bursts of energy as "manipulative" or "attention seeking." Over time these labels can become a part of the mask they wear to get by. It can also make it difficult for an Autistic person to have their need for alone time or other social boundaries respected. For example, Timotheus told me that since he can come across as an affable "life of the party" type, it can be hard for his friends and family to understand that he sometimes also needs to recharge alone.

"My grandparents originally came from the deep South, so in that cultural sense it was important nobody gets left out," he explains. "If you feel sad, then it's best to be in a group. But in my case, I need to be left alone. But if I say to peers or even family members, *I need my alone time,* they say *no no no, you can't be alone.* I'm damned if I do, damned if I don't."

In many different ways, masking as outgoing and sociable can lead to an Autistic person's struggles being underestimated or erased. My friend Bethy is energetic, wears lots of eye-catching, bright clothing, and is covered in some of the coolest tattoos I've ever seen. They've been active in Chicago's theater and circus arts communities for years, and when they're excited, they jump and down squealing with delight. Bethy also loves modeling, and is very in tune with their body and sensuality. They treat their personal style and physicality as a full extension of their selfhood. For many, these qualities would be a bit surprising to witness in an Autistic person. So many of us have poor coordination and feel at odds with our bodies,[62] and we're stereotyped as uncool nerds with no sense of style. Bethy is pretty visibly Autistic, but they're also very charming. If I didn't know better, I'd assume their sunny, graceful personality meant they had an easier time socializing than more withdrawn, shy Autistic people do.

But because I know Bethy well, I realize none of that is true. While they found it easy to make surface-level friends at the bar where they use to work, they say that bonding with someone in a deeper way proved very difficult. They second-guess themselves, and are constantly running an algorithm in the back of their mind about how their actions and words will be received by others. They think a lot about how they're perceived and rarely feel at home in any community. Their immaculate style is also an effort to have their personhood and individuality recognized by other people. They've always been misunderstood, and every day is a fight to communicate who they really are. Bethy is masking, and putting extensive energy into doing so—just like inhibited, quiet me.

Just as some Autistics desire a lot of social contact, some seek out a high degree of stimulation and sensory input. Contrary to popular belief, Autism doesn't make a person's hearing super sensitive or their eyes super responsive to light. What Autism actually does is influence how our brains filter through the information taken in by our senses, and how we combine all that data into a cohesive whole. That can manifest in us being either *sensory seekers* (sometimes called sensory inattentive types)[63] or *sensory avoiders*—and most of us are a combination of both, depending on the sense.

For various reasons I outlined in Chapter 1, neurotypical brains tend to dismiss small details that might detract from the "big picture" their brain believes it sees.[64] Metaphorically, when a neurotypical person sees a "forest," their minds start glossing over the dead, bare trees and clumps of hedges that complicate the view.[65] In contrast, Autistic people perceive all the individual trees, and stumps, and rotting animal carcasses. The thousands of small features don't effortlessly combine into something larger for us,[66] so we have to process all of it separately. It's exhausting.

When I walk into my apartment building at night, I'm hit with a wave of discordant sensory information. It's particularly bothersome if I've already had a stressful or emotionally taxing day and my energy is depleted. There's the frenetic chatter of my neighbors, and the chaotic slamming of doors all along the hall. I can hear the elevator groaning to the ground level, my neighbor's music thudding below me, and ambulances blaring in the distance. Each piece of sensory information vies for attention, and doesn't blend into uniform background noise. In fact, the longer I have to endure it, the more annoyed I become. One way I can cope with this is by blocking out the world and dampening all the stimuli that are distracting me. But another, equally effective way to cope with sensory challenges is by seeking out really strong, bold sensations that overpower all that white noise.

When an Autistic person is a sensory seeker, they might crave loud music, spicy food, blazing bright colors, or plenty of activity and motion. They don't wear headphones in public to drown out the overwhelming noise of other people, but because a thumping synthpop track helps keep them engaged and grounded. The goal is the same in either case—to make sense of a barrage of data that's hard to process. A sensory seeking, fun-loving persona makes for a very effective Autism mask; no one sees you as an "overly sensitive" disabled person if you're constantly traveling the world and thrashing to the music at your local bar's metal night. It might even be an enjoyable mask to wear, though needing to constantly seek out stimulation can prove limiting. In their essay "Autistic People Party, Too," the writer Jesse Meadows describes how a drinking, drugging party-girl persona helped them fit in with other people and find a modicum of sensory comfort.[67] Eventually, though, that lifestyle proved unsustainable, and they had to learn to seek novelty and stimulation in healthier ways.

Logan Joiner is a teenager who has been sharing his passion for roller coasters with the world since he was eight years old. On his two YouTube channels (KoasterKids and Thrills United), he has a combined viewership of nearly thirty-five thousand subscribers. He shares videos of himself bungee-jumping from bridges, cliff diving into open bodies of water, and racking up amusement park visits. Logan's Autistic, and he got into roller coasters because they help him regulate how his brain processes sensory information.

"I'm not a big fan of unexpected surprises," Logan has explained.[68] "But if you think about it, roller coasters aren't really like that . . . so they're not scary because they're predictable."

Despite how messy and noisy they can be, amusement parks can actually be quite comforting to Autistic people. Amusement parks offer predictable social interactions and prepackaged experiences that rarely change. The layout is clearly marked, the food is bland yet filling, every attraction is over in a matter of minutes, and the signage is big and clear. Once you get used to a roller coaster, it provides consistent stimulation at expected points in time. For sensory-seeking Autistics, the rushing wind and vibrations of the track can provide relaxing physical input, just like a weighted blanket or fidget cube, only more forceful. There are statistics to memorize, development and launch history to learn about, and a whole community of nerdy online creators to share coaster and attraction lore with. Plus, on a roller coaster you can shout and flail your arms without anyone giving you funny looks. Since many of us have trouble regulating speaking volume and love to arm-flap, roller coasters, concerts, and other noisy, raucous spaces can be unexpected refuges from social judgment.

I have known Autistics who are DJs, salespeople, team managers, nonprofit fund-raisers, and aerialists. The more outgoing and sensory seeking among us love anime conventions, house parties, political campaigning, and competitive sports. It's often very difficult, though, for these kinds of Autistic people to get their disability taken seriously, because they can be so outspoken and charming. When they do have trouble socializing or they fall behind at work, their loved ones accuse them of "faking" that they're having a hard time, because they found it effortless to go out and party at a burlesque show the evening before. It's an all-too-common experience for disabled people, being told that your skills in one area are proof that you're "not trying hard enough" in another.

Very few people would guess these outspoken, high-energy folks are Autistic, particularly during their rambunctious childhoods. If anything about them seemed unusual, ADHD was probably what people guessed. Incidentally, Autism and ADHD co-occur at very high rates, and are diagnostically quite difficult to untangle.[69] Psychologists often call them "sister conditions" because both of them impact things like distractibility, sensory seeking, and being deeply pained by social rejection. This brings me to the next group of Autistics who often get overlooked: those with comorbid and overlapping conditions.

Autistics with Other Conditions

When it comes to mental illness and disability, diagnostic categories are really flawed things. A disorder is a cluster of symptoms and traits that tend to go together, but don't always, and the way those clusters get organized tends to change over time. Psychologists have been debating for decades whether anxiety and depression should be considered elements of the same disorder, for example, or looked at as separate conditions that are just correlated.[70] Psychiatrists in the 1940s believed Autism was a form of childhood schizophrenia,[71] but they certainly don't see it that way now. Our understandings of these labels are constantly in flux, and who gets stuck with a particular label varies across time and cultural context.

Often, a person exists somewhere on a spectrum between multiple disorders, or has a unique combination of traits from multiple conditions. If you have ever had a single manic period in your life, you may get diagnosed with Bipolar Disorder rather than Major Depressive Disorder, for instance, even if the depressive episodes massively outnumber the manic ones. On the flip side, if you don't meet the low weight requirement for Anorexia, you may never get your disorder recognized no matter how much anguish it presents in your life. This dynamic is particularly challenging for people with Autism Spectrum traits, because our neurotype is so multifaceted and so easily mistaken for other conditions.

People with post-traumatic stress disorder, for example, can look very similar to Autistic people. PTSD sufferers tend to be afraid of large crowds, are easily rattled by loud noises, and become more reserved when placed in hard-to-read situations. PTSD-fueled hypervigilance can look a lot like masking: you're constantly scanning your environment for threats, and modulating how you present yourself, so you can stay safe. To complicate matters, many Autistic people experience trauma at a young age, and have PTSD symptoms from that. It's common for us to be mistreated by parents and caregivers, bullied by classmates, or seen as "easy prey" by abusers. The leading treatment for Autism in children, Applied Behavioral Analysis therapy (or ABA for short), has widely been criticized by Autistic people as being traumatic to endure.

For all these reasons, it's not always possible (or helpful) to try to untangle which of a person's traits are Autistic and which are caused by the trauma of being neurodiverse in a neurotypical world. Daan is a forty-year-old man living in the Netherlands, and in addition to being Autistic, he was abused by both his parents. He tells me his diagnosis of complex PTSD effectively masked his neurodivergence for many, many years.

"I assume everybody is talking about me and is a hair's breadth from blowing up and calling me a horrible person," he says. "And is this Autism and not having a good theory of other people's thinking? Or is it that my mother would hurl invectives at me if I so much as put the sponge on the wrong side of the sink? There is no answer."

Daan's first trauma therapist tried to teach him that his fears were irrational; his mother was long dead, she told him, and could never hurt him again. She believed that she could help him question the "illogical belief" he had that people were unsafe. But Daan was still actively being hurt and rejected almost every day of his life because he was Autistic. His perceptions of the social world as menacing were realistic, not illogical.

"I would make observations that were just, literal facts, like *oh hey you got a haircut*, and people would think I was making fun of them," he tells me. "My boss screamed at me for that. Girls would go out with me and then berate me for not acting the way they expected a grown man to act. It was like my mother attacking me all over again. And then I would go to the therapist and she'd say I was reliving my trauma with my mother and seeing her in other people. It was horrible, crazy-making stuff really."

Clinical studies show Daan's experiences are far from abnormal. Therapy that is focused on battling "irrational beliefs," such as cognitive behavioral therapy (CBT), doesn't work as well on Autistic people as it does on neurotypicals.[72] One reason for that is many of the fears and inhibitions of Autistic people are often entirely reasonable, and rooted in a lifetime of painful experiences. We tend to be pretty rational people, and many of us are already inclined to analyze our thoughts and feelings very closely (sometimes excessively so). Autistics don't need cognitive behavioral training to help us not be ruled by our emotions. In fact, most of us have been browbeaten into ignoring our feelings too much.

Recently, Daan switched therapists. His new therapist had only taken one continuing education course on Autistic adults in her entire career, but that still made her better informed than most providers. She sent Daan to get assessed, and began to read up on how to alter her therapeutic practice to fit him better.

"My new therapist admits there isn't much research on helping Autistic people work through trauma," he explains. "But she at least got me evaluated. And that has unlocked a world of understanding for me, because it's helped me talk to other Autistics online."

Autism can also look a lot like an anxiety disorder. Most of us are anxious nearly every moment we're around other people, after all. Overstimulating, unpredictable surroundings will tend to activate our fight-or-flight response. The rituals and repetitive behaviors we develop to cope with stress can look a lot like Obsessive-Compulsive Disorder. Autistic burnout presents very much like a major depressive episode. All too often, these negative mental health consequences of masking are what a therapist recognizes, rather than the untreated disability that's caused it.

Some undiagnosed Autistic people (particularly women) identify as "highly sensitive persons."[73] Highly sensitive persons are generally described as intuitive, emotionally astute, and easily overwhelmed. Even the creator of the term, Elaine N. Aron, has revealed that some of the highly sensitive family members she has described in writing later found out they were Autistic.[74] The stigma that comes with Autism (and its very male, standoffish associations) may be part of why so many women on the spectrum find labels such as *anxious* and *highly sensitive* to be far more resonant.

In some cases, marginalized Autistic people get stuck with mental health diagnoses that are even more reviled and misunderstood than Autism is. It's quite common for adult Autistic women to be incorrectly labeled with Borderline Personality Disorder, for instance.[75] This is a really disastrous diagnosis. Borderline Personality Disorder is many therapists' least favorite condition to work with.[76] As a group, they're commonly viewed as overly dramatic, needy, attention seeking, unreliable, and even abusive.[77] When I've taught psychotherapists in training, many of them have shared with me that their supervisors taught them to avoid BPD sufferers like the plague, and to never even befriend a person with BPD traits.

Though it's called a disorder of "personality," BPD could perhaps be more correctly described as a disorder of attachment and emotional processing.[78] People with BPD fear rejection very intensely. They have an unstable sense of self that's highly dependent on the acceptance of others. They're often described by loved ones and therapists as having extreme emotions that seem inappropriate or manipulative.[79] If these sound eerily similar to the "female Autism traits" from the table earlier in this chapter, that's not a coincidence. Many women (and other gender minorities) who have been repeatedly rejected and traumatized for being Autistic develop an insecure sense of self, a (reasonable) fear of rejection, and big "overly sensitive" emotions that reflect the distress they almost constantly feel.

Nylah is one such woman who was incorrectly labeled as BPD before finally arriving at an Autism diagnosis. She had all the traits that tend to overlap: insecure self-esteem, fear of being abandoned that would prompt emotional meltdowns, and an unstable sense of who she was.

"I used to pretend to be whoever my boyfriends wanted me to be so they wouldn't leave me. And that was supposedly so manipulative and evil of me," she says.

In actuality, Nylah was trying desperately to not be alone. If a partner was into hockey, she filled her wardrobe with hockey jerseys. If a guy liked women who dressed up, she started getting weekly manicures. It didn't work great, but it was all she knew.

"Living so falsely made me feel suicidal, and what do you know, attempting suicide when you have Borderline means you're manipulating people for attention," she says. "I was the one constantly setting myself up to be taken advantage of, but with the Borderline target put on my back, I was a hysterical villain in people's eyes."

Nylah only began to question this narrative about herself when a relative received an Autism diagnosis. At age sixty-five, her mother got assessed—after many decades of carrying an equally stigmatizing Narcissistic Personality Disorder diagnosis.

Nylah says, "My mother is very self-involved, but that's because she literally cannot understand what's happening in others' brains and she can get so locked into her own view. Her actions can seem selfish because Autism gets in the way of her empathy. I have really intense empathy, it is painful almost, and she is the flip side. She just doesn't have it. But is that evil? She literally cannot help it."

Nylah shares with me that though her mother is inconsiderate and stubborn, she is also a woman who cares deeply about the world. Anything that gets in the way of her activism is a threat to be excised from her life. Recognizing that about her mom, and admiring that passionate, dedicated side of her has helped Nylah feel more at peace about their relationship.

"She cares very much about feminism and saving the environment. Her heart is big and it is wounded. She's a difficult person doing her very best, which in a Black woman seeking therapy in the 1970s meant you were a narcissist, apparently."

An article by psychiatrists Meng-Chaun Lai and Simon Baron-Cohen, published in the medical journal *The Lancet*, has proposed that an entire generation of Autistic people were misdiagnosed as having personality disorders.[80] Unsurprisingly, they propose that most of the misdiagnosed were marginalized women. Usually, I find a lot of problems with Baron-Cohen's work; he has long been an advocate for the view that Autism is best understood as an "extremely male brain."[81] Yet in this research, he seems to acknowledge that the reason many women are not diagnosed as Autistic is because they're labeled as Borderline, Histrionic, or Narcissistic instead. Getting stuck with a personality disorder diagnosis also makes it very difficult for a patient to find affirming, compassionate mental health care, particularly if that stigma interweaves with sexism or misogynoir.[82]

As I briefly mentioned above, Autism and ADHD co-occur and overlap immensely. Both disabilities relate to a person's "executive functioning," meaning their ability to plan ahead, divide large goals into smaller steps, sequence tasks in a logical order, and self-motivate to complete them. Yet even the fact that we struggle with these activities is contextual, and cultural: in a world where rugged individualism wasn't prioritized, it might not be a disability to need help finding your car keys. Both Autistics and ADHDers are easily distracted by stimuli, yet also prone to hyperfixating on activities we find enjoyable, getting engrossed for hours without remembering to pee or eat. Generally speaking, Autistics tend to perceive themselves as having more control over what they hyperfocus on than ADHDers do. ADHDers are more likely to describe boredom and understimulation as *painful*, where as some Autistics really enjoy stillness and quiet. Both neurotypes are underdiagnosed in women and people of color, and those who aren't diagnosed at a young age typically wind up masking for decades before figuring their identity out.[83]

Though ADHD is not believed by professionals to affect emotional processing and social skills development directly, one prominent experience among ADHDers is *rejection-sensitive dysphoria*, feeling intense panic and distress when receiving negative (or even neutral) social feedback from other people. Because ADHDers find rejection so terrifying and painful, their social behavior can be just as restrained and people-pleasing as that of masked Autistics. Autistics may have trouble guessing what other people are feeling or understanding unspoken social norms, but ADHDers may also be accused of being "oblivious" too, talking at length without picking up on others' boredom, or getting so lost in a video game or favorite hobby that they miss their roommate frustratedly doing all the cleaning. The underlying mechanisms might be different, in other words, but many of the struggles are the same.

While ADHDers don't appear to process information in as bottom-up a fashion as Autistics do, the high energy and anxiety associated with the neurotype can look incredibly similar to how Autistics react to overwhelming sensory information.[84] And while some masked Autistics may generally be better at staying on task, maintaining a consistent schedule, and keeping organized compared to the average ADHD, many of us are so chronically exhausted and burnt out that we experience the same struggles with daily life that people with ADHD do. Plus there are plenty of non-masked Autistics who require daily assistance, so it's not fair to say that Autism is a more functional or organized neurotype—however, Autism is often stereotyped to be the "order" to ADHD's "chaos."

Though we have many experiences in common, there are some differences between ADHDers and Autistics worth noting. First, an ADHD diagnosis is easier to receive as an adult, though it comes with the very stigmatizing assumptions that patients' brains are "broken" and require stimulant drug treatment.[85] Second, the accommodations many people with ADHD require can be incompatible with what Autistic people need. As an Autistic person without ADHD, I need a quiet, private, clean space in order to feel calm and focused. I also need silence and darkness in order to sleep. Many people with ADHD, in contrast, require stimulation, novelty, and sensory input. They may need the television blaring while studying, for example, or may be unable to sleep without music on. Clutter and mess overwhelms many Autistic people; for many ADHDers "visual noise" is easy to ignore, so much so that messes can "disappear" from their field of view. ADHDer friends often enlist my help looking for their phones and keys because they can't scan through their piles of stuff to find it. To them it's all just a morass of white noise, but I can instantly locate specific objects at a glance.

Many ADHDers that I know describe themselves as "time blind," or as perceiving time as moving in a spiral or series of waves. I experience time quite linearly, and rigidly, and have never been late to an appointment or missed a deadline in my life. Writers and creatives who have ADHD tend to work in big bursts of late-night passion, and put their work together in an associative, big-picture way. I work on a consistent schedule, analyzing sources and putting them together piece by tiny piece. But I also have an impulsive and chaotic streak, which might have gotten me labeled ADHD (or Borderline, or something else) if I hadn't been better at hiding it when I was young.

A number of the Autistic people I interviewed for this book are also ADHDers. So are many of the writers, mental health providers, and activists I quote. Within the Autistic self-advocacy community, people with ADHD are usually treated as honorary members by default. And the more we learn about the two neurotypes, the less they seem like distinct categories. They are, in every sense, sibling disabilities, two highly similar groups who belong in community with one another.[86]

In addition to overlapping with many mental disabilities and disorders, Autism also co-occurs frequently with physical disabilities like Ehlers-Danlos syndrome (EDS),[87] gastrointestinal disorders,[88] and epilepsy.[89] Heather Morgan, who has physical disabilities as well as Autism, says we can think of some conditions as sharing Autism's genetic markers.

"I think there are more of us in that category than we necessarily realize," she tells me. "[P]eople with disabilities that maybe aren't typical Autism, but have Autistic characteristics in their genetic sequence."

When Autism intersects with other disorders or disabilities, traits can take on new forms or be hidden entirely. I'm close friends with the family of Angel, an Autistic teenager with traumatic brain injuries and intellectual disabilities. If Angel hadn't been diagnosed with Autism prior to the car accident that caused his brain injury, doctors might never have recognized him as Autistic at all. They might have believed, for example, that he couldn't speak because of neural damage caused by the car accident. If that had been the case, Angel wouldn't have gotten his augmented communication device, or the iPad he uses to chat with friends on social media. Thankfully, Angel's family and care team figured out that his lack of verbal communication wasn't caused by an inability to express himself, but by an Autistic need for nonverbal methods of self-expression.

Angel is a rare example of a masked Autistic person who isn't viewed by the people around him as "high functioning" or high in intelligence. Of course, the very idea that certain Autistic people function more highly than others, or that functioning status is a binary quality you can catch at a glance, is problematic in its own right. That kind of thinking leads to many of us having our disabilities erased, and the private suffering that makes public "functioning" possible is ignored. It also perpetuates the idea that the only disabled lives worth living are those that can still manage to be productive or impressive in some conventional way.

"Highly Functioning" Autistics

Neurotypical people are obsessed with functioning levels. If you tell a nondisabled person that you're Autistic, but you're able to hold a conversation or maintain a job, they'll immediately start gushing about how functional you are. Usually, that remark comes with the implication that you don't really count as disabled because you can fake a nondisabled status (if only for a moment). When I was doing press for my first book, I received a fair share of comments like the following, which was left on a YouTube livestream in which I appeared:[90]

"If Dr. Price is autistic then they are extremely high functioning. Most people with autism spend their whole lives barely able to hold down a job because they're unable to meaningfully or appropriately interact with others, nor are they able to focus on anything intently for any extended period of time or if they do, it's something that's extremely trivial and irrelevant."

There is a lot to unpack in this comment. First is the commenter's assumption that because I seem to function "highly," my being Autistic is somewhat dubious to him. He says "if" I'm Autistic I must be high functioning, not that I am Autistic and capable or accomplished. He sees the two things as incompatible. Furthermore, he seems to think I don't really count as Autistic, because I can feign normality so well during an hourlong conversation. Another thing that jumps out is the way he equates holding down a job with having a life of value. In this commenter's view, I am a high-functioning Autistic because I can hyperfocus on something that makes money. Autistic passions that aren't moneymaking are, as he says, "trivial" and "irrelevant." That word *irrelevant* is also particularly striking—it's as if the Autistic person's own feelings and pleasure do not matter at all, only how their life is received by others.

When neurotypical people equate "functioning" with being less disabled, they fail to recognize the immense, hidden labor that goes into appearing normal. It also misses just how oppressive having to seem normal is by itself. It's reminiscent of when I see a fat person proudly identify themselves as fat, only to be corrected by a thin person with a dismissive, "You're not fat! You're just curvy! You're so pretty!" That kind of response betrays discomfort with fatness and fat pride, and reveals a latent belief that one can't be fat and beautiful at the same time. But a person can be both fat and beautiful, the two attributes are completely independent of one another. On top of that, it's insulting that a person's beauty is part of how their value is defined. Conversely, an Autistic person can function in one (or many) realms of public life, while being significantly disabled in others. Furthermore, some people don't "function" independently in any area of life at all, and that shouldn't detract from their value and the respect they receive, either.

The Instagram account @MyAutisticNurse documents the life of one "high functioning" Autistic person, a nurse who goes by the nickname Boo.[91] By all accounts, Boo is a fantastic nurse; her mind is a repository of medical facts that she can call from memory at will. She's excellent at working with pediatric patients and putting them at ease. She also has days when she is completely unable to speak. After an especially stressful shift at her hospital, she spends hours on the floor, lining up her favorite toys over and over. Like any other Autistic person, she has meltdowns and low-energy days, but because she's intelligent and capable, her Autism doesn't fit the "typical" mold.

Until 2013, the *Diagnostic and Statistical Manual of Mental Disorders* drew a distinction between Autism and Asperger's Syndrome. Autism was more profoundly debilitating and associated with major communication deficits and intellectual challenges. Asperger's, on the other hand, occurred in people with high intelligence, and was associated with well-spoken, emotionally frosty math geniuses and computer nerds. The 2013 edition of the *DSM* folded both labels into one: Autism Spectrum Disorder, or ASD. Today, instead of talking about how Autism differs from Asperger's, clinicians discuss whether someone is "high or low functioning" or what level their "support needs" are.

The Autistic Self Advocacy Network (or ASAN) and other organizations led by Autistic people reject terms like *high functioning* and *low functioning*. Those words oversimplify how a disability affects a person's life, and equates their productivity with their value as a human being.[92] A person who can speak, socialize, and hold down a job may strike outside observers as very "high functioning"; in private, that same person may need help getting dressed, or may require people to remind them when to eat. Boo's husband, for example, has created an easy-to-read chart listing all the snacks they have available at home, to help Boo process what to do when she is feeling hungry and run-down. He also helps motivate her to do things like brushing or washing her hair, activities that are both necessary and painful for her.

Conversely, a seemingly "low functioning" Autistic person who cannot speak or dress themselves may be able to excel in school or solve complex math equations, so long as they are provided with accommodations. The writer and activist Ido Kedar spent much of his early life unable to communicate with anyone. He couldn't speak verbally, and his motor control made it difficult to write. Then he learned to type on an iPad, and his blog "Ido in Autismland" was born. Ido has written two books, given countless interviews, and continues to post regularly about Autism and disability justice to his blog. He also graduated from high school with a 3.9 GPA and is currently working his way through college. Academically and intellectually, Ido functions at a very high level, now that he has the support to make that possible. Yet because he can't speak and lacked that support for a long time, he occupied a "low functioning" position in society for many years.

Cases like Ido's and Boo's really highlight how superficial functioning labels can be. Still, they shape how psychiatrists, teachers, and parents think about Autism, and it does tend to be the people consid-ered "high functioning" who can mask the most readily, and who therefore miss getting diagnosed. Generally speaking, if an Autistic person was verbal from a young age and could fake some social nice-ties, they were likely to either be considered "high functioning" as kids, or they weren't identified as Autistic at all. This is a bit ironic, because learning to speak at an early age was an early indicator of Asperger's Disorder.[93] My mom claims that I said my first word at six months old, and was speaking in sentences by the time I was one. I supposedly shocked a department store clerk as a one-year-old by greeting him and declaring "I believe I smell potpourri." My whole family has tons of stories like these. Many people who either were labeled as having Asperger's in the 1990s or are considered "high functioning" now have similar stories of being hyperverbal toddlers. It often led to us being filtered into gifted education programs rather than special education, which came with both advantages and its fair share of poorly bound-aried, objectifying experiences.

For me, and for countless "high functioning" Autistics, communi-cation and intelligence become an essential part of our masks. I never could fit in with other kids, but I could impress teachers with my grasp of big words and my sophisticated-sounding opinions. Though my language was highly developed, my social and emotional life was not. I annoyed other kids by talking too much about subjects that didn't interest them. I clung to adults who found me "impressive" and equated being well-behaved with being mature and worthy of their respect. I also absorbed the idea, common to many "gifted" children, that a per-son's intellectual potential belongs to society, not to themselves, and they owe the world greatness to justify their oddness. In my adoles-cence, English teachers adored my papers, and I excelled on the debate team, but I was brittle and distant to my friends and made all kinds of reckless personal decisions (such as shoplifting and skipping classes that I didn't like) to the point where I nearly got arrested and expelled. I got so attached to seeing myself as smart and accomplished that I neglected my physical health in the pursuit of success, too. Until I was in my mid twenties and realized I was Autistic, I was basically a perpetual adolescent, performing intelligence for praise but mismanaging my personal life and not connecting with anyone in a deeper way.

Nylah had a similar experience. "I was a fantastic saleswoman when my life was at its most dysfunctional," she tells me. "I could charm anyone if they didn't get to know me, really know me, and see how much I was drinking and lying to prop that life up."

Hiding self-destructiveness behind a mountain of achievements isn't functioning, not really. The very concept of "functioning status" is predicated on the logic of capitalism and the legacy of the Protestant work ethic, which both have trained us to believe that a person's productivity determines their worth.[94] No one is more harmed by this worldview than the disabled people who cannot work and produce value at all, and are the most likely to wind up abused, forcibly institutionalized, or homeless as a result. Equating a person's social value (or even their right to exist) with their productivity is sadly a common outlook, but it's also a profoundly alienating and ableist one. It harms the Autistic people who are able to "play the game" and mask as productive and respectful; for the Autistics who cannot play along, that game can quickly turn dangerous, even deadly.

Meeting Masked Autistics and Finding Your Place in the Community

Spaces like the Autistic Self Advocacy Network and Autistics Against Curing Autism embrace self-realized Autistics, because the community recognizes not everyone will have the chance to get a fair or affordable assessment. Plus, many people with subclinical Autistic traits may share common struggles and goals with us, and deserve to be included in our ranks. This includes the parents or relatives of diagnosed Autistic children who come to realize they're on the spectrum as well, and people with "sibling conditions" like ADHD or PTSD.

I want Autistic people to experience less shame about who they are, and to learn to take off the restrictive masks that have trapped us for decades. The first step to unmasking is accepting who you are, and finding others with similar experiences. You don't need a piece of paper from an assessor to begin to do that.

If you suspect you are Autistic, I encourage you to find a local Autistic Self Advocacy Network (ASAN) chapter, and begin to read writing and watch videos Autistic people have posted online. Learn a bit about just how varied our experiences and identities are. As you learn more, you may find you feel at home among us. Or you might find out some other community (such as the ADHDer community, or the broader Mad Pride movement) is a better fit. Both outcomes are perfectly okay. Even if you conclude you are not Autistic, your self-exploration will mean you've learned a whole lot about a group that could use more understanding allies.

When I was first exploring an Autistic identity for myself, I checked out videos by Autistic creators and activists, who showed me just how varied Autistic people can be, both in terms of personality and interests. The more Autistic voices I read and listened to, the less Autism felt like a curse. The shame I felt about my identity began to ebb, and pride in who I was gradually replaced it.

Once I had enough confidence to say I resonated with Autistic experiences, I put effort into meeting fellow Autistic people in the flesh. I met people at a local group, Autistics Against Curing Autism, run by Timotheus Gordon Jr. I also attended a local genderqueer support group and where nearly half the attendees were neurodiverse. I posted on Autism support groups online, like the subreddit r/AutismTranslated, and got to know others like me in those ways. These connections to the Autism self-advocacy world wound up doing far more for me than the psychological establishment did. Establishing official recognition of my disability was challenging, bureaucratic, and ultimately felt very hollow and meaningless—much like getting legal recognition of my gender. I was Autistic long before any professional recognized it, just as I was trans long before the state acknowledged it. However, nothing aided me in accepting myself and unmasking quite like finding my "people" and seeing proof positive that there was nothing wrong with us.

If you suspect you might be Autistic, I hope you can seek out similar spaces and resources for yourself. ASAN has chapters in many major cities, and online Autism groups are filled with supportive people who love to answer questions and share their own stories. On most social media sites, the #ActuallyAutistic and #AdultAutistic tags are filled with useful posts. You might also wish to seek out tools created by Autistic people, for Autistic people. For example, weighted blankets or fidget toys sold by sites like Stimtastic might help soothe your anxiety. Or the social skills toolkits offered on blogs like RealSocialSkills .org may help you develop greater confidence in interacting with people, disabled and neurotypical alike. It is not cultural appropriation or "faking a disability" to try out these tools. If Autism-friendly resources and adaptations prove helpful to you, that's another key signal you belong in our spaces, or at the very least have a great deal in common with us.

Ultimately, I can't tell you if you are Autistic, and I don't necessarily think it's something we have to discuss in a binary or categorical way. Autism is a spectrum, a rainbow of different shades and hues that thrive when they stand beautifully together. For too long we have hidden what makes us unique, fearing we're broken or unlovable. Embracing Autism means shedding that mask and finding safe ways to share our vibrant colors with the world.

In the next chapter, I'll explain how the ableism, sexism, and white supremacy lurking behind early Autism research created the pressure for so many of us to "mask." I'll outline what the gradual development of the mask looks like over the course of an Autistic person's early life, and discuss the science on what masking really is and what psychological processes undergird it. I'll provide some tools and exercises for investigating your own mask, and where it might have come from. We'll also reflect on the psychological and emotional costs of masking. In the chapters that follow, I'll introduce you to Autistic people who are slowly unlearning Autism stigma and taking their masks off, and provide some tricks and tips developed by Autistic coaches, counselors, and activists. We'll also discuss some public policy changes that would help Autistic people and other neurodiverse groups attain justice. As the next portion of the book will outline, masking is just as pervasive as Autism is. It's much more than faking a smile—it impacts how we identify, how we dress, the careers we choose, our relationships, and even how we lay out our homes. When we unmask, we get to reexamine every choice that we've made to "fit in," and begin to construct more authentic and affirming lives. A world that is more tolerant of difference is a safer and more nourishing place for everyone. And we can begin to build that world today, simply by questioning the ways we've been forced to live, and choosing instead to exist proudly as ourselves.

CHAPTER 3

The Anatomy of the Mask

Undiagnosed and clueless about the root of her challenges, Crystal had to suffer in silence throughout childhood. As her grandfather observed, she was a well-behaved, sweet kid, and a total teacher's pet. Yet behind her smiling, agreeable façade, she was coping with constant social confusion and loneliness. In classes where instructions weren't always clear, like science and math, she floundered. At school, she socialized with other girls, but she rarely got invited to sleepovers or outings to the mall or skating rink. She kept her head down around other people, and at home complained of frequent stomachaches and threw "tantrums" out of stress. By middle school, it was impossible for her to ignore how difficult she found regular life.

"Once you get to middle school, you have this really complicated class schedule you have to follow. All these transitions, bells going off, everyone switching classrooms every hour, after school-activities, busy busy busy. I don't do well with shifting gears; it takes a ton of energy for me now and I was suddenly having to do it all day."

Many Autistic people find it challenging to transition between activities. Each change requires a lot of what psychologists call executive functioning, a skill linked to planning and initiating behavior.[1] Most Autistics find it relatively easy to give a task we enjoy our unbroken attention, but we find it challenging to gear shift. Crystal could sit reading a book for hours without interruption, but in middle school classes switched so often that by the time she adjusted to a new room and settled into paying attention, it was time to move again. Middle school was also socially overstimulating: she went from sharing a classroom with fifteen children she'd known all her life to suddenly having to learn dozens of new names, faces, and interlocking social dynamics.

Friendship gets way more complicated and fraught as a preteen, and so do all the expectations placed on you. The adults aren't as kind and gentle as they once were. If you take a long time to figure something out, they assume you're dragging your feet out of adolescent apathy rather than executive functioning differences. If you have problems making friends, it's because you're a moody teen, not because neurotypical conversation rules are inscrutable to you. For Crystal, and for a lot of masked Autistic people, middle school is when a lot of struggles really come to the fore. Then puberty hits, and you have to get used to a shifting and unfamiliar body, and a whole new slew of disturbances follow.

All Crystal knew at the time was that the school bells stressed her out and everything was moving too quickly. She felt like she was moving at half speed, while everyone around her was a blur. It was hard for her to keep track of which interests she had faked around which people, and which personality she'd adopted to win over each teacher. She began to burn out, so her cognitive and social functioning declined even more.[2] Now she couldn't even push herself through the school day. All she wanted to do was find a private place to lie down and vegetate. No one had noticed yet that she needed help. So, she started begging her mom to let her skip school.

"It was really hard to convince my mom to let me stay home that much," Crystal says. "And eventually I hit the limit of how many sick days I could have without getting in trouble. But for as long as I could I got 'stomachaches' and stayed home, which really kept me sane."

For Crystal, faking sickness was an essential part of her mask. It could get her out of the overstimulating classroom and provide her some much-needed rest. Mirroring her female classmates and pretending to like what they liked was an act of masking, too. And as school became more and more challenging, Crystal started masking in new ways, like pretending she didn't care about "boy" subjects like science and math.

"There were girls around me who were getting interested in makeup and fashion, dating boys, celebrity gossip," Crystal says. "I could play along with that too. . . . The cool vapid girl vibe was a shield for being confused by all the random symbols in algebra that no teacher explained to me and just assumed I'd figure out. Instead of admitting I didn't understand what the hell was going on I could flip my hair and say *this is so boring, let's talk about something that matters, like Mariah Carey dating Eminem.*"

Crystal had already observed that if she asked for help with something that neurotypical people found "obvious," she wouldn't get assistance. They'd just find her exhausting, or think she was asking questions just to waste time. But Crystal genuinely didn't know what role x played in a linear equation. She didn't understand what "show your work" meant in a math context, so she'd write long paragraphs explaining her thought process in words, and describing exactly which buttons on the calculator she'd pressed. Her teacher took this as some kind of personal insult, and wrote Crystal up for it. She cried in the detention hall the entire time, baffled that her best attempt at showing her work had somehow been rude.

There were also elaborate rules about how middle-school-aged kids were supposed to act, but Crystal only ever found out about these rules when she'd broken one of them egregiously. Like the time she wore a painfully uncool tie-dyed T-shirt from JCPenney to school and the other girls wouldn't quit laughing at it.

Crystal says, "I had to become almost a cartoon of vapid femininity to explain why I was so out of it. I couldn't be good at being a person, but I could be good at being a *girl*. And my girly-ness could explain why I was so dumb at math and so bad at people. *She's just a ditz.*"

Timotheus Gordon Jr. tells me that when he was a child, he had to learn to mask his youthful sensitivity and hide his nerdier interests, presenting as tougher and cooler than he actually felt inside.

"In my community, crying is a sign of weakness, and I could be targeted for being weak, so early on I had to mask my sadness with aggression and learning how to fight," he says. "When it came to having interests like social sciences, history, and more geeky stuff like Pokémon, I had to hide it because that was considered to be uncool and a weakness."

As was true in Crystal's case, gender roles and ableism both conspired and pushed Timotheus to hide the parts of himself that his neurotypical peers would look down on and punish. He could play up his more gender-normative interests, such as his love of football (with all its statistics and player trivia to memorize), but anything that marked him as too sensitive, odd, or not sufficiently masculine was risky.

Unlike Crystal, however, Timotheus's experiences as a masked Autistic are also inseparably tied to anti-Black racism. Though he now has many authentic relationships rooted in like-mindedness and shared nerdy interests, he still has to worry about being perceived unfairly as he moves throughout the world. He doesn't just have to worry about being seen as weak as he did as a child—out among white people and in white institutions, he has to fear being seen as too aggressive.

"Even my mannerisms like speaking bluntly or directly, or matter-of-fact. I still have to mask because I want to tell the truth. But it's not about what I say, it's about what people interpret. And I have gotten into trouble because of what people interpret."

I think for most masked Autistic people, there are key moments in childhood or adolescence where we learn we are *embarrassing* or *wrong*.

We say the wrong thing, misread a situation, or fail to play along with a neurotypical joke, and our difference is suddenly laid bare for all to see. Neurotypical people may not know we're disabled, but they identify in us some key flaw that is associated with disability: we're childish, or bitter, self-absorbed, or too "angry," or maybe we're just awkward and make people cringe. Avoiding being seen in these ways becomes our core motivation in life, each day a battle between the heavy armor we wear and the embarrassing characteristics that armor was designed to cover up.

For me, masking was always about not seeming childish. When I was a kid, I was forever getting corrected for acting like a baby, and that mortified me. When I was disgusted by the textures of the unfamiliar food at sleepaway camp and went into a full-blown, sobbing meltdown over it, I got reprimanded for being a picky eater and a crybaby, and was forced to sit at the table all evening, until I gulped some cold ravioli down. When I failed to learn how to ride a bike at the "correct" age because I had poor balance and motor control, my dad shamed me for my immature clumsiness (perhaps because it reminded him of his own masked motor disability). As an adult, I would cuddle with stuffed animals at night with the blinds pulled down low and my bedroom door double locked, fearing that someone might walk past the house or into my room and discover the terrible fact that holding soft, cute things brought me comfort.

The fear of seeming childish wounded me in a profound way, as it does many Autistic folks. One of the major ways abled society dehumanizes the disabled is by calling our maturity into question. "Adults" are supposed to be independent, though of course no person actually is. We all rely on the hard work and social-emotional support of dozens of people every single day. You're only seen as less adult, and supposedly less of a person,[3] if you need help in ways that disrupt the illusions of self-sufficiency.

Needing help with toileting, for example, reminds abled people of the fact that they once wore diapers, too, and that one day they might need diapers again. People who need help toileting are vulnerable, and reliant on others. That fact distresses and repels the nondisabled, and they cope with their hard feelings by framing those who wear diapers as essentially different from themselves. They're perpetual children, inhuman incompetents, not someone to empathize with. My own "childishness" reminded allistic people that much of what we call maturity is a silly pantomime of independence and unfeeling, not a real quality of unbreakable strength. Abled people hated seeing my awkward softness and confronting the fact they might be sensitive and needy in their own ways, too. So they acted like I was invisible, or that my childlike habits were perverse. I learned that feigning maturity would be my sole salvation, the only way to ensure my humanity got recognized.

As I grew older, I overcorrected for secretly being "childish" and "embarrassing" by adopting a façade of jadedness and hyperindependence. Though it manifested in a slightly different way than it did for Timotheus, I made it my goal to always seem tough. I made fun of my friends, rolled my eyes a lot, and acted like I was too cool to care about anything. I tore down other people for liking "babyish" things, like boy bands and cartoons. I refused to cry in front of anybody, and resented anyone who did express emotions openly. I told myself I'd never get caught being a baby ever again. That commitment meant never asking for help at all.

If you're a masked Autistic, or suspect you might be, you probably can recall experiences like Crystal's, Timotheus's, and mine. I think examining the origins of your mask can help you identify some of the deep-seated fears that drive your need to wear it. Are you afraid of seeming stupid? Or childish? When you were young, did people accuse you of being cruel? Did you come to believe you were finicky, or selfish?

Autistic people frequently are stereotyped as immature, unintelligent, cold, or out of touch. And each of our masks helps to cover up the Autism stereotypes we felt we needed to resist the most. Behind each mask, there sits a deep pain, and a series of painful beliefs about who you are and what you must never allow yourself to do. Consequently, a big part of unmasking will mean facing those qualities you loathe the most in yourself, and working to see them as neutral, or even as strengths.

Here's an exercise to get you thinking about where your mask comes from. Many of the negative qualities associated with Autism that we explore here will come up again later, in exercises focused on reexamining your self-concept and practicing unmasking.

Reflecting on the Need to Mask:
What Does Your Mask Protect You From?

1. Try to recall a time early in life when you felt intense embarrassment or shame. Describe that situation here.

2. When you recall this experience, what emotions do you feel?

3. Complete the sentence by checking off as many adjectives as you like:

   "In that moment, everyone could see that I was _____."

   ____ Selfish   ____ Robotic

   ____ Awkward   ____ Immature

   ____ Childish   ____ Disgusting

   ____ Self-absorbed   ____ Embarrassing

   ____ Cold   ____ Clueless

   ____ Stupid   ____ Cruel

   ____ Weak   ____ Pathetic

   Other: _____

4. Of the words listed above, which one is the most *painful* to hear associated with you?

5. List some actions or habits that you associate with that word.

6. Complete this sentence: I pretend to be _____ so that people will tolerate me, but deep down I know that I'm not.

___ Independent   ___ Happy

___ Cool   ___ Confident

___ Generous   ___ Caring

___ Mature   ___ Organized

___ Warm   ___ Smart

___ Impressive   ___ Powerful

___ Helpful   ___ Worthy

Other: _____

7. Complete the sentence:
"If I want people to like me, I can't let them find out that I _____."

Now that we've explored what Autism really is, gotten the chance to meet some masked Autistics, and reflected on the social and structural forces that drive the need to mask, let's dive into the science behind what masking really is.

What Is Masking?

In the psychological literature on the subject, Autism masking is said to consist of two classes of behavior:[4]

Camouflaging: attempting to hide or obscure Autistic traits in order to "blend in" with neurotypicals. The main goal of camouflage is to avoid detection as disabled.

Compensation: using specific strategies to "overcome" challenges and impairments related to disability. The main goal of compensation is to maintain the appearance of high, independent functioning.

When Crystal attempted to disappear into the social background by making herself agreeable and passive, she was camouflaging how confused and overwhelmed she was. When she studied up on celebrity gossip so she'd have things to discuss with her friends, she was compensating for her comparative lack of neurotypical conversation skills. Some of Crystal's masking behaviors were a blend of both compensation and camouflage: faking being sick allowed Crystal to hide how exhausted and overloaded she was (in other words, it camouflaged these needs), but it also provided her a neurotypical-approved excuse for getting the breaks she required (which allowed her to compensate for her exhaustion). Camouflage is all about obscuring one's unique qualities and struggles as a disabled person; compensation is all about crafting little hacks and cheats to help you get your needs met because you can't request the accommodations you require. Playing up an interest in football because it was socially acceptable and gender conforming, for instance, was a compensatory strategy that served Timotheus well.

All masked Autistics employ both compensatory and camouflaging strategies to help us get by, and apply them to a wide variety of tasks we find challenging. Someone might verbally camouflage by forcing themselves not to speak too much about their special interests,[5] for example, and socially compensate by researching a friend's Facebook posts before meeting up with them, so they'll have a good idea of what to chat about.[6] A person might camouflage their auditory sensitivities by gritting their teeth through the pain and never complaining about it, or they might compensate for it by wearing subtle noise-canceling earbuds that don't stand out as unusual.

When I introduce neurotypical people to the concept of Autism masking, they usually understand it as a social process or performance. It's true that masking involves things like memorizing social rules and feigning friendliness, but that's really just the most obvious form it takes. Most of us have to mask everything from our information processing style, to our lack of coordination, to our limited food preferences, to the fact that we require more rest than neurotypical people are expected to. Masking shapes the fields we work in, how we dress and carry ourselves, where we live.

Many maskers choose careers that allow them to hide their

executive functioning issues. Or they realize they have no choice but to freelance because they can't keep up with all the meetings and socializing a full-time job requires. I was initially drawn to academia because I believed it was a place where I could dress however I liked, keep my own hours, and be eccentric without consequence. I knew I'd never have the energy or patience to fake being professional by corporate standards, so I compensated by developing skills and credentials that would allow me to be valued for my mind rather than my looks or poise. Many Autistic people who work in tech gravitate to the field because Autism spectrum traits are somewhat normalized there. Multiple neurodiverse people who do sex work reported to me that the flexible hours and the potential of making rent within a few days of work made the career a good fit for them.

Masked Autistics tend to arrange our lives around our limitations and needs, and sacrifice anything that might demand too much energy out of us. An impressive resume or academic transcript might hide the fact our homes are messy, our hair is unbrushed, and we haven't socialized with anybody recreationally in months. In a few key areas we may appear to be functioning highly, but that façade requires we let everything else in life fall apart.

My friend Jess once described their compensation this way: "It's like going to the grocery store, but only being able to bring home what you can sneak into your pockets when nobody is looking. And everybody else gets to just go through the checkout and buy as much as they want, so they don't understand why you find shopping stressful."

Jess has ADHD, but their description of how challenging it is to lie, cheat, and steal your way through a neurotypical-looking life when you lack the accommodations you need is just as relevant to life as a masked Autistic person. Regular life is more cognitively and emotionally demanding for neurodiverse people than it is for neurotypicals, but we have to hide that fact from other people on a daily basis. To prop up our façade of being "high functioning," we build a messy, unstable scaffolding of flawed coping mechanisms. It's no wonder we report anxiety[7] and depression[8] at elevated rates. If the only food you ever get to eat is what you can steal, you're gonna move through the world feeling undernourished and hypervigilant.

Though masking is incredibly taxing and causes us a lot of existential turmoil, it's rewarded and facilitated by neurotypical people. Masking makes Autistic people easier to "deal" with. It renders us compliant and quiet. It also traps us. Once you've proven yourself capable of suffering in silence, neurotypical people tend to expect you'll be able to do it forever, no matter the cost. Being a well-behaved Autistic person puts us in a real double bind and forces many of us to keep masking for far longer (and far more pervasively) than we want to.

The Double Bind of Being "Well-Behaved"

Psychiatrists and psychologists have always defined Autism by how the disability impacts neurotypical people. A more "severely" Autistic person is not necessarily a person who experiences more interior suffering, but rather someone who suffers in a more disruptive, annoying, or disturbing way. The Autistic children who present the biggest hassle are the ones most likely to be referred to services, whereas those who can conceal their struggles are granted tentative approval—but risk never being understood or empathized with.

Researchers Zablotsky, Bramlett, and Blumberg set out to understand how parents perceive the "severity" of their Autistic kids' symptoms.[9] They surveyed nearly a thousand families raising Autistic kids, and also measured the Autism symptom severity of the children themselves. What the researchers found was that parents did not accurately perceive the level of their kids' suffering. Instead, parents based their ratings of Autism "severity" on how much their kids' behavior bothered them and required a lot of their time and attention. Many children described by parents as "high functioning" were quietly coping with debilitating sensory pain, or were falling behind academically or socially in significant ways. This carries over to how Autistic adults are perceived, and the expectations that neurotypical institutions place on us to appear "normal."

This desire to make Autistics compliant and nondisruptive is a large part of why the prevailing treatment for Autism in children is Applied Behavior Analysis (or ABA) therapy. ABA is focused on training Autistic kids to fake a neurotypical personality. It's a behavioral therapy, not a cognitive or emotional one. As long as the Autistic child's outward actions change and become less "disruptive" or more "normal," it doesn't really matter to the ABA therapist what's going on between the kid's ears.

ABA therapists train children to camouflage their Autistic traits using a system of rewards and punishments. ABA patients get sprayed in the face with water (or on the tongue with vinegar) for failing to make eye contact, or for talking too much about their special interests. If a child engages in echolalia (phrase repeating), chews on their fingers, or flaps their hands, they'll be punished, even if they find these impulses painful to restrain. ABA patients are also forced to rehearse compensation strategies. They're made to sit still for hours until they parrot back a conversational script correctly, and aren't allowed to get up and play until they provide an "adequate" amount of eye contact.[10] They may be asked to repeat conversational niceties like "please" and "thank you" over and over until they hit on the correct tone of voice, or be told to stand up and sit down repeatedly while the therapist snaps their fingers at them like they're a trained dog. When Autistic kids act out or demand attention, ABA therapists are supposed to withdraw, leaving the room or ignoring their distress. This teaches the Autistic child not to expect any help from the outside world.

ABA therapists also punish children by electrocuting them.[11] The electroshock devices used in ABA therapy were briefly banned by the Food and Drug Administration 2020,[12] before being reinstated in 2021.[13] Today, the Association for Behavior Analysis still vocally supports the use of such "aversives" to discourage visibly Autistic behavior. In 2012, an ABA-trained special education teacher came under fire for coating her young students' crayons in hot sauce, to discourage chewing.[14] That case wasn't a random act of violence. It reflects the core philosophy of ABA. The founder of ABA, Ole Ivar Lovaas, used to coerce children into providing hugs and kisses to their therapists by giving them candy.[15]

Forty-six percent of Autistic adults who underwent ABA therapy as kids report having Post-Traumatic Stress Disorder (PTSD) as a result of the experience.[16] Many experience deep shame even naming the subjects they feel passionate about, because they've been punished for having special interests. Some are unable to appreciate the emotional and psychological benefits of fidgeting or stimming because the importance of having "quiet hands" was so deeply drilled into them. Many don't know how to refuse an unreasonable demand, or how to express emotions like anger or fear. One former ABA therapist confessed on an anonymous blog that she worries she conditioned her patients to be easy to manipulate and abuse.

"Upset about being treated like a circus animal? Not my problem, kiddo," she writes. "I'm here to lure you with candy and manipulate you into doing my bidding, no questions asked. Which will make you excellent prey for sexual predators, abusive teachers, caregivers, and partners later in life."[17]

Despite how loathed ABA is by Autistic people, the parents and teachers of Autistic kids tend to love it, and research broadly deems it "effective." This is because the efficacy of the program is based on the neurotypical gaze, not how the Autistic child feels. ABA does teach Autistic kids to quiet down and be less annoying and "weird." The problem is, it does so by training them to hate themselves and obey all adults. It's akin to evaluating how "effective" a depression treatment is by asking the depressed person's boss how they are performing, rather than checking in with the depressed person themselves. Sadly, the comfort and convenience of the neurotypical teachers and parents are prioritized, so ABA remains the one and only "evidence-based" treatment for Autism that most insurance plans will cover. Becoming "well behaved" is more important than being psychologically well.

For many Autistic kids, learning to obscure your pain often becomes a primary survival strategy; for masked Autistics, this isn't taught within ABA therapy, but as part of regular life. I didn't go through ABA, but friends' parents did yell at me for squirming awkwardly in my seat. No one forced me to rehearse "normal" conversational scripts, but kids laughed and walked away from me when I spoke in an inappropriately loud voice or quoted movies to express how I felt. My Girl Scout leader shamed me in front of the whole troop for years because I always sat with my knees pressed to my chest. My body craved the pressure of sitting in a curled up, "gargoyle" posture (many Autistic people enjoy sitting this way), but the group leader found it so irritating she couldn't help but berate me for it in front of the whole troop every single time it happened.

Autistic educator and social equity consultant ChrisTiana Obey-Sumner has written about an eerily similar experience of having her Autistic traits publicly shamed in Girl Scouts.[18]

"One of my stimming activities is that I suck my thumb, and put my forearm to my face to both smell my natural scent and feel the soft hairs brush up against my nose," she writes. "For some reason, this rubbed my scout leader the wrong way when I was around 7 or 8 years old. She called all of the other children to circle around and hurl insults at me."

Every masked Autistic person has a litany of experiences like this. Most maskers dodge the massive psychological bullet that is ABA therapy, but we still receive endless conditioning that says our unfiltered selves are too annoying, unusual, awkward, nonconforming, and cold to fit in. We also witness how other nonconforming bodies and minds are treated. When the entire world shames people for being into "childish" things, having odd mannerisms, or simply being irritating, you don't need ABA to program you into compliance. Everyone around you is already doing it.

I still remember the first time I consciously compared myself to a more "typically" Autistic person, and realized I needed to hide who I was. It was middle school, and I was sitting in the cello section a few feet away from Chris, a percussion player.[19] Chris and I were both in the same special education gym class; I was there because I was uncoordinated and had abnormally slow reaction times, and my muscles were incredibly weak, though no one figured out this was due to Autism. Chris, on the other hand, had been diagnosed when he was very young.

Chris was smart and chatty. He loved sharing World War II trivia with people. He'd ask questions in class that seemed to come out of nowhere, and sometimes would involuntarily do a stiff-armed wave to stim, which (because of his World War II obsession) people read as a Nazi salute. Kids laughed at him, teachers condescended to him, and school administrators treated him like a problem to be contained. He was the first Autistic person I ever knew, and how he was treated was instructive to me.

That day in orchestra class, I was already on edge and annoyed by how loud everyone was. Percussionists were whipping drumsticks around; viola players were gossiping and laughing; violinists were tuning their instruments, filling the air with screeching, high-pitched peals. I coped by folding my arms tight across my chest and screwing a pissed-off expression onto my face. The grimacing, somewhat irritated expression that Autistic climate activist Greta Thunberg is now famous for[20] is very similar to how I used to react to loud noise and social chaos. I had already started to cultivate a grumpy, goth persona to protect me from seeming weak. Instead of showing that I was overwhelmed, my mask told other people to stay far away.

Chris didn't have that option. He couldn't mask how upset he was by the noisiness of the orchestra room. He was jittery and visibly agitated, slamming his music stand up and down on the ground, trying to get his anxiety out. People laughed at his unease and tried to provoke him by asking him questions they knew he wouldn't understand.

"Hey Chris," an older boy hollered. "Do you spit or swallow?"

Chris kept slamming the music stand up and down while he looked off into space and pondered. "I guess I do both," he answered sincerely, not grasping the sexual implication. He interpreted it as a literal question about whether he ever spit or swallowed at all. People cackled and looked away. Chris's whole body was tense. He knew he'd stepped on some conversational land mine the older boys had planted.

Then some prankster pulled the fire alarm, and the already loud room filled with clanging bells and kids yelling. There was laughter and mayhem as everyone headed for the door. I felt sick to my stomach and furious, but able to hide behind my mask of wincing pissed-off-ness. Chris, on the other hand, had booked it out of the room. School administrators found him circling the track outside, dashing and breathing heavily. Through the windows, we watched as the adults tried to reassure him there was no fire, that he was safe. But it wasn't the fire that was bothering him. It was the noise, and the people. It took them an hour to coax Chris back inside.

Though everyone at school knew Chris was disabled, they had no patience for his actions. Administrators groaned as they tried to get him to calm down; my classmates and I joked while he kept awkwardly circling the track. We all saw him as hopelessly immature and embarrassing. I recognized a much-loathed, deeply buried part of myself in Chris, and I hated him for it. I thought I was better than Chris. I could "keep it together." I took pride in the fact that no one would ever catch me being nervous and weak. I remember being disgusted and fascinated by Chris in equal measure. I kept my attention pinned to him during every orchestra class after that, picking apart every quality in him that I needed to hide. I began to surround myself even more thoroughly in a camouflage of frostiness and rage.

Masking as Overcorrection

For many masked Autistics, the best way to camouflage a socially undesirable quality is to rebound into the complete opposite direction, and overcorrect for anything neurotypical people and institutions have taught us to hate about ourselves. An Autistic person who was mocked for being needy and intense as a child may camouflage as hyperindependent and emotionally avoidant, for example. On the flip side, an Autistic person who has repeatedly been told they are selfish and robotic might instead wear a mask of helpful friendliness, and become a compulsive people-pleaser or teacher's pet. We internalize many of the values of the ableist society we're living in, and project those values both at other disabled people and at ourselves.[21]

After the incident with Chris, I put excessive effort into hiding everything about me that might reveal I was disabled. I avoided showing enthusiasm or strong emotions for fear of seeming "cringey" and immature. I shut up about my obsessive interest in fruit bats and video games. I put on headphones and sunglasses when I went out in public, and didn't look anybody in the face. I impressed teachers with my wit and racked up debate trophies and merit-based scholarships, which fed into my sense that I was better than other people, and that my intelligence was the real reason I was alone. I dished out so much forceful social aggression that no one could think about challenging me. In old home movies from that time, I mock my friends and upbraid them for showing excitement or innocence. It was a cruel act that only made me harder to love, but I performed it perfectly. Until, like many masked Autistics, I finally realized the mask was taking far more from me than it ever gave, and that if I wanted to stay alive, I'd need to let it drop.

In the table on the next page, I've listed some of the most common negative stereotypes of Autistic people, and the opposing qualities often used to camouflage and overcompensate against them. As you read through the list, you can reflect a bit on the traits that were encouraged in you as a kid, and which qualities you did your damnedest to avoid. I've also listed some common behaviors that go along with each masking strategy, and left some blank space, so you can fill in your own examples. You may want to revisit your responses to the exercise at the top of this chapter, to help you reflect on which needs and fears shaped your own need to mask.

I was taught it was bad to be:	So I had to pretend to be:	I did this by behaving this way: (add your own using the blanks)
Arrogant	Humble	• Pretending I didn't know the answers to questions . • Keeping silent when people said things that weren't true • Softening statements with phrases like "if that makes any sense" or "maybe" to make myself sound less certain • • •
Cold & Unfeeling	Warm & Friendly	• Smiling all the time no matter how I felt • Asking people about their feelings and not talking about myself • Taking care of other people whenever they were upset • • •
Annoying & Loud	Agreeable & Quiet	• Only experiencing big emotions in private • Solving problems by myself • Not getting "too excited" about anything, including good things • • . •

Childish	Mature	<ul><li>Serving as a confidant for adults and authority figures</li><li>Carrying myself in a restrained, "proper" way</li><li>Acting like a "teacher's pet" or "little professor" and distancing myself from my peers</li><li></li><li></li><li></li></ul>
Awkward	Cool	<ul><li>Withdrawing from any activity I wasn't instantly good at</li><li>Pretending to be aloof and uncaring</li><li>Rehearsing fake conversations in my mind so I could make talking to people seem effortless</li><li></li><li></li><li></li></ul>
Clueless, Pathetic.	Independent	<ul><li>Nodding or laughing, even when I have no idea what's going on</li><li>Developing unique, private habits and "hacks" that make it possible for me to hold my life together</li><li>Making sure my life looks "put together" on paper, even at the expense of my health or happiness</li><li></li><li></li><li></li></ul>
Sensitive	Strong	<ul><li>Not voicing my needs</li><li>Feeling ashamed whenever I wanted to cry or express anger</li><li>Fighting internally with every "disruptive" emotion I felt</li><li></li><li></li><li></li></ul>

I was taught it was bad to be:	So I had to pretend to be:	I did this by behaving this way: (add your own using the blanks)
Weak	Tough	• Mocking or being aggressive with other people • Thinking of myself as superior to others • Showing distaste for anything society considers feminine, soft, or tender • • •
Weird	Normal	• Studying what other people like in a systematic, analytical way • Imitating people or characters' mannerisms, style of dress, tone of voice, etc. • Mocking those who are more obviously "weird" than I • • •

There are massive psychological consequences to adopting strategies like these, which go way beyond the anxiety, depression, and burnout we've already discussed. To maintain their masks and compensate for the challenges they're facing, many Autistic people fall back on an array of destructive and compulsive coping mechanisms, including substance abuse, calorie restriction, excessive exercise, emotional co-dependency, and even joining cults. I think if we want to really confront the role the mask has played in our lives and work on parting with it, it's important we face just how unsustainable and costly masking has been. We sacrifice a lot of our well-being and individuality in order to seem "normal." In the next chapter, I'll review the research showing how damaging that is, and share the stories of a few Autistic adults who've begun to question whether all the effort they've been putting into compensation and camouflage has really been worth it.

CHAPTER 4

The Cost of Masking

"I'm pretty sure my dad was Autistic," Thomas tells me. "I think his drug use was a way to blunt the world's edges."

Thomas is a programmer and he was diagnosed as Autistic a few years ago. For much of his life before that, he relied on alcohol just as his father had relied on drugs. Getting drunk was the only way he could move through the world with any degree of comfort.

"When I was in my teens, I found that having a couple drinks in me allowed me to perceive myself differently. I had more confidence and felt more social. But more importantly it dulled the razor-sharp edges of reality enough where I could be in a crowded loud area. Because I really couldn't bring myself to do that without alcohol."

To neurotypical people, Thomas often seems like a "high-functioning" person. But there has always been immense turmoil simmering beneath the surface. In college he nearly attained a 4.0 GPA—then dropped out very suddenly, because he couldn't handle the social aspects of school. A few years later, he had a good job and could maintain a sixty-hour workweek, but was sneaking drinks and coming to work hungover. He had a partner, but they barely spoke to one another. His home life was a mess. Through it all, he remained convinced that alcohol was the only thing keeping him sane. He couldn't fall asleep without it, desperately needed it to prop up his otherwise unsustainable life masquerading as a neurotypical person. Soon that life would all begin to crumble, and he'd be forced to finally confront why he (and his father) had always fallen back on substances in order to make life bearable.

Research shows that Autistics who mask tend to suffer from intense social anxiety,[1] and some of us learn to self-medicate that anxiety with drugs or alcohol. We may also reach for substances to help blunt our sensory issues or help us pretend to be more confident. Alcohol, weed, and other depressants are also an appealing and socially acceptable way of unwinding after a stressful day of constantly gaming out how every move we make will be received by other people.

Masked Autistic people fall back on a variety of flawed strategies in order to relax, mute our most disruptive behaviors, or conform with neurotypical standards. Some use compulsive exercise or calorie restriction to make their jittery, unruly Autistic bodies settle down or shrink into a more convenient shape. Some self-harm in order to regulate their anxiety or sensory overwhelm. Others become so lonesome they seek out approval from high-control groups and cults, or find themselves trapped in abusive domestic relationships they are unable to escape. Even many mental health professionals are unaware that these disorders and self-destructive behaviors are highly comorbid with Autism. The stereotype that Autistic people are withdrawn "losers" who just sit at home on the computer all day runs very deep, and it prevents many of us from recognizing ourselves and understanding the roots of our struggles. It's hard for many masked Autistic people to recognize that being a hard-drinking party animal who routinely gets swept away in abusive relationships can be a sign they are struggling with an unrecognized disability. When we compensate in those ways, we often believe it's because we're just toxic, weak-willed people.

Below is a table listing some of the problematic coping strategies that research shows masked Autistics fall back on, and a few bullet points explaining why we tend to reach for them.

Propping Up the Mask: Problematic Coping Strategies and Why Masked Autistics Use Them
Problem Drinking or Substance Use
• Dulls sensory sensitivities
• Provides "liquid courage" for intimidating social situations
• Relaxes inhibitions and filters
• Provides energy to get through an overly demanding world
• Stimulates the senses
• Entertains an anxious or preoccupied mind
• Silences the inner critic
Eating-Disordered Behavior
• Grounds life in daily goals and rituals
• Provides physical stimulation via hunger, exercise, purging, etc.
• Distracts from social struggles by focusing on the body
• Defines "goodness" and "worthiness" in terms of behavior or appearance
• Gives the Autistic person a sense of self-control or discipline
• Explains away feelings of gender dysphoria or physical dissociation
Detachment and Dissociation
• Prevents rejection by disengaging first
• Blunts painful emotions such as grief, sorrow, and regret
• Allows the Autistic person to focus only on what they're naturally "good" at
• Removes the pressure to learn challenging emotional or social skills
• Silences needs and emotions others find bothersome
• Preserves limited energy

Adherence to Rigid Rules and Belief Systems

- Makes a confusing reality feel more understandable and concrete
- Translates vague social norms into specific expectations
- Creates an in-group to which the Autistic person can belong
- Provides daily structure and soothing rituals
- Soothes self-doubt and fears about being a "bad person"
- Promises salvation from the present, unjust world

"Fawning" and Compulsive People-Pleasing

- Earns the Autistic person praise
- Offers a false promise of acceptance
- Simplifies complicated relationship dynamics
- Flattens social interactions into one easy rule: always say "yes"
- Validates the Autistic person's belief they should ignore their feelings and needs
- Minimizes conflict and reduces anger

As you look over this list of behaviors, bear in mind that the line between "good" coping and "bad" coping is often blurry, and there's no shame in having used imperfect strategies in order to survive. A method that may have worked pretty harmlessly for a while, like drinking a beer before going out with friends, may sometimes morph into something more compulsive, like sneaking drinks at work. Or drinking might only become a problem during times of high stress. Excessive exercise can be both a useful way to calm yourself down when you're on the verge of a meltdown, and a compulsive habit that is damaging your joints. These things aren't binary. Sometimes we are forced by circumstance to ignore our physical and mental health because maintaining our job or housing situation is the most pressing thing. When we lack a clear understanding of our disability, and no one around us recognizes us as disabled, we make do the best we can.

In this chapter, we'll get to meet a variety of masked Autistic people who have used elaborate, at times flawed strategies to maintain their masks. They've overexercised or drugged their way into social acceptance; some of them have spent years detached from other people, or sought out belonging in reactionary groups. These individuals have come to recognize that in addition to protecting them from social rejection, masking has gotten in the way of them leading authentic, happy lives. They've also begun to reexamine their coping mechanisms, aiming to identify the unmet needs they can satisfy with more appropriate disability accommodations, rather than self-destructiveness and denial.

Problem Drinking and Substance Use

As he grew older and he became even more reliant upon alcohol in order to "stay sane," Thomas's life began unspooling. He had grown resentful of his partner, and they were looking into breaking up. Around this same time, Thomas quit his job, and attempted suicide. Then he moved across the country for another job, but quit it pretty shortly thereafter. He kept fantasizing about death, seeing it as the only way out of an existence that had become utterly unmanageable. The therapists Thomas saw during this period diagnosed him with Bipolar Disorder and Borderline Personality Disorder, because his relationships were unstable and his emotions sometimes became explosive, in addition to him experiencing long periods of depression. He kept trying to get sober but couldn't make it work.

"Literally, it took me six months to get my first thirty-day coin [in Alcoholics Anonymous]," he says. "And even then, I was still very unhappy. During that crazy summer of repeated relapse and plotting of my own death, my ex put me in contact with a new therapist."

Thomas's ex-partner was a social worker and had recently attended a panel about Autism Spectrum Disorder while at a conference. He was struck by how much one panelist's description of Autism mirrored his experiences being with Thomas. The panelist turned out to be a therapist, and Thomas's ex put the two in touch. With the help of a therapist who actually understood the comorbidity between Autism and alcoholism, Thomas was finally able to make progress in dealing with his addiction.

"I came to figure out I have had massive social anxiety and sensory issues all my life, and I was using alcohol to numb them," Thomas explains.

One of the most common and subtly debilitating experiences Autistics have is sensory overwhelm. I've already described how the bottom-up nature of Autistic sensory processing leads to us being overstimulated and easily distracted by things like ambient noise and visual clutter. There is an additional neurological feature of Autism that contributes to our sensory issues and meltdowns in a significant way— our difficulty adjusting to a stimulus over time.

Neurotypical brains engage in *sensory adaptation* and *habituation*: the longer they are in the presence of a sound, smell, texture, or visual cue, the more their brain learns to ignore it, and allow it to fade into the background. Their neurons become less likely to be activated by a cue the longer they are around it. The exact opposite is true for Autistic people: the longer we are around a stimulus, the more it bothers us.[2] As I've already mentioned, our neurons are also "hyperexcitable," meaning our senses get set off more easily by small input that neurotypicals don't even notice, such as a hair falling into our face or a pile of mail being left on our desk.[3] We're better at noticing small details and changes in our environment,[4] which can be a real advantage for meticulous work (like programming, Thomas's profession), but we are also more prone to being startled or distracted.[5]

When an Autistic person is flooded with upsetting sensory information for too long, they enter a state of *sensory overload*. Sensory overload can look like a temper tantrum or a crying fit, it can take the form of a shutdown or meltdown, or it can present as the Autistic person becoming confused and responding to questions in routinized or nonsensical ways. Sensory overload makes it hard to complete complex tasks, think through things rationally, or manage emotions. When we're overloaded, we become irritable, or filled with despair; we might even start self-harming to get an endorphin rush or ground ourselves.

Our bodies are visibly tense with anxiety, and we're difficult to engage with during these times. What non-Autistic folks often don't realize is that Autistic people experience intense sensory input as if it were physical pain.[6]

Unfortunately, when an Autistic person complains about the sensory pain they're in, people think they're being overly dramatic, needy, or even downright "crazy." I can't fully convey how frustrating it is to be in deep distress over a persistent noise my boyfriend can't even hear. When I find myself stomping around the house anxiously, pounding on the floor with a broom to get my neighbor to turn down her music, I feel like I'm being "crazy." My partner knows I'm not making this stuff up, and he tries his best to be accommodating and patient. But for most of my life, people were unsympathetic to my sensory complaints. They acted as if I chose to be distracted and furious every day.

In response to sensory overload I've yelled, and sobbed, and needed to be held; I've tried punching pillows, hitting myself on the arms and legs with a hairbrush, running away from people, and hitting myself in the head. Very few of these reactions are socially acceptable, so I've mostly resorted to them in private. In recent years, I've learned how to prevent these meltdowns before they occur, by giving myself lots of quiet time alone, and extricating myself from stressful situations before they make me bubble up with anxiety. The second I feel myself suppressing frustration that I feel I don't deserve to voice, I know I need to get out of the area. However, once a true meltdown hits there's very little I can do—I need to either escape the situation, or find an outlet for all my energy. Drinking is really the only release valve neurotypical people can respect—as long as you present it as a fun habit, rather than a compulsion.

Many Autistic adults report problematic drinking habits, or substance use disorders.[7] Dulling our sensory sensitivities is one of the key reasons for this link.[8] Another reason is that substances assist us with social regulation. When you're used to carefully monitoring and modulating your actions all the time, a stiff drink can help you let your guard down, and momentarily relax.[9] Social norms are loosened when people are drinking. Drunk allistic people talk for too long and interrupt one another, too! If you say something weird at a party, drunk people might forget it even happened. The ease of being around other drunk people can itself be kind of intoxicating. Unfortunately, relying on substances in order to feel at ease or connected can rapidly become self-destructive.

The 2020 Netflix series *The Queen's Gambit* depicts the life of Beth Harmon, a fictional chess prodigy living in the mid-twentieth century. Beth is heavily coded as Autistic.[10] She's blunt and analytical, with little time for other people's emotions. She confronts her opponents with a cool, almost reptilian stare, and rattles off chess facts and move sets in an obsessive, flat monotone many Autistic viewers instantly found recognizable. She's also addicted to sedative pills, and drinks heavily. Unlike most Autistic characters on TV, Beth isn't just a hyper-competent nerd; she's a wild, free spirit who compulsively uses drugs, shoplifting, and sex to keep herself stimulated. Her self-destructive habits are also part of her mask: she disarms her chauvinistic male competitors and superficial classmates by seeming cool and wild.

I've never related to an Autistic character quite as much as Beth. Like her (and like Thomas) I spent my teen and early adult years racking up achievements while absolutely wrecking my personal life. In high school I'd black out drunk during the day sometimes, slipping vodka into my Gatorade in the high school parking lot to win the approval of my friends. I skipped class, forged early dismissal paperwork to get out of orchestra, and shoplifted frequently. At one point I was nearly expelled, but I was spared when a sympathetic school administrator "lost" my expulsion paperwork with a wink.

I didn't get in much trouble for my bad behavior because I was earning A's and was a nationally ranked debate team competitor. The same insouciant, smart-but-self-destructive energy carried me through my early twenties. In early adulthood I got into a lot of messy, destructive relationships and self-harmed with nicotine, anorexia, and random hookups. It was all part of the jaded, "mature" mask I'd started wearing all the way back in middle school. I thought if I was excelling on paper, and living a cool, glamorous life, there was no way anyone could ever say I was "childish" or "pathetic." No one could accuse me of being too sensitive if I hid my sensory issues by pouring Amaretto into my coffee and drinking during developmental psych. I never had the alcohol tolerance to become an addict (I threw up far too easily for that), but if that hadn't been the case, I might have easily ended up on the same path as Thomas.

Eventually, Beth Harmon's drinking turns from glamorous to grim. She uses some of her closest male friends for sex and then dismisses them; she alienates her entire support network, botches a few crucial chess matches because she's hungover, and resigns herself to padding drunkenly throughout her filthy home, overlining her eyes with kohl while taking pulls from a wine bottle. The partying and self-destruction that was once her social crutch slips out from under her, just as it did for Thomas and myself. Unlike us, though, Beth's fictional downward spiral doesn't lead to seeking out therapy or arriving at an Autism diagnosis. She's a beautiful, accomplished, unhappy woman living in the 1950s. No one knows how to name her troubles yet.

Understanding the physical, sensory, emotional, or psychological needs that you've been trying to meet with your substance use may help you identify other, more beneficial coping strategies. A survey of more than five hundred Autistic adults published in the journal *Autism in Adulthood* found that the most commonly reported reasons for binge drinking were social reasons, and to boost positive feelings.[11] Alcoholism and substance use can mask Autism super effectively, because most people still believe Autistics are buttoned-up geeks who prefer to stay home. If you've been unaware of your disability for a long time, or been in denial about it, you may have used getting high or drunk to cover up your suffering, or to give you the energy to socialize. You may believe, for example, that you can't be interesting or fun without the aid of substances. If you have trauma related to abuse you've endured as a masked Autistic person (or from other sources), you might use substances to self-medicate post-traumatic stress.

When a substance use disorder co-occurs alongside other mental health conditions, such as post-traumatic stress or depression, research shows most patients prefer and benefit from an integrated treatment approach that addresses the multiple, interlocking issues at the same time.[12] Autism isn't a disorder that needs to be treated, but most Autistic people do have mental health struggles related to living in an unaccepting neurotypical world. For Autistic people who do have substance addictions, exploring an integrated treatment program is likely to be a good fit.

If you suspect you have an unhealthy relationship to drugs or alcohol, it will be important to identify a treatment method that suits your neurotype, or find a mental health provider who has experience with Autistics. Since a growing body of research suggests cognitive behavioral therapy (CBT) approaches don't work as well for Autistics as they do for neurotypicals,[13] CBT-based addiction treatment might not be a good fit—at least not without modifications. One exploratory clinical study published in 2019 did find that when mental health providers were taught about how to communicate effectively with Autistic patients (a skill set most providers lack), the cognitive behavioral therapy they offered did help Autistic adults with their substance use disorders.[14]

Unfortunately, most care providers are not well informed about how Autistic people think and communicate, and there is very little published research into which addiction treatment programs consistently work best for adult Autistics. Many of the effective treatment plans that do assist Autistic adults involve making sure our health care, housing, and other material needs are also being met, in addition to ensuring we are plugged into a network of supportive people. Often the fears that CBT therapists train their patients to view as irrational (*if I say the wrong thing, I'll lose my job and wind up on the street!*) are completely rational for Autistics, and rooted in genuine experience.

In Thomas's case, cutting back on alcohol laid bare the sensory sensitivities and anxiety that lingered underneath. It also rapidly became clear that he couldn't maintain a high-stress, high-stimulation job that would be more likely to provoke him to drink. Today he manages his sensory issues using noise-canceling headphones, and he forces himself to take regular breaks away from busy, noisy settings. He's working from home, and learning to recognize when he's getting overloaded by anxiety or noise. There's less need for him to camouflage his Autistic traits now, and thus less desire to drink. He's now been completely sober for several years.

For many Autistic people, taming a fraught relationship with substances may necessitate getting comfortable with being more visibly Autistic, which can be a very slow process. In their essay "Alcohol: An Autistic Masking Tool?"[15] Jesse Meadows describes their relationship to unmasking and sobriety this way:

"I made friends by drinking. Alcohol gave me dating and adventures and sex. Without it, all of these things are much harder, some of them impossible. I don't leave the house very much anymore. In a lot of ways, I became a more autistic person when I got sober."

The flip side of this can sometimes be true. In order to get sober, sometimes you have to be willing to be more Autistic.

Eating-Disordered Behavior

Dorian Bridges is a horror writer and YouTuber whose channel, Of Herbs and Altars, features discussions about early 2000s alternative fashion and culture, eating disorder and drug addiction recovery, and issues in the Autism and Asperger's communities. In the early 2000s, Dorian was an undiagnosed Aspie[16] teenager who was struggling socially and in school. In one especially poignant video, Dorian describes how growing up without a diagnosis fundamentally changed the course of their life.[17]

"I knew innately from a very young age I find life harder than other people," they say, "but there was never any reason. It was always just *you are lazy; you are being lazy.*"

Dorian says they had many clear Asperger's Syndrome traits. They inhaled books and sat off alone in the corner at family gatherings. They spoke "like a thesaurus" and did well on IQ tests, but found daily classwork hard to keep up with. But like so many other masked Autistics, they were seen as a "girl," and were assumed to be gifted and a little weird, rather than disabled.

"My parents were told, there's nothing wrong with your kid. . . . Your child is going to go far! Your child has nothing that's going to ever get in their way."

Many masked Autistics are sent to gifted education as children, instead of being referred to disability services.[18] Our apparent high intelligence puts us in a double bind: we are expected to accomplish great things to justify our oddness, and because we possess an enviable, socially prized quality, it's assumed we need less help than other people, not more. Dorian couldn't handle the pressure of such high expectations, or the lack of compassion. So they began to self-harm. At age thirteen, they happened upon a magazine article about a girl with anorexia and felt incredibly envious. This visibly sick girl was being showered with affection and care. She wasn't expected to excel at anything but staying alive.

"What I got from this article was this girl made herself so close to death that her family were afraid they were going to lose her, and now she has all this love and support around her. And she doesn't have to achieve anything, because she nearly died," Dorian says.

Dorian held on to this article for years, rereading it until they had it nearly memorized. They began to starve themselves, hoping that if they looked like they were dying, people would finally go easy on them. They also started frequenting pro-anorexia (or "pro Ana") forums, where they befriended other eating disordered teens and traded weight loss strategies and "thinspiration" photos. Eventually they began meeting up in person and having binge-purge parties. Dorian says this community was filled with self-destructive people who were often a bad influence on one another, but also that it was the only nonjudgmental place they had access to, the only space where they could truly let their pain show.[19]

My own eating disorder had different motivations than Dorian's did, but it was no less tied to my Autism. From age fifteen until about twenty-five, I denied myself food because I wanted to look "androgynous," and I believed that meant looking thin. I overexercised because I thought it proved I was strong. The pain of an empty stomach was physically satisfying to me; the throb in my legs after two hours of playing Dance Dance Revolution on calorie counter mode made me feel like I'd finally reined in an out-of-control body. Unlike Dorian, I didn't want people to know I was having a hard time. Ever. I wanted to be an otherworldly creature, free from silly human needs. I pulled a lot of all-nighters, thinking that staying up late exercising was a better use of my time than rest. When a friend on the debate team told me that I seemed like a "robot" because I never seemed to sleep, eat, or like people, I felt an immense sense of triumph. My mask was solid steel.

Autism and eating disorders are highly correlated, especially among women,[20] trans people,[21] and maskers diagnosed late in life. A lot of factors account for this. Some maskers believe that being conventionally pretty and thin will help them blend in. Others neglect their physical needs because they've mentally detached from their bodies. Purging can be used to self-harm, or to regulate a disrupted sensory system. It floods the body with endorphins, which can be calming and addictive. In one video, Dorian describes how a friend from the pro-Ana forums used to pace her hallway all night, every night, in a desperate bid to burn calories. This sounds a lot like a repetitive self-stimulatory behavior,[22] in addition to a purge. My compulsive DDR playing was absolutely a sneaky way to self-stimulate, as well as an attempt to lose weight.

Some masked Autistics are drawn to the structure and sense of control that an eating disorder can provide. We often seek out clear "rules" for good behavior, which we then adhere to rigidly, hoping they will keep us socially safe and finally render us worthy.[23] When I was an undiagnosed Autistic teen, my brain was constantly buzzing with vague anxiety. Calories, checking my body in the mirror, and weighing myself were concrete things I could focus on instead of inchoate fear. The fatphobic society I was living in had taught me that being thin was superior to being fat, and I attempted to follow that rule with fervor. Running myself ragged with exercise meant I'd eventually be able to fall asleep. The online eating disorder community gave me routines to craft my day around.

It was all quasi-religious. I didn't believe in God, but I could worship at the altar of Dance Dance Revolution every night, sweating and gulping down ice water while my brain floated above me in a nutrient-deprived haze. Exercise bulimia also gave me a way of connecting with the girls around me. Wanting to be thin was one of the few gender-conforming traits I had.

Clinical research has found that somewhere between 20 and 37 percent of diagnosed anorexia nervosa sufferers are Autistic.[24] Since Autism is underdiagnosed in the populations who are most likely to be diagnosed with eating disorders (women, trans people, and gay men), the actual rate of co-occurrence might be much higher. In conventional eating disorder treatment, Autistic patients have worse outcomes: they require longer hospital stays, are less likely to reduce their eating disordered behaviors, and experience more depression and social isolation in recovery groups.[25] However, eating disorder clinics and inpatient programs have started taking steps to accommodate their Autistic patients, with some promising results. Here's how Tchanturia and colleagues (2020)[26] described their newly Autism-friendly eating disorder ward:

> We invested in materials necessary to create a more [Autism-] friendly ward environment, including redecorating the ward to create a neutral colour scheme, developing a "sensory box" for patients with items such as weighted blankets and sensory toys, and we began hosting wellbeing groups for autistic patients and for those without autistic traits together with members of the multi-disciplinary team to support sensory difficulties and enhance social communication (e.g., introducing communication passports and other strategies).

Tchanturia and colleagues found that Autistic patients on this accessible ward had significantly shorter stays, and follow-up research suggests Autism-friendly eating disorder treatment does result in better outcomes.[27] Since eating-disordered behavior is at least partially socially motivated for many Autistic people, it may also be beneficial to seek belonging and social structure in new ways that feel less performative and most authentic. In their videos, Dorian says that their health was at its worst when they tried to seem like a normal, perky, preppily dressed woman.[28] Presenting as a transmasculine goth with loud outfits and intense makeup helps them feel far more at home in their body, and hanging out with other "weird" alternative types gives them the sense of belonging they once sought in pro-Ana groups. Now that they know they're Autistic, they're also able to be more vulnerable about when and why they're struggling, so they don't have to use a shared compulsion to bond with other people.

Detachment and Dissociation

To cope with the pressure of masking, many Autistics disappear into our own heads. I can't tell you how many times I've heard an Autistic person say they wish they could just be a floating brain in a jar, or a dark, sentient mist with no physical form. It's a common neurodivergent fantasy, because our bodies can seem so at odds with what the world wants them to be. Dissociation is also a means of controlling the social and sensory data we're taking in, ignoring inputs that have become too intense. For example, when there are too many people around, my friend Angel says he goes away into "Angel World" in his head, and everyone around him becomes blurry. He has some relatives that he has never seen the faces of, because he's only ever met them at big family gatherings where everyone blends into a sea of muddy, vague shapes. When he's dissociating, he can still go through the motions of eating, bathing, and walking around, but mentally he's not really there.

The only thing that brings Angel back is having plenty of time to rest and disengage. For other Autistic people that I know, including myself, having to mask and socialize for an extended period increases the odds we'll begin to dissociate or shut down. People don't literally become "blurry" for me when I'm overwhelmed, but I do stop gazing at people's faces and often fail to recognize people I know or hear their voices unless they get in my face and wave their hands. Putting less cognitive effort into masking can help, as can escaping the overloading situation that was provoking me to detach in the first place.

In the short term, mentally detaching works great. It frees up a lot of energy and attention, so we can focus on activities we're good at, or think only about the ideas that capture our interest. But in the long term, retreating inward alienates us from our needs even more. Some research suggests that Autistic people have a diminished *sense of agency*; in other words, we feel less in control of ourselves and our bodies than non-Autistic people do.[29] A lifetime of being corrected for incompetence and childishness affects our self-concept, and makes it hard for us to develop basic skills of self-advocacy or assertiveness.

In one study of Autistic agency, Autistic and non-Autistic people were both asked to manipulate a cursor on a screen as part of a computer game.[30] Random time lags and movement glitches were added to the game, so that players didn't always have full control over what the mouse was doing. Players were told to attempt to win the game, and were also asked to report when they thought they had control of the mouse and when they didn't. Neurotypical people were pretty accurate in judging when they had control of the mouse. They could tell when a mouse movement was caused by a lag or glitch rather than their own hands. Autistic players instead struggled to tell the difference. They tended to believe they were more in control of the game when they were winning, and that they were not in control when they were losing, even when the two were unrelated. In particular, this result appeared to be driven by Autistic people trusting internal cues less: they didn't trust their own feelings of whether they were in control or not, so much as external benchmarks of success in the game.

This may be a bit of a contrived example from a laboratory setting, but it points to a tendency many of us have to view ourselves as powerless, and fundamentally detached from our bodies and the broader world. We rely on external signs of success (winning a game, getting praised by another person) to guide us, rather than trusting our perceptions and power of discernment.

Unfortunately, when we disengage from our bodies, we miss out on a lot of valuable self-protective physical signals. Research shows that most Autistic people have a reduced sense of the body's warning signals, or *interoception*.[31] Most of us tend to feel like our bodies are not really our own, and struggle to draw connections between the external world and how we feel inside.[32] For example, a neurotypical person might notice that their coworkers are leaving for lunch, and then check in with their own body and recognize they're hungry, too. An Autistic person might instead be lost in their own head, and fail to draw a connection between their coworkers departing and the need to check for hunger within themselves. It's unclear how much this is caused by a neurological feature of Autism, and how much it's a by-product of masking and social pressure. After all, masked Autistics are socially conditioned to silence the physical needs we do notice. If I have to suppress my desire to pace around the room and sing songs to myself because doing so makes me look like a "freak," how am I supposed to know that listening to hunger or tiredness is fine?

Though Autistic people tend to be hypersensitive to sensory input, most are relatively numb to physical pain.[33] It may sound paradoxical, but it makes sense when you recall the research showing that Autistic brains are generally detail oriented and hyperexcitable. When my shirt gets untucked, I cannot stand the little burst of cool air I feel hitting my belly. It's a persistent, small stimulus that is too annoying to ignore. Yet I've walked for miles with bleeding fissures on my heels and barely felt a thing. Masking also tends to involve swallowing your anguish in order to keep the neurotypicals around you happy. Complaining about discomfort that no one else is experiencing can make you seem "crazy" or "demanding." Many of us become quite adept at ignoring pain, just as we neglect our own hunger or thirst.

Unfortunately, this isn't just true of physical pain. It extends to emotional pain, too. Research by psychologist Geoff Bird indicates that about half of all Autistics suffer from *alexithymia*,[34] or the inability to recognize and name emotions.[35] For those of us with alexithymia, we may know in a vague way that we're distressed, but might not be able to name a specific feeling like jealousy or resentment. We also struggle to figure out *why* we're feeling emotions. This trait is yet another reason that neurotypicals stereotype us as unfeeling and detached.

Alexithymia may arise, in part, because Autistics aren't given the tools to understand how emotions feel in our bodies, and because we are taught to prioritize others' feelings above our own. Growing up, we're told how neurotypical emotions look and feel. We're encouraged to track other people for signs of discomfort or disapproval, so we can change our actions and become more pleasant or compliant. Our own facial expressions, nonverbal signals, and perceptions of our bodies and surroundings are different, and neurotypicals frequently ignore them. So when we're upset or uncomfortable, we often fail to recognize it until we're nearly on the verge of a complete meltdown. As we begin to unmask, we stop monitoring the reactions of other people so closely and with so much hypervigilance; this allows us to check in with our bodies more. Our reflexive self-censorship may begin to reduce, allowing us to notice our discomfort and honor it. However, many Autistic people (myself included) still need time alone to reflect on how we're feeling, because the social information given off by other people is so distracting. Today I'm sometimes able to notice in the heat of the moment that I'm uncomfortable with the topic of conversation, for instance, or the way someone is pushing me to do something I don't wish to do, and I can tell them to stop; other days I simply feel panicky and frantic, and can't figure out what's wrong until hours or days later.

Because Autistic people often struggle to look after our bodies or to recognize and advocate for our needs, work, school, and other social settings can be incredibly painful for us to navigate. An oft-cited statistic claims that 85 percent of Autistic adults are unemployed,[36] though higher-quality cross-sectional research puts the number closer to 40 percent.[37] Some research suggests that Autistics who disclose their disability at work often regret having done so, because they don't get many useful accommodations and may be underestimated or othered.[38] For these and many other reasons, Autistic people often have no choice but to work from home, and as a population we're digitally self-employed at high rates.[39] Work-from-home and consulting positions frequently undercompensate and overwork us, but they offer a level of flexibility and privacy that more stable jobs lack.

In addition to compensating by working from home or pursuing digital work, a significant percentage of Autism maskers disengage from reality via internet and gaming.[40] Digital work and gaming are incredibly appealing to Autistic people's brains. Online and in games, cause and effect are clearer than in "real" life.[41] It's easy to ignore subtext or nonverbal cues and focus only on shared tasks and clear, measurable outcomes. In digital communication, Autistic people get the time we need to carefully process a message, google any terms that are unfamiliar, and carefully reflect on how we might want to respond.

There's nothing innately wrong with using the internet to help meet your need for social contact and structure. Disabled people have found community and shared resources on the internet for decades. However, excessive and compulsive internet use and gaming can prove damaging to Autistic people and inhibit our social connections and development.[42] When we spend too much time online, it can limit how much practice we get interacting and communicating out in the world, contribute to feelings of loneliness and depression, and further the detachment so many of us feel from our bodies. Hiding our struggles away from the world is not a productive means of gaining acceptance, and there's a difference between using the internet as a way to develop a sense of fluency and competence, and retreating into it because we feel we have no other choice.

Thomas tells me that as he's come to understand his own Autism and work on unmasking, he's gotten better at noticing how he feels and figuring out how to care for himself. For many years, particularly before his diagnosis, he would just push his emotions and desires away.

"This week I noticed my energy replenishment was at a standstill," he says. "I couldn't focus on data work, which is normally one of my passions. I journaled about it a bit and realized my girlfriend has been home more than usual lately. I love her, but being around her all day was overstimulating me. The next day the weather was beautiful, and all I did was sit outside and read. It felt wonderful, there wasn't all this stimuli hyper-activating me."

Thomas still carries the baggage of being fully masked and undiagnosed, and thinking he was simply a difficult or angry person. Over the years, though, he's learned to push past this cultural programming and actually construct a life that's authentic to him. Building that kind of self-knowledge and acceptance has been vital to his happiness and his sobriety.

"I enjoy hanging out in train yards, and learning ridiculous amounts of useless knowledge, and I'd rather work on jigsaw puzzles than watch TV. Because my life is aligned with who I am now, I have much less need to drink. Recovery is predicated on aligning your life with your values, and you aren't going to be able to align anything until you know who you are."

This is just as true of Autistics who reflexively detach from reality because they're so accustomed to camouflaging their every feeling and need. You cannot craft a comfortable or worthwhile life if you don't know who you really are, or if your self-image is shaped entirely by rules imposed on you by other people. Thankfully, it is possible to step away from defining yourself by the approval of other people, and by your adherence to society's rules. In later chapters, we'll explore how that process can look, and hear from several people who have walked away from a life defined by seeking approval and masking.

Adherence to Rigid Rules and Belief Systems

Masked Autistics sometimes find structure and belonging in "high control" groups, such as radicalized political organizations, religious communities with very restrictive beliefs, and cults. High control groups famously prey on people who are lonely and desperately seek a sense of purpose. Their repetitive rituals, seemingly close-knit social bonds, and ironclad rules about who is "good" and who is "bad" appeal to isolated people who yearn for connection and structure.

I've spoken to a wide array of masked Autistic adults, and over a dozen have shared stories with me of belonging to fringe religious communities, conspiracy theory groups, multilevel marketing schemes, and other high control organizations. There isn't any empirical research I can find that documents just how prevalent this is for our population. However, recent research by Griffiths and colleagues (2019) does describe Autistic adults as having an elevated vulnerability to financial exploitation, domestic violence, relational abuse, and emotional manipulation.[43] These are the precise qualities that define cults—and they're part of what makes such spaces alluring to us.

We're susceptible to manipulation for tons of reasons. Autistic adults tend to be in socioeconomically precarious positions, which can make it hard for us to escape people who mistreat us. When you're unemployed or underemployed, you're going to be more willing to move in with a romantic partner, or become dependent on an extremist religious group quickly, as a matter of necessity. Our yearning to be accepted and tendency to downplay our own feelings also leaves us prone to mistreatment. ABA therapy and social masking instruct us to be compliant and conformist. Orthodoxy and rules about how we're supposed to act can feel grounding and "rational."

Growing up Autistic in the rural western United States, Andrew found himself lured into a controlling religious community. He says members of the church quickly identified him as a potential mark.

"I was living alone, clearly one of the only nonwhite people in a very white small town, depressed, anxious all the time, drinking coffee all day at the diner, and they started talking to me, saying they just wanted to get to know me."

He was getting "love bombed," a common technique in cults where new members are showered with excessive affection and special attention.[44] Love bombing trains a person to let their guard down and relax their boundaries around the new group. For Autistic people who have been on the fringes of society all our lives, it can be exhilarating to suddenly, inexplicably be adored.

Once Andrew decided to join the church, things began to change. Members kept him up on the phone late at night, asking intense questions about his family, from whom he was estranged. One of the church's leaders interrogated him about his bisexuality, and how he could reconcile it with their faith's teachings. Andrew stopped going on dates with men, because that stopped all the questions. Expectations continued to ramp up: volunteering to help church members with babysitting once a week ballooned into a nightly commitment.

"I still blame myself for falling for these tactics, because it's not as though they had a gun to my head," he says. But, he explains, it was controlling behavior, nonetheless. "They're hugging you and joking with you one day, they won't even look at you the next, and it shapes how you think and act over time."

Controlling and dogmatic groups promise a life filled with meaning, and a new family who will never leave you. In reality, they entrap people in a complex web of sometimes incompatible expectations, with rejection forever looming. Since many of these organizations rely on their members' devotion, free labor, and donations in order to function, they have a vested interest in making people feel like their efforts are never enough.

Andrew says it took him a couple of years to figure out he was being played. The stress of being in the church began to give him panic attacks, but members saw it as a betrayal of their "family" for him to seek group therapy. That made him begin to question their beliefs. It's also when he sorted out that he was Autistic.

Some of the Autistic people I spoke to had less dramatic

experiences that were still damaging. Things like becoming unhealthily attached to graduate student advisors, or devoting years to nonprofits or activist groups whose goals they truly believed in, but which had really unhealthy boundaries or a toxic, workaholic culture. Other Autistic people I interviewed became adherents to rigid belief systems of their own making, without the influence of anyone else. They wanted to make their own worlds predictable, easy to make sense of, small. It began as a way to take charge of their lives, until the number of self-imposed rules they followed spiraled out of control.

Some Autistic people end up being radicalized by far-right online communities, which tailor themselves to appeal to lonely, frustrated men.[45] Groups like QAnon, the Proud Boys, and Men Going Their Own Way provide a sense of belonging to people who have persistently been alienated. They offer friendship and a place where it is safe to ask taboo questions and say offensive things without fear of social consequences. These communities also prey on the Autistic tendency to fixate on a narrow array of topics. They bombard members with propaganda, teach them obscure language that no one outside of the group will understand, and desensitize them to bigotry using jokes and memes. Once deeply embedded within these subcultures, it's very difficult for an Autistic person to claw their way out; their extreme beliefs and hyperspecific way of communicating make it harder than ever to get a job or make friends.

Neurodiverse women and gender nonconforming people are similarly preyed upon by "gender critical," transphobic communities, which use many of the same thought-controlling tactics. A former member of one of these groups, the writer Ky Schevers, says they were basically subjected to anti-trans conversion therapy by fellow group members.[46] They were taught to censor their own feelings of gender dysphoria, and to view the desire to transition as a betrayal of the group and of womanhood in general. I've read up on these groups extensively and followed a lot of anonymous "gender critical" accounts for years, and it's shocking to me how many of its members are Autistic. This fact has even become a part of their ideology: they claim to be protecting Autistic women from being lured into the "trans cult." In actuality, they're the culty ones, seeking out vulnerable, gender-dysphoric people and working to isolate them from the broader trans community.

In the list below I've listed a few attributes common to high-control groups, which were originally observed by psychiatrist Robert Lifton in his classic text, *Thought Reform and the Psychology of Totalism*.[47] Lifton's research focused on manipulation techniques pushed on political prisoners and prisoners of war, but subsequent work has found similar processes being invoked by American extremist groups,[48] as well as groups that might not qualify fully as cults but still exert a strong pull on their members, such as many evangelical faith communities.[49] Abusive, manipulative dynamics appear on a smaller scale in multilevel marketing schemes,[50] exploitative workplaces, and even communities that pride themselves on being progressive bastions of free thought, such as academia.[51] It's important for Autistic people to be aware of the warning signs of psychological manipulation, because we are at an elevated risk of being targeted by organizations (and even informal social groups) that employ such methods.

Warning Signs of a High-Control Group

1. The group promotes an antagonistic view of the outside world and nongroup members: "It's us versus the world."
2. Group members constantly feel insecure about their position within the group; members may be punished for any small mistake or failure.
3. Personal boundaries are discouraged; people are expected to view the group as a "family," and sacrifice as much as they can for it.
4. Any perspective that challenges the group's orthodoxy is unspeakable; members feel shame about thinking or feeling the "wrong" things.

5. Repetitive language and group jargon are used to dismiss criticism. Group members repeat empty clichés in order to silence difficult conversations.

Most Autistic people never become radicalized by hate groups, of course, and it would be both ableist and ethically troubling to claim someone's disability excuses their adopting a racist, sexist, transphobic ideology. However, it's important for each of us to recognize how a mix of social exclusion, Autistic hyperfocus and rule-abiding, and cultlike programming can blend to taint a vulnerable person's thinking. When you have never been able to move through the world comfortably, you'll seek relief and meaning where you can get it. For a subset of Autistic people, that means falling into abusive, cultlike communities. For others, it takes the form of rationalizing or excusing abuse in private relationships. Many of us mask through compulsive people pleasing and compliance.

Fawning and Compulsive People Pleasing

The Big Bang Theory is one of the most popular sitcoms in TV history, which makes the show's character Sheldon perhaps the most famous Autistic-coded character around. He's infamously curt and socially detached, a jerk who gets away with being inconsiderate because he's such a know-it-all. Lisbeth Salander from the Girl with the Dragon Tattoo series is another classic example of the asshole Autistic genius trope. She uses her almost robotic perceptiveness and rationality to upbraid and insult people, as well as solve crimes. Rick from *Rick and Morty* is another standout example. He's actively abusive to his grandchildren, and a total slob who frequently destroys his adult daughter's home, but his entire family (and most of the show's fandom) look up to him because his brilliant, no-nonsense analytical mind invented portal technology.

As real, living people, Autistics are forever running away from the "asshole genius" trope. In a 2016 survey of college students' attitudes toward Autistics, psychologists found that people associated the neurotype with introversion, social withdrawal, and having a "difficult" personality.[52] These stereotypes of Autism existed before shows like *Big Bang Theory* and *Rick and Morty*, but those portrayals certainly reinforced biases that were already there. In the average person's mind, there is a singular image of how Autism presents in adults: a genius, almost always a man, who is blunt and direct to the point of cruelty.

To avoid embodying this trope, Autistic people fold ourselves into all kinds of accommodating shapes. We do what we can to not seem difficult, cruel, or self-absorbed. We internalize the message that talking about ourselves and our interests bores other people, that we're socially inept and bad at reading emotions, and that our sensory needs make us big babies who never stop complaining. For fear of becoming a Sherlock, we morph ourselves into Watsons: agreeable, docile, passive to a fault, always assuming that the larger personalities around us know what's best.

Masked Autistics are frequently compulsive people pleasers. We present ourselves as cheery and friendly, or nonthreatening and small. Masked Autistics are also particularly likely to engage in the trauma response that therapist Pete Walker describes as "fawning."[53] Coping with stress doesn't always come down to fight versus flight; fawning is a response designed to pacify anyone who poses a threat. And to masked Autistics, social threat is just about everywhere.

"Fawn types avoid emotional investment and potential disappointment by barely showing themselves," Walker writes, "by hiding behind their helpful personas, over-listening, over-eliciting or overdoing for the other."[54]

Walker notes that by never revealing their own needs or discomfort with other people, fawners spare themselves the risk of rejection. But they also fail to connect with people in any meaningful way. It's a lonesome state to live in. It's also deeply draining. Many masked Autistic adults struggle to balance full-time work with social lives or hobbies at all because maintaining a conciliatory mask for eight hours per day is just too labor intense to have energy for anything else.[55] The connections we do form may never feel satisfying or authentic to who we truly are, because they rely on us meeting people's needs reflexively and always telling them what we think they want to hear.

Autistic wellness coach Samuel Dylan Finch has written a lot about why Autistic people fawn, and how fawning frays our relationships. He's also a fawner himself, though it took some time to recognize this.

"I am a people-pleaser," he writes on his blog.[56] "It took me a long time to realize this, though. Because I'm opinionated! And I speak my mind!"

Finch writes that when he really wants to connect with another person, his instinct is to censor his real self and "mirror" the other person: "The more invested I was in an emotional connection, the less likely I was to criticize that person, vocalize when my boundaries were crossed, express unhappiness with their behavior, or share anything that I felt might damage that relationship."

Here are some of the signs of having a "fawning" response to stress and social threat, inspired closely by Finch's work and writing.

Fawning and People-Pleasing Reflection Tool[57]

Consider each statement and reflect on how true each one is for you.

1. It doesn't feel like anyone knows the "real" me.
2. I don't know how to say no to people.
3. I feel responsible for managing other people's feelings and reactions, even when they don't involve me.
4. I sometimes feel like I'm betraying myself by going along with things I don't agree with.
5. I closely monitor social situations to see when conflict is brewing, and try to stop it before it starts.

The impulse to fawn that Finch describes is very familiar to me. I find it easy to correct a coworker if they make a factual statement that's wrong, but when I was trapped in an abusive relationship with a person I deeply loved, contradicting him terrified me. Just the idea of telling him that he'd treated me unfairly made me want to sputter and flee the room. Years later, I still have trouble criticizing people, including those who make me feel safe and accepted. My brain knows better, but my body expects a rage outburst all the same. Autistic people are at an increased risk of domestic abuse, in part because we tend to be a bit gullible or overly trusting, and are quick to alter ourselves to placate others.[58] When you're trapped under the mask, all love feels conditional. It's hard to know which needs are acceptable to voice. It's also easy for us to feel responsible for serving as an intermediary or peacekeeper when any tension arises between other people, because for us, conflict can be very dangerous.

Some psychological research suggests that there are heavy emotional and relational costs to constantly aiming to please other people and project back at them the emotions and responses they wish to see. One common fawning tactic among Autistics is mirroring: lightly mimicking the actions and emotions of another person, trying to meet the energy they are giving off so that they view us as normal and similar to themselves. However, paying close attention to a person's actions and feelings and then mimicking it as best you can is a very cognitively draining and distracting endeavor. A study by Kulesza and colleagues (2015) found that when experimental study participants were asked to subtly mimic the behavior of a conversation partner, the mimicker actually had a harder time recognizing the emotions of the person they were mimicking.[59] Even though the (neurotypical) participants in the study were successfully imitating the emotional displays of their conversation partners, they were so focused on the performance that they stopped really thinking about what those emotional displays meant. This study has not been replicated in an Autistic or neurodiverse sample, but if mirroring other people is so mentally labor-intensive that it reduces the empathy of neurotypicals, it's likely true of Autistic people as well. In fact, these results suggest that all the attention we put toward masking our own emotions and mirroring another person's contributes to our struggles with empathy in the first place.

Since Autistic people often struggle to identify our emotions as well (particularly in the heat of a stressful social interaction), we often have a hard time recognizing when someone's actions have hurt us or made us uncomfortable. It takes time for me to reflect on how and why someone's actions might have hurt me. Autistic sex educator and writer Stevie Lang has observed that Autistic people sometimes find it challenging to negotiate sexual consent as well, because we can't always tell the difference between wanting something, and *wanting to want it* in order to make someone else happy:

"Our aversion to rejection and desire to be accepted may make it difficult to know when we are experiencing consent," he writes, "and when we are trying to conform to social expectations to be liked or to avoid rejection."[60]

Ultimately, all masking is about setting our feelings aside so we can focus on pleasing others or conforming to social norms. This is always going to be a self-destructive values system to live by, regardless of the coping mechanisms we use to prop it up. Whether we use alcohol, excessive exercise, overwork, social isolation, codependency, or some other self-destructive strategies to help us blend in, it's always going to be damaging to put social approval and "passing" as neurotypical above our actual needs.

We don't actually have to live this way. Autistic people can learn to listen to ourselves again, challenge the shame society has pushed on us, and become radically visible and outspoken about the accommodations we require and deserve. It may be challenging and daunting to detach from years of reflexive, self-protective masking, but a life free from its confines is possible for us. In the next few chapters, we'll review the research on how Autistic people can accommodate their neurotype in all facets of their lives, hear from coaches and specialists who are helping fellow Autistics learn to unmask, and meet several masked Autistic people who have begun to embrace who they are, and question the forces that taught them to hide themselves away.

CHAPTER 5

Rethinking Autism

Let's start at the beginning: the first step of the unmasking process is realizing you're Autistic. It might not feel like it's an active step toward self-acceptance or authenticity, but coming to understand yourself as disabled is a pretty dramatic reframing of your life. Almost every neurodiverse person I've spoken to for this book shared that discovering they were Autistic was a powerful aha moment, one that prompted them to rethink every narrative they'd believed about who they were. Painful labels they'd carried around inside themselves for years suddenly didn't seem as relevant: it wasn't that they were stupid, or clueless, or lazy, they were just disabled. It wasn't that their efforts had never been enough, or that they were fundamentally wrong or bad. They simply hadn't been treated with the compassion they deserved, or given the tools that would have allowed them to flourish. Naming their position in society as a disabled person helped them to externalize that which had long been internalized. It proved that none of their suffering had been their fault.

Of course, adopting an Autistic identity doesn't instantly undo the habitual camouflaging and compensation that so many of us have had to default to. Much like the hypervigilance that's common to trauma survivors with PTSD, masking is a reflex that comes out most intensely when we experience uncertainty or social threat. And recognizing oneself as a disabled person certainly doesn't make the world seem any less confusing or threatening. However, accepting ourselves as Autistic does free many of us (perhaps for the first time) to question whether it's fair that we be expected to live in such a concealed, apologetic way.

The process of unmasking is all about rethinking the beliefs and behaviors that seemed normal prior to discovering we were Autistic. It means reexamining the stereotypes about Autistics (and other disabled people) we've been exposed to via media, education, and formative experiences in our youth. It requires we question society's most deeply cherished values, and notice where there are gaps between what we've been told we *should* be, and how we'd actually like to live. Finally, unmasking demands that we look back on our past selves with a spirit of grace, gradually learning to see that the sides of ourselves that we were told were too loud, too stilted, too weird, or too much are actually completely fine, even wonderful, and absolutely deserving of love.

Reframing Autism Stereotypes

A few years ago, Trevor was out camping with his friends in the Ozarks. Everybody was getting a little drunk, whipping one another with T-shirts and goofing off. Somebody suggested the group hold an impromptu "forearm beauty" pageant. Everyone laughed and stared at Trevor. A hush settled over the group.

Trevor pretended to be bashful, then slowly strutted to the center of the crowd. He rolled up his sleeves slowly, almost seductively, and then struck a dramatic pose like something straight out of a comic book, putting his disproportionately large, muscular forearms on display for everyone to see. People oohed and aahed at the sight, and Trevor's roommate fanned himself as if he was going to faint.

"It's an in joke in the friend group," he explains. "I have really huge forearms. Like Popeye. From flapping my hands all the time."

Trevor has always regulated and expressed his emotions by flapping and fluttering his hands. Hand flapping is one of the most common Autistic stims. It's such a well-known, visible sign of Autism that training children to have "quiet hands" is one of the foremost goals of ABA therapy.[1] Though hand flapping is harmless and not disruptive, neurotypical people recognize it instantly as a sign of disability—and therefore punish it harshly. People imitate Autistic hand flapping when they want to imply a disabled person is stupid, annoying, or out of control. Donald Trump famously did a cruel imitation of hand flapping during his 2016 campaign, while criticizing a physically disabled reporter. But in recent years, despite all the social baggage, Trevor has learned to embrace his flaps.

Trevor came out as Autistic to his friends a few years ago. He's forty-five now, but has known about his disability since he was twelve. When he was diagnosed, Trevor's mom told him it had to remain a secret for the rest of his life. She believed that people would underestimate him and exclude him if they knew he "lacked" many of the skills neurotypical folks had. For decades, Trevor dutifully hid his stims and tendency to overthink things. In college, he took improv classes to help seem more outgoing. He read books on manners, and left dates early, so the guys he was seeing wouldn't notice he had a hard time speaking when he was tired.

Eventually, as the Autism acceptance movement became more visible, Trevor began questioning his mother's old advice. He poked around forums like reddit's r/AutismTranslated and read the stories of people who'd come out as neurodiverse. On the website Stimtastic, he found chewable rubber jewelry (or "chewelry") designed for stimming, and secretly ordered some for himself.

Telling his friends about his Autism ended up being kind of anticlimactic.

"They were not surprised," he said laughing. "At all. They really know me."

Before coming out, Trevor couldn't explain to people why his forearms were so beefy. It was just another odd thing about himself that he felt self-conscious about. He wasn't a muscular guy. Like many Autistics,[2] Trevor had a reduced muscle tone relative to most of the neurotypicals he knew. He walked with a hunched posture and had reedy upper arms. Big button-up shirts helped hide his uniquely Autistic body.

But once Trevor was "out," he could let people admire and joke about his buff arms. He was shocked that people actually found them attractive. He's not self-conscious about his body or his stimming anymore. All the mental energy he once placed on obscuring his disability is freed up to focus on other things. And the fear of detection that his mother imbued in him has proven to be entirely misguided.

In previous chapters, we've reflected on the common reactions neurotypical people have when they first encounter visibility-disabled traits in a child and contemplated the many negative stereotypes about Autism that cause us shame and drive us to mask. Here we'll reexamine those early experiences and stereotypically Autistic traits and consider whether they can be viewed in a more neutral or even positive light.

In the book *Raising Your Spirited Child*, author and parent educator Mary Sheedy Kurcinka encourages frustrated and exhausted caregivers to rethink negative impressions they have of their children.[3] Kurcinka wasn't specifically discussing Autistics when she coined the term *spirited child* in the early 1990s, but it's pretty clear that her own spirited son has a lot in common with Autistic kids. Much like the term *indigo child* (which has been popular with New Age parents for decades),[4] *spirited child* refers to a somewhat vague constellation of behaviors and traits that overlap a great deal with Autism and ADHD. Parents of children with Autism-spectrum traits often try to find (or invent) a softening euphemism for their child's differences. It's label avoidance, with a bit of a spiritual sheen. In Kurcinka's case, branding her son as spirited was an attempt to resist the stigmatizing attitudes that doctors and psychiatrists had about him and his future.

Professionals viewed Kurcinka's spirited son as stubborn, difficult, and strong-willed; he was prone to loud shrieking and intense reactions to stimuli, and defiant in the face of instructions he didn't want to follow. Kurcinka did some research of her own and found that all the writing available to parents about kids like her son focused on how challenging they were to raise, and the toll they had on their caregivers. The early 1990s were an era when people commonly believed that a kid's Autism ruined their family's lives. An oft-quoted (and entirely incorrect)[5] statistic from that period claimed that parents of Autistic children had a divorce rate of 80 percent.[6] Neurodivergence was a horror that visited families, and disabled children were resented for bringing it into the home. Dismayed by the poor quality of information available, Kurcinka set out to create resources that were more compassionate and looked to the behavior of spirited children with curiosity instead of condemnation.

Kurcinka asked that parents try to reframe their kids' "problem" traits as positives. Many of a kid's most disruptive behaviors were signs of their independence and will. As disability advocate Rabbi Ruti Regan writes on the blog Real Social Skills, "noncompliance is a social skill."[7] It's only "bad" if you're looking at it from the outside, from the perspective of someone who seeks to control or restrict. Though Autistic people are stereotyped as lacking empathy, it's frequently non-Autistic teachers and caregivers of Autistic children who fail to reflect on their interior experience, and the motives and feelings that make their behavior make sense. A noncompliant child may be stressful to raise, but if you want your kid to become a strong, healthy person with the power to self-advocate, it's crucial they know how to stand up for themselves and say "no."

Here are some of the old, stigmatizing labels of "spirited" children that Kurcinka set out to challenge, and the more positive alternatives she recommended:

Old Label	New Label
Stubborn	Assertive, Persistent
Wild	Energetic
Distractible	Perceptive
Picky	Selective, Discriminating
Demanding	Knows clearly what he wants
Inflexible	Traditional; does not like change
Manipulative	Knows how to get needs met, charismatic
Anxious	Cautious
Explosive	Dramatic
Nosy	Curious, Inquisitive
Loud	Enthusiastic, Zestful
Argumentative	Opinionated, Committed

You might have noticed that some of the traits listed in Kurcinka's table were also in the lists of negative Autism stereotypes earlier in this book. I developed the tables in Chapter 3 long before reading Kurcinka's book, based on feedback from a large pool of Autistic adults. It turns out many Autistic adults' least liked personal qualities are the exact same traits caregivers were complaining about in their children thirty years ago, at the time Kurcinka was writing. These tables might have been developed independently of one another, but they are clearly in conversation. When many of us were growing up, adults saw us as loud, stubborn, uncaring, overly reactive, and burdensome. We've grown up believing we truly are hard to be around, and to love.

When a person from a highly stigmatized group absorbs and believes some of the negative stereotypes applied to their group, they're suffering from what researchers call *self-stigma*. Self-stigma is heavy;

people high in it experience reduced self-esteem and see themselves as less capable than other people, and they're often afraid to seek help.[8] Psychologists have studied how to reduce self-stigma in people with mental disorders like depression, anxiety, and schizophrenia for decades; however, there is essentially no research into how to reduce self-stigma in Autistics. What little data does exist is on helping the abled family members of Autistic children to feel less shame about being *related to* someone disabled.[9]

Since there's a dearth of research examining self-stigma reduction in Autistics, we have to look to the data on treating internalized stereotypes in other populations. A review by Corrigan, Kosyluk, and Rush (2013) concluded that for a variety of people with mental illnesses, coming out proudly about one's disability and presenting it as a valuable part of one's identity helped reduce self-stigma's impact.[10] A more recent experimental study by Martinez-Hidalgo and colleagues (2018) paired people with stigmatized mental illnesses with neurotypical conversation partners for a series of workshops, where they discussed mental health as well as other topics like creativity.[11] At the end of the intervention, participants with mental illness reported less shame about their conditions, and their neurotypical partners' biases against people with mental illness went down a bit, too. This study did include some Autistic participants, though the sample was a very diverse array of people of other neurotypes as well, but the results are promising. In general, most research does show that proudly owning one's disability can have a big impact on how people feel—and it can change the attitudes of the neurotypical people around us.

It's heartening to witness how fellow masked Autistics take proud ownership of traits they once deeply disliked and were taught to loathe: childishness, selfishness, stubbornness, being a robot. Looked at from another angle, childishness is joy and open curiosity. Selfishness is a vital protective skill. One interviewee told me that his stubbornness and moral clarity is what allowed him to be a whistle-blower when he discovered his company was violating customer privacy protections. There is some research suggesting that people who are used to being disliked and going against the social grain are more likely to speak out and blow the whistle on injustice.[12]

Bobbi, the "gender failure" I spoke to in Chapter 1, tells me they have learned to see their unique combination of rashness and sensitivity as a real superpower. Bobbi is an occupational therapist who works with young children. They say connecting with frustrated kids comes naturally to them because of their past, and their Autism.

"When kids get told that they're too sensitive, that their reactions to things are wrong, that really messes with them. But sensitive is not bad. If we were talking about a metal detector, sensitive would be good. Or a bomb-sniffing dog. You want a good instrument to be sensitive. Why is it bad to be very skilled at sniffing out the emotional bombs in the environment?"

Bobbi was emotionally astute, even as a child. Their family disliked how skillfully they picked up on emotional manipulation, neglect, and abuse. "Sensitivity," despite being a sign of attentiveness and discernment, is frowned upon when you're good at detecting things people would rather you not see. Today, Bobbi is in a place where their sensitivity is seen as the boon it really is. They help children by using that sensitivity to recognize and resonate with their pain.

Some Autistic experiences are unpleasant no matter how you look at them. Gastrointestinal issues are painful. Sensory overwhelm is an absolute torment. It's very understandable that many Autistic folks (myself include) resent having these features of the disability. However, no personality traits or modes of thinking and feeling associated with Autism are innately bad. Usually we internalize messages that we're bad, immature, cruel people only because the neurotypical people around us lacked the tools to look at our Autistic traits from the proper angle.

In the table on the opposite page are all the "negative" Autistic traits we explored back in Chapter 2, reframed to center on the Autistic person's perspective. You can try adding your own reframes, or your own examples of how your "worst" traits have served your best interests.

Reframing Autistic Stereotypes		
I was told I was:	**But actually I am:**	**I value this quality in myself because:**
Arrogant	Confident Principled Independent	• It helps me stand up for what's right • I'm often the first person to speak out about a problem • I can set a positive example for others • • •
Cold & Unfeeling	Analytical Rational Thoughtful	• I notice things others miss • I don't get swept away in the heat of the moment like others do • I'm good at noticing connections and systems others can't see • • •
Annoying & Loud	Enthusiastic Alive Outspoken	• I am my own best advocate • I raise other people's energy levels • I experience intense happiness and recognize beauty • • •

I was told I was:	But actually I am:	I value this quality in myself because:
Childish	Curious Open-minded Joyful	• I'm great at learning and growing • I experience the full range of human emotion • I take pleasure from the small things in life • • •
Awkward	Authentic Unique Don't Blend in with the Crowd	• If something is hard for me, other people probably need help with it, too • My way of moving through the world is entirely its own • I don't conform to unfair standards • • •
Clueless, Pathetic	Reflective Unassuming Open About Vulnerability	• I recognize we all need one another • I know how to ask for the help I need • I value my connections to other people • • •

I was told I was:	But actually I am:	I value this quality in myself because:
Sensitive	Perceptive Emotionally Attuned Compassionate	• I recognize mistreatment very well • I'm good at taking the emotional temperature of the room • I'm in touch with my feelings and with the feelings of others • • •
Weird	One of a Kind A Trailblazer Unconventional	• I make the world a bigger, broader place • I challenge old conventions and unfair rules • I'm the ultimate authority on how my life should be • • •

Quite frequently, the traits that inconvenience or weird out neuro-typical people are the very same ones that define who we are and help keep us safe. When we stop taking an outsider's perspective of our own disability and instead center our own perspectives and needs, this becomes clear. It's not actually a bad thing that we are spirited, loud, intense, principled, or strange. These traits are merely inconvenient to systems designed by abled people that don't take our unique way of being into account. But the more we work to normalize our neurotype, and the more we loudly, proudly take ownership of our Autistic identities, the more institutions will be forced to change to accommodate us and others who have been repeatedly shut out.

Another powerful step in the unmasking process is learning to reclaim our passions and special interests. Most of us have been stifling all our large feelings for years—not just distress and discomfort, but joy as well. By happily delving into our special interests and reveling in our Autistic capacity to hyperfocus, we can help retrain our brains to see our neurotype as a source of beauty rather than a mark of shame.

Celebrating Special Interests

Clara is obsessed with new wave and pop musicians from the 1980s. Her bedroom is packed floor to ceiling with old records; her walls are covered with concert posters from long before her birth in 1993. Clara has candy-apple red hair, and she wears thick leather platform boots, torn-up acid-wash jeans, thick pink lipstick, and flowy, androgynous black asymmetrical shirts. Clara's favorite musician is the late Pete Burns of the band Dead or Alive, most famous for the song "You Spin Me Round (Like a Record)." She met Pete and got his autograph multiple times, and has watched every concert recording, interview, and reality TV show he ever appeared in.

Clara has an Autistic special interest in Pete Burns, and engaging with that interest brings her immense pleasure. When she really likes someone, she opens up to them by reciting facts about Pete Burns's many cosmetic surgeries and media controversies. When she gestures with her arms, a tattoo of Pete Burns's face peeks out from under her T-shirt sleeve.

When Clara went away to college a few years ago, she decided to hide her obsession with Pete Burns from her new classmates. She wanted to start out on the "right" foot, and not weird anybody out by being too fixated on the singer and reality TV star. So, she didn't bring any of her records or posters with her. She covered her tattoo up with long-sleeved sweaters. All buttoned up and masked, she found it very difficult to make friends.

"Every day was sort of empty," she says. "Just going through the routine with nothing to land on."

After a year of this, Clara was painfully depressed and listless. Her grades were terrible and she had no appetite. With her parents' encouragement, Clara transferred to a school closer to her childhood home, so she could go back to living in her bedroom, with access to all her Pete Burns stuff. She reconnected with online friends who were just as passionate about music and alternative fashion as she was, and gradually her life began to improve.

"It was like coming back to life," she says, "like a little plant standing up once it's in the sun."

When it comes to special interests, Autistic brains are total sponges, absorbing facts and figures at a rate that seems kind of inhuman to neurotypical people. We can develop a special interest in nearly anything. Some of us learn to speak fluent Klingon; others memorize algorithms for solving Rubik's cubes. My sister's brain is a compendium of movie trivia and dialogue. My own special interests have included everything from bat biology to the history of the Tudor dynasty, to personal finance, to subreddits run by so-called men's rights activists.

Though the *Diagnostic and Statistical Manual of Mental Disorders* states that Autism is defined by having a "restricted" range of interests, some Autistic folks cycle through new special interests every couple of months and become polymaths in a variety of subjects. Others are steadfastly dedicated to one topic their entire lives. We don't have control over what our special interests are, or when they appear or recede in our lives. Being obsessed with a person or topic isn't a choice, and does not necessarily reflect our values or beliefs, hence my former classmate Chris's experience of being bullied for being obsessed with World War II. I often find my special interests are a perverse fascination with a person or movement I find morally abhorrent. Though others might find it disturbing to read (for example) transphobic blogs for hours on end, I've found that studying such subjects is empowering and informative.

Autistic people find it rejuvenating and stimulating to spend time learning about our special interests. In studies that examine the lives of Autistic adults, engaging with special interests is positively associated with subjective well-being.[13] When we get to appreciate our hyperfixations, we feel happier and more satisfied with life. But for a long time, neurotypical researchers viewed special interests as an impediment to having a "regular" life. ABA therapists penalize Autistic children for speaking about them,[14] withdrawing attention and affection when the subjects come up. This trains Autistic kids to hide their deepest joys, and avoid cultivating their passions.

Punishing Autistic children for talking about their special interests is perhaps the most arbitrarily cruel element of ABA therapy. Most children have fanatical interests at one point or another, and in an adult, having an intense passion can bring a great deal of meaning and pleasure to life, as well as an opportunity to connect with like-minded people. However, ABA therapy is rooted in reinforcing the narrowest of social standards and pushing them on Autistic children, in hopes that a high degree of conformity will keep them "safe." Being too passionate about a video game, comic book, or wild animal species is often viewed in society as childish or limiting, and so Autistic children are expected to hide their enthusiasm.

Interestingly, adults are only shamed for having an obsessive interest if that interest is a bit too "strange," and doesn't come with the opportunity to rack up a lot of achievements or make a lot of money. People who routinely complete eighty-hour workweeks aren't penalized for being obsessive or hyperfixated; they're celebrated for their diligence. If an adult fills their evenings after work learning to code or creating jewelry that they sell on Etsy, they're seen as enterprising. But if someone instead devotes their free time to something that gives them pleasure but doesn't financially benefit anyone, it's seen as frivolous or embarrassing, even selfish. In this instance, it's clear that the punishing rules imposed on Autistic children reflect a much broader societal issue: pleasure and nonproductive, playful time are not valued, and when someone is passionate about the "wrong" things, that passion is discouraged because it presents a distraction from work and other "respectable" responsibilities.

The mental health costs of preventing Autistic children from enjoying their special interests are immense. Having the freedom to develop and express special interests is linked to improved social, emotional, and even fine motor development.[15] A survey of Autistic young adults by Teti and colleagues (2016) found that many use their special interests to develop emotional awareness skills and coping strategies.[16] This frequently plays out in fandoms and nerdy communities, where neurodiverse people with mutual special interests find one another, socialize, and sometimes begin to unmask. In a study of internet habits, researchers Johnson and Caldwell-Harris (2012) found that Autistic adults actually had a greater variety of interests and more numerous interests than their non-Autistic peers, and made far more social media posts about their interest that were designed to provoke conversation, compared to neurotypical people.[17] Autistic people are also a foundational part of most fandoms and conventions centered around shared hobbies—we devote a lot of energy to finding and creating spaces where we can interact with people who share our interests, and within nerdy fandom spaces, social norms tend to be more forgiving and relaxed. It turns out that special interests aid us in becoming more outgoing, well-rounded individuals.

In 2020, Autistic self-advocate Jersey Noah developed Special Interest Week, a weeklong series of reflection prompts posted to social media, which were designed to help Autistic people reflect and share about the things that bring us joy. So much of the writing Autistic people post online focuses on our frustrations and experiences of being excluded and misunderstood. Online, Autistic adults are commonly expected to educate non-Autistic people about what our neurotype really is like, and to debunk all the misinformation allistics have passively absorbed (and projected onto us) all our lives. Jersey created Special Interest Week in order to give Autistic people a bit of a breather from all this heavy educational and emotional lifting. In essence, they were creating a kind of anti-ABA therapy, encouraging neurodiverse people to infodump about our obsessions as loudly as we wanted without worry about neurotypical people's expectations or needs.

I consulted with Jersey when they were developing the prompts for

Special Interest Week, as did several other Autistic creators, including Matt and Brandy Haberer, who host the disability podcast *The Chronic Couple*. In October 2020, the first Special Interest Week ran on Instagram, with the accompanying hashtag #AutieJoy. Hundreds of Autistic people participated, posting photos of their hat collections, video game achievement spreadsheets, and beaded earrings they had made. It was cathartic to read these stories and share how my hyperfixations shaped my life for the better, too.

Below is an adapted version of Jersey Noah's Special Interest Week prompts, which you can use either privately or on a blog or social media platform, to reflect on your own passions and what they've meant to you.

Special Interest Week:[18]	
Seven Prompts to Help You Reflect on Autistic Joy	
Instructions: Every day for a week, set aside some time to reflect on one of the prompts below. In the fields provided, you can doodle, write about the topic, or even paste in photos relevant to the special interest. You may also wish to track down physical reminders of these special interests. Try listening to a record you used to love, for example, or sorting through an old drawer of collectibles. Whatever helps you connect to a powerful sense of Autistic Joy!	
Day 1 Your Oldest Special Interest	
Day 2 Your Most Recent Special Interest	
Day 3 A Special Interest That's Changed or Grown Over Time	
Day 4 A Special Interest That Is Collected/ Collections	
Day 5 The Special Interest That Has Shaped Your Life the Most	

Day 6 A Special Interest You Share with Someone	
Day 7 A Day for Embracing and Celebrating Special Interests. What's something positive your special interests have brought to your life?	

Reflecting on your special interests may leave you feeling exhilarated, empowered, or hopeful, just as Heather Morgan's Key Moments exercise (provided in the introduction to this book on page 14) was also designed to do. Masking is a practice of silencing ourselves and letting neurotypical expectations dominate our actions, rather than being guided by our core personal values. But when we drill down into what makes us feel happy, stimulated, and fully alive, we can identify who we really are, and what our lives ought to look like. In the next section, we'll revisit our Key Moments from that earlier exercise, and see what those moments have to say about who we are and what we value most.

Rediscovering Your Values

"Autistic people absorb a lot of messages that tell us, *oh, that's not allowed, I can never be good enough, the rules are different for me than for anyone else*," Heather Morgan says. "And we can deconstruct those messages by asking, well, what do my values have to say about that?"

For a long time, Heather believed the rules other people were expected to follow were fundamentally different than the rules that applied to her. She was trying to fit within the lines neurotypical people had drawn for her, but her efforts all seemed to fail. The instructions she was given didn't line up with people's actual (unspoken) expectations. It was paralyzing. Eventually, she decided to stop focusing on what others desired from her, and let her life be guided by her actual values. That's when she first developed her Values-Based Integration exercise, which she's now led many Autistic clients through.

In the introduction of this book, I encouraged you to complete the first stage of the Values-Based Integration process, conjuring up the memory of five "key moments" in your life where you truly felt alive. One of the goals of this exercise is to help you nurture a sense of trust in your instincts and desires. The unique qualities and feelings associated with each of your key moments can also help you figure out what it is that you value most in life. In order to name what your values are, you can look back on these memories and try to articulate exactly why each of them was so special.

"Once you have finished telling each of your five stories," Heather Morgan writes,[19] "go back and look for the key words that describe each story. Most stories will have at least two or three key words, and some key words will be repeated between stories."

Suppose, for example, that one of the key moments that came to mind for you was your wedding day. What felt especially poignant about that day? Was it being surrounded by all of your loved ones? Was it the connection you felt toward your partner? Did you enjoy the attention? The celebration? Try to identify what made that time really stand out and do so without passing any judgment. Notice any words that appear multiple times, across multiple memories. Try to dig a little deeper and use values-based words (such as *connection, family, creativity,* or *generosity*) to describe those special experiences.

Values-Based Integration:[20]
Identifying Your Values

Instructions: To complete this activity, you will need to refer to the Key Moments exercise you completed in the introduction of this book (page 14).
Review those memories and try to list key words that describe each moment and why it was special to you. Most stories will have at least two or three key words, and some key words will be repeated between stories. Feel free to list as many words as you like, until you identify ones that really capture your feelings.

Moment 1:	Key words that describe why this moment was special:

Moment 2:	Key words that describe why this moment was special:
Moment 3:	Key words that describe why this moment was special:
Moment 4:	Key words that describe why this moment was special:
Moment 5:	Key words that describe why this moment was special:
Try to identify which of the words you listed above are the most important or resonant. Look to see if any words can be grouped together, or if there is a single word that sums up an idea for you. You can list key words and try grouping them together here:	

Our key memories and the words we use to describe them can help us understand what matters most to us and offer up a valuable contrast between the way we currently are living and the life we'd like to build.

To help illustrate this process and some of the conclusions that can come from it, let me offer one of my own key moments. In the summer of 2019, I was walking home through Wrigleyville, the sports-bar-laden Chicago neighborhood surrounding the Cub's Wrigley Field. There was a pub crawl going on, so a lot of drunk people were ambling from bar to bar. As I walked past a quiet side street, I saw a woman walking away from a visibly drunk, staggering man. She kept nodding and smiling but trying to walk away, and seemed deeply uncomfortable. The man kept stumbling toward her and yelling for her attention. I decided to stop what I was doing and follow the pair down the street.

I watched for a while as the woman tried to put some distance between herself and the man, who keep towering over her and asking her questions. Her mannerisms were placating and disarming. He kept putting his arms around her shoulders and she kept slipping out from under him. After a few moments, I saw the man escalate, and put his hand on the woman's lower back. She tensed up. His hand wandered lower onto the seat of her jeans. My instincts kicked into gear.

"Leave her alone, dude," I yelled out, racing up to meet them. The man stiffened. "Let her go."

He looked back at me, his eyes bleary, and slowly said, "We're fine."

"You need to stop touching her," I said in a low, authoritative voice. I put my body between hers and his. "You just stay here with me until she has gone on her way."

He grimaced at me and slurred the words, "You leave us alone."

"No, dude. You're going to leave her alone. You're going to stay here, with me, until she gets far away."

He was visibly angry and for a moment I thought I was gonna get punched. Yet I had no fear. I felt totally in control of the situation. I continued telling him to stay put, my voice now at full volume so others in the neighborhood could hear. The guy was definitely furious, but he stood there with me, staring me down, swaying menacingly, until the woman got to her apartment about a half a block away, closed the door, and locked herself inside.

"Get out of here," I told the guy when it was over. "You go walk the other way." I stayed put until he was long gone.

Most of my life, I have lacked courage and clarity of purpose. I hesitate, second-guess myself, worry that I'll embarrass someone. I often tell myself I'm misreading the situation I'm in, or that I don't have the power to fix the injustices I see around me. I also tend to put my own well-being before that of others, because I don't trust that anyone else will ever value me. In this instance, I wasn't burdened with any of that doubt, or that cowardice. I stood up for what was right, even though doing so was "awkward" and also might have gotten me hurt. I made a judgment call and used my wonderful Autistic arrogance to take charge.

When I contrast that strong, confident version of me with the nervous, smiling, restrained-to-a-fault person I often am when I'm masking, I can see exactly where my values lie, and how my mask blocks me from being my authentic self. When I let the fear of seeming "weird" or "rude" drive me, I fail others as well as myself. When I focus only on protecting myself, I forget how strong I am, and how wonderful it feels to care for other people. That experience taught me that I value *protecting other people* and being *principled* and *courageous* more than I value fitting in or being invisible—but that I am often tempted to succumb to those desires anyway. When I listen to my values, my life is more fulfilling and meaningful. I feel more powerful, and less stuck. This memory also illustrates for me that it's my Autism, not my mask, that helps me live in accordance with my beliefs. I was able to step in and help that woman because I was willing to make the situation awkward, and I was stubborn and forceful enough to stand my ground in the face of aggression and intimidation. These qualities might at times make me inconvenient to neurotypical people, but sometimes getting in the way is exactly the right thing to do.

Feeling Gratitude for Your Autism— and Your Past

So far in this chapter, we've worked on rethinking unfair beliefs we have internalized about Autism, and about ourselves. This can be an empowering process, but it comes with some melancholy as well. You might find yourself looking back on all the years you "wasted" masking and regret how you let shame and social judgment shape you. To help work through those challenging feelings, it's useful to extend a little *self-gratitude* your own way, and take stock of the positive impact Autism has already had on your life. Being Autistic in a neurotypical world is often traumatizing,[21] and being forced to mask is essentially an experience of society-driven abuse. Though you may sometimes wish that life had been different or that you hadn't been made to suffer, your disability isn't to blame for what happened, and neither are you.

It was a far-reaching, centuries-old system of injustice that left you in such a difficult spot. Even knowing that, you might feel immense regret about the way life has gone so far. But psychological research shows that extending gratitude to your past, trauma-surviving self is a powerful means of healing.[22]

Quite often, people who have coped with trauma in imperfect ways experience a *fragmentation* of selfhood. They see different feelings and behaviors as almost distinct parts of themselves, rather than an integrated whole they can make sense of and have control over. The person they were at school may not line up with who they had to pretend to be at home. They may have needed to create a complex tapestry of social fictions to keep their lives together. It's easy to feel shame about having coped in that way. But extending gratitude to your past self and taking stock of how Autism has shaped your life (even when you were trying to hide it) may help you to feel more unified, as well as more accepting of the way things were.

My friend James Finn is a novelist, former Act Up activist, and retired defense analyst with the U.S. Air Force. He's worn many hats in his fifty-eight years of life, and all of them have been well suited to his focused, observant Autistic nature. He was only diagnosed ten years ago, so for most of his life he didn't know *why* he was so adept at scanning through facts and developing systems that helped organize them, or why he could absorb new languages like a sponge. He just naturally gravitated to work that gave him ample time to sit alone, processing information.

"The Air Force is probably going out and recruiting Autistic analysts," he tells me. "I mean if they're not, they ought to be. I could geek out on studying data sets and making connections and just live in my office, it was wonderful. If it weren't for the FBI coming in and doing random polygraphs one year and me having to lie about being gay, I probably would have stayed in the military."

After leaving the Air Force in the 1980s, James took a job doing translation work for the United Nations. As the AIDS crisis began to intensify, he became involved with an HIV/AIDS service agency, where he got to help queer people and intravenous drug users. He lived in New York and remained highly engaged in Act Up activism until the late 1990s, when the fight against AIDS was finally beginning to look less bleak. From there, James moved to Montreal to live with a boyfriend, and began working in sales. He spent his downtime learning French, obsessively writing and rewriting translations in a notebook.

"And that is actually one of the things that tipped my therapist off I might be Autistic," James says. "I had five notebooks that were filled with French phrases on one side, translated three different ways into English on the other side. I told my therapist this and he gave me this look and raised his eyebrows like, *I'm sorry, what?*"

James got assessed pretty quickly thereafter, and found out that he was, in fact, Autistic. The previous forty-eight years of his life instantly made sense. At his sales job, James used to spend hours typing out transcripts of hypothetical dialogue, gaming out every possible way the conversation might go. That way, no matter what someone said, he'd have prepared a way to respond. Today, his fiction readers tell him he's fantastic at writing dialogue, and really understands how other people speak and feel. But it's not because these things come naturally to him. He devoted thousands of hours to picking conversations apart to make sense of them.

"Autism has caused me a lot of challenges throughout my life and a lot of times I don't like it," James says. "But without it I wouldn't have been the manager of an HIV service organization. I wouldn't have written novels. I wouldn't have learned French. So, even though sometimes I feel lonely and even though sometimes I feel like people misjudge me, it's all kind of worth it, too."

I hear this kind of thinking expressed by Autistic people a lot, especially those who have found community alongside other neurodiverse people and have had time to make peace with who they really are. After the initial shock of realizing you have a hidden disability, there are often waves of acceptance and relief.

In Autistic self-advocacy circles, the question of whether we'd take a pill that magically "cures" Autism often comes up. The vast majority of people in our community reject that question out of hand, because Autism is a core part of who we are, impossible to separate from our personalities, talents, preferences, and general outlook. We wouldn't be the same people without it. Being Autistic has fundamentally shaped James Finn's life, his career, where's his lived, his relationships, and his passions, just as being a gay man has. It's not really possible to imagine a James Finn that lacks these traits and is still recognizably him.

For my part, I know that without Autism I wouldn't have completed my PhD at age twenty-five; I wouldn't have memorized thousands of song lyrics, befriended dozens of genderqueer weirdos with nerdy interests, or written anywhere near as many words as I have. If Autism hadn't made it hard for me to drive, I might not have moved to Chicago. I might have chosen to live in a city without public transit, and wouldn't have met my partner of over a decade. Each aspect of who I am is tightly interwoven with the rest, and on good days I love myself enough to be grateful for almost every single one.

To wrap up this chapter, I'd like to ask you to reflect on the meaningful things Autism has already brought into your own life. These positives don't have to be respectable by neurotypical standards. Most of us aren't genius savants, and our worth should not be measured by our ability (or inability) to meet conventional benchmarks of success. What's really important here is to focus on how neurodiversity has brought pleasure, connection, and meaning to your life. Autism cannot be "cured," and most people in the Autism self-advocacy community eventually come to see that fact as a blessing, because Autism is so core to their existence, and integral to becoming the wonderful people that they are.

Thanks to Autistic hyperfocus, I've developed these skills:	
Thanks to my special interests, I've learned a lot about these subjects:	
If I wasn't Autistic, I never would have gotten to know these people who are important to me:	
If I wasn't Autistic, I never would have had these experiences:	
If I wasn't Autistic, I wouldn't have these awesome personality traits:	
Being Autistic is hard, but it has made me resilient in these ways:	

Self-stigma is a liar; you're not cringey, "too much," a baby, or a cold-blooded creep. You're a marginalized person with many beautiful and unique qualities. Your needs are value-neutral, and your emotions are helpful signals to respond to that don't merit any shame. Autism has always been a powerful driving force in your life, often for the better, even when you did not know that it was there. Now that you do know it's there, you can work on accepting and loving the person you have always been beneath your mask, and practice sharing that version of you with the world. Unmasking doesn't happen in one big burst of confidence; it's a gradual process of relaxing your inhibitions, trusting your feelings, and letting go of compensatory strategies that no longer suit you. In the next chapter, we'll look at ways you can reduce the camouflaging and compensating that you do, reject neurotypical expectations, and construct a lifestyle that centers your neurotype instead of downplaying it.

CHAPTER 6

Building an Autistic Life

"Over the last year I've lost over 10,000 followers. And I think that's because I've gone from being an aspirational version of myself, and now I'm just doing what I want."

Moorea Seal is a Seattle-based author and entrepreneur, and for many years she was a digital curator and influencer as well. She's best known as the author of the bestselling *52 Lists* journal series, which provides a year's worth of weekly writing prompts around a specific topic or theme. There's *52 Lists for Happiness, 52 Lists for Bravery*, and *52 Lists for Togetherness*; there are *52 Lists* branded planners, postcards, and to-do lists. Each book is beautifully designed, both soothing and stimulating to look at, with graphics set against backdrops of earth tones and photos of plants. The prompts are broadly useful, but also reflect the mental health and self-exploration journeys Moorea has been on over the years.

The store Moorea used to own in Seattle was much the same: a carefully arranged, inviting space filled with stylish dresses and jewelry, bags and heels, and ball cacti planted in glossy white, geometric dishes. Moorea first became internet-famous on Pinterest because she had such a preternatural talent for pulling visual elements together. Her eye and taste also led to success on Instagram. Moorea's digital brand became so recognizable that fans began seeking out her store, which she named after herself so it would have recognizable branding. Over the course of a few years, Moorea became a massively successful author, small business owner, and influencer. She went to conferences and had business meetings with large brands. She signed deals with Gap and Nordstrom, and was profiled by outlets like Amy Poehler's *Smart Girls*. She navigated all this as an undiagnosed Autistic person, wearing a mask of sleek, feminine beauty. The larger her brand became, the more confining it felt.

"I've had so much pressure to be the face, to wear certain things, to do a *performance* of Moorea," she tells me. "I want to be Moorea. I want to be me. I don't want to have to put *this* on all the time."

At the height of her success, Moorea was in an unfulfilling marriage and beginning to question her sexual orientation. The constant grind of running a business and representing her company was wearing her down. She started having panic attacks. Her brain, desperate to protect her from the overload she was experiencing, would shut down during meetings and high-stress situations.

"I would be in meetings and I'd have, you know, business partners yelling at me like, *Moorea, pay attention. Do this thing, you're late on this.* I would just start bawling crying, and then they would say I was being emotionally manipulative. And it was just that I had no words left."

Moorea had always felt a tension between her internally "weird" self and the attractive, put-together woman people expected her to be. She was an outspoken ally to LGBTQ people, but didn't acknowledge her own queerness. Professionally, people valued her mind, and the unique images she could create, but they didn't want her to push the envelope by posting about her political views. She followed the rules, tried to strike the right balance between being herself and being an influencer, but it left her trapped in a horribly inauthentic, exhausting position.

So, Moorea began to let things go. She closed her store and pared down her partnerships to just a few key collaborators. She and her husband separated, and she came out as queer. She started boxing, and getting more muscular, and began dressing in baggy, masculine clothing more often. On Instagram her follower count dropped. She started posting about Black Lives Matter, her struggles with depression, and her queerness, and more followers disappeared. Many of the white, straight women who loved Moorea's old brand were put off by the real her.

The more Moorea embraced her true self, the more she lost. But it didn't exactly feel like a loss. She had gained a greater understanding of who she really was. Several months into the pandemic, a friend of Moorea's suggested she get assessed for Autism. She received a diagnosis very quickly thereafter.

"I was just happy in that moment," she tells me. "I was just, *ahhh. That makes sense.*"

Moorea's story is a bit different from what we've heard so far. She had begun unmasking herself months before figuring out where that mask had come from in the first place. The dissonance in Moorea's life was so stark she didn't need an Autism diagnosis to let her know things were unsustainable and needed to change. Being a queer, androgynous influencer in a hyperfeminine, conformist industry was obviously untenable. As soon as she acknowledged this, and began to walk away from it, all Moorea's hidden facets began to shine. And when she did discover that she was Autistic, Moorea wasn't shocked or embarrassed. She'd always had Autistic friends, as well as friends with intellectual disabilities, so in many ways the revelation felt like coming home. By the time Moorea came out as Autistic on her Instagram, anyone who was going to be alienated by her had pretty much already left.

"I'm gonna keep being brutally open about myself," she says. "People are going to respond however they choose."

Moorea has gone through a lot of change in the past few years, and at times it's left her emotionally reeling. But she's approached these changes with radical acceptance and trust in herself. She knows that being Autistic has been a positive force in her life, and listening to herself has allowed her to zero in on which kinds of life are fulfilling and sustainable for her. I think that ultimately, that's what every masked Autistic should be shooting for. To trust and unconditionally accept ourselves enough that we can accept the rejections and losses that sometimes come by living as we really are. We can't please everyone. Unmasking means we stop trying to be an appealing "brand."

Moorea had camouflaged and compensated for her Autism beautifully for many years. But she learned, at a certain point, that it was better to live on her own terms than it was to appeal to the masses. At the time I interviewed her, she was living in a guest house on her sister's property, and working according to her own schedule. She found lots of time throughout the day to play with her sister's toddler-aged kid, and to take restorative walks and baths. A few months later, she moved into a cheap, yet comfortable micro-studio apartment, and stripped down to the basics even further. She still does creative, curational work, but she's learned to let a lot of things go. This life isn't as fast-paced and achievement oriented as Moorea's old life was. But it is more her.

In this chapter, we'll take a look at a few evidence-based ways that Autistic people can build our lives around our strengths, values, and needs. We'll also hear from several Autistic coaches, activists, and mental health providers who have devised ways of accommodating neurodiverse bodies and minds, and learn a bit more about people like Moorea, who have stopped defaulting to neurotypical scripts about what a home, career, or life "should" look like. Recall that masking consists of both camouflage and compensation. It's a complex system of behaviors, performances, and even life decisions. It follows then that unmasking Autism goes a lot further than just lowering our inhibitions. It means rethinking the entire shape of our lives. When we trust ourselves and get in touch with our values, everything from how we dress, to how we lay out our homes, to how we conceive of time itself may change.

Divergent Design

Marta Rose is an educator and Autistic peer counselor, and online she writes regularly as @divergent_design_studios. Some of her most groundbreaking work is around the concept of *divergent design*—the idea that the physical spaces we inhabit as Autistic people ought to prioritize our sensory health, and work with the actual patterns of our lives.

"When designing an interior space," Marta writes,[1] "design for how you actually live, not how you aspire to live . . . your space must be designed to accommodate the reality of your life, without shame or judgement."

Before living by this principle (and coaching other Autistic people on it), Marta used to beat herself up for things like leaving her clothes in a pile on the floor at the end of the day. She put a hamper near her closet to make staying organized easier, but at the end of the day, she was always too exhausted to sort between the clothes that were clean enough to be put away and which ones needed a wash. She had a dining room table covered in junk and berated herself for never using it to actually have family meals. Her home design was aspirational, but not at all practical.

"My new plan is to put some hooks on the wall right beside my bed, so I don't have to take even one extra step to hang up clothes that aren't dirty yet," she explains. Dirty clothing can go in the hamper, or just be tossed on the floor and gathered up later. This approach keeps Marta's room reasonably organized, but she doesn't put stress on herself for not keeping things perfectly organized and clean.

Mariah, a designer who recently discovered that she's Autistic, says that redesigning her home and workspace has been a foundational part of her unmasking.

"I am a designer by day, so I've learned a lot of 'design rules,' but I really broke a lot of them when considering my desk setup," she says. "Working from home helps me be able to unmask in a lot of ways that many people don't even see. But I'm unmasking to myself, and that feels extraordinarily liberating."

Mariah keeps sensory and self-care tools in a box near her desk, so she can reach for them and fidget whenever she needs. A massage roller sits beneath her desk, so she can stim with it using her feet. She wears industrial-strength noise-canceling headphones (the kind landscapers use) and keeps plastic toy wands filled with glitter within arm's reach to fiddle with. Her desk layout doesn't look like what she was taught a well-designed space "should" be. Living by her own rules has had a massive positive effect. She's constantly making adjustments, finding new ways to make herself more comfortable.

"Everything feels different, it really does impact everything. Like my body was masked!" she says. Now that her daily environment works with her body rather than against it, she feels physically and mentally free.

Marta Rose writes that divergent design should honor the unique relationships Autistic people have to objects. Some of us are very stressed out by visual clutter, because it creates sensory "noise," and that means home décor and staying organized can be very challenging for us. If anything new enters my apartment, I notice it instantly, and it bugs the hell out of me. Sometimes I throw necessary things away on impulse, because looking at them makes me so stressed. A university once sent me a huge recording kit in the mail, in preparation for a virtual event. It freaked me out so much I nearly returned the box to UPS and lied that it had gotten lost in the mail. That's how badly I wanted it out of my house. I have had to work around this trigger; when I helped organize a trans clothing swap, for example, I asked a friend to hold on to all the clothing donations. I knew if I had a bunch of trash bags of clothing in my apartment, I might throw them away impulsively one evening.

Experimental research shows that many Autistic people have trouble ignoring visual "noise," to the degree it really disrupts our processing.[2] Clutter can erode our focus, making it hard for us to think clearly or regulate our emotions. A study of Autistic schoolchildren found that many had trouble paying attention in classrooms where the walls were covered in distracting, bright posters, and the shelves were stuffed with books and toys.[3] Most children's spaces are very busy and bright, despite how negatively this impacts Autistic kids' processing. It's no wonder that Moorea Seal became known for her minimalistic, sleek aesthetic. Lots of neurodiverse people crave spare or even Spartan surroundings. It's less to keep track of, less to clean every week, and less to pack up when it comes time to move. It's also very on-trend: minimalistic design, capsule wardrobes, and throwing away items that cause clutter and fail to "spark joy" (à la Marie Kondo) have all become immensely popular in recent years because it is so visually soothing and practical.[4]

That said, not all Autistic people are well suited to minimalism. Marta Rose observes that objects carry a very strong significance for Autistic people, so tidying our living spaces up and throwing things away can be very difficult.[5] Many of us identify with the items we love, and even feel a degree of empathy for them, as if they were alive. Psychologists call this phenomenon *object personification*, and Autistics exhibit it at an elevated rate compared to the neurotypical population.[6] We also tend to connect emotionally with animals more readily than people, which can also influence how our home environments should be arranged.

Autistic people frequently rely on beloved objects to provide consistency, familiarity, and emotional grounding.[7] Cleaning and getting rid of unnecessary things causes decision fatigue for many of us,[8] because we have to think really effortfully about why we might want to hold on to something, and game out every possible scenario where it might come in handy. We also have to battle against social programming in the process: do I really want to throw out my action figure collection, or do I just think doing so will make me seem more adult?

Do I never wear these boots because they are loud and impractical, or because they're buried under a pile of t-shirts and I forget they exist?

To manage these competing needs, Marta Rose has a few suggestions. First, you can display one item that represents a larger collection that's become unwieldy. If you have dozens of collectible toys, for instance, you could put up a single shelf featuring your current favorites and store the rest away. Selecting which toys to "feature" each week or month can itself be a fun way to look through your whole collection and express yourself. You can also take photos of the objects to catalog them and throw some actual items away. Sometimes, old junk can be repurposed: old makeup and jewelry can be used to make visual art; holey T-shirts can be sewn together into a quilt. This often makes the pain of throwing away a beloved inanimate friend a little bit less painful, because they get to become part of something else that you'll use and cherish.

If you want to hold on to an entire collection but find it distracting to look at every day, you can hang a curtain over your shelves, or place things into closed bins. Marta also recommends Autistic people consider hiring someone to help them tidy and keep their spaces clean. Hiring a house cleaner or tidier is reaching out for an accommodation that you need, though Marta observes many Autistic people (particularly women) feel shame about enlisting that help at first. Additionally, some Autistic people might feel agitated or dysregulated by having a stranger in their home rearranging or cleaning their things, or they may need cleaning tasks to be done in a very particular way, and managing that can be frustrating for everyone involved. For many Autistic people, affording regular house cleaning visits may be out of reach. Some find a workaround by enlisting the help of friends or romantic partners, or by trading skills on local exchange and marketplace groups. I know one Autistic person who loves organizing homes and finds cleaning soothing, so she actually tidies other disabled people's houses for free, or in exchange for supplies she needs or home-cooked meals.

Algedra Interior Design is a Dubai-based interior design firm that has consulted with Autistic people and families to develop a handful of divergent design best practices.[9] Their tips are pretty unsurprising, in light of all the research we've reviewed thus far: stick to clean lines and muted colors, such as pastels and earth tones; avoid loud patterns, bright lights, or ornate details. If you self-stimulate in ways that might cause physical harm (for example, swinging your arms around), avoid furniture with sharp corners. If your body craves movement, you can lay down a soft mat to flop onto. Algedra also recommends using insulation, rugs, and decorative soundproofing panels to dampen noise in an inobtrusive way.

Of course, these principles do not apply to everyone. Autistic people's needs and preferences are incredibly varied, as we've already discussed throughout this book. Unmasking in one's living environment means detaching from expectations about how one "should" live, first and foremost. Some Autistics are sensory seekers and crave bold, bright lights, or lots of sound, and their homes reflect that. Honoring the need for stimulation and excitement is just as important as providing quiet and stillness, and so for some Autistic people, unmasking your home may mean simply giving yourself permission to keep your space as cluttered as you like. Clara, the Pete Burns superfan, knows that she feels best when she's surrounded by all her favorite records, concert posters, makeup, and loud accessories.

"I need color and stuff, and a place to play my music as loud as I want," she says

Here are some questions to get you reflecting on what you need out of your home and workspace, and how you might make your own environment a little more affirming:

Divergent Design Questions

- What are some textures that ground you or your senses?
- Do you enjoy a minimalistic, spare space, or a cozy space filled with familiar objects?
- What smells do you find relaxing? What smells invigorate you?
- Do you enjoy dim light, colorful lights, or bright, white lights?

- What objects do you enjoy holding or having near you?
- Do you need background noise in order to focus? Is there ambient noise in your surroundings that you need to block out?
- Do you hold on to any objects or furniture out of a sense that you "should" appreciate them? If you could let go of those things, what might you want to put in their place?

One of the core elements of Marta Rose's divergent design approach is to look at lived experience as data. The best predictor of how you will use a space (and what you need a space to be able to do) is how you already use it. If you never eat dinner in the dining room, maybe that space can become a game room instead. If putting on a fitted sheet is so frustrating that you never make your bed, you can just lay a top sheet directly onto your mattress. In fact, this is how most humans have handled bed dressing throughout history![10] You don't need to live like a "presentable" adult. You can do your own thing in your own unique way—and that means you can reexamine your habits, your living space, and even your approach to time.

Reimagine Success and Time

"I don't understand why the workday is eight hours," Sue tells me. "I can get everything done in about three."

Sue is in her early fifties and works in tech. She only figured out she was Autistic a few years ago, when her teenaged son was assessed. Unlike many formerly masked Autistics I spoke to, Sue didn't view it as a major revelation. It's just given her a new vocabulary for why she finds other people so confounding.

"I've come to understand that neurotypicals need time talking, arranging papers, opening and closing their email over and over and not getting much done," she says with a shrug. "I believe that some of them actually enjoy being at the office all day, and they'd rather take all day to plod through something than hunker down and finish it."

Sue has been able to shape her life around the fact she's very efficient, and has little patience for activities she perceives as a waste of time.

"I get the day's [work] tasks done with by about lunchtime usually, then I go run errands and exercise. By mid-evening, I'm ready to do work again, so I knock out a whole bunch of emails or whatever else. My coworkers always wake up to a ton of Slack messages from me about what needs fixing."

Years ago, Sue's manager learned that by giving her flexibility, the organization gets to benefit from her natural productivity and thoroughness. As we've repeatedly discussed in this book, research shows Autistic people pay much closer attention to small details than neurotypical people do, particularly when they have the cognitive energy to do so, and in the workplace that can have real benefits.[11] Many tech companies actively recruit Autistic employees because we have a reputation for doing thorough work.[12] This can create an exploitative workplace culture, though, where our disabilities are only valued insofar as they generate profit for somebody else. It's a highly conditional form of acceptance, one only reserved for the apparently "high functioning" and those willing to define their lives by their productivity. However, the tech sector does tend to be a place where being direct or socially awkward is a bit more accepted, and in Sue's case, it's been a good fit. She appreciates she can be her authentic, brusque self at work.

"I don't have a lot of patience for inefficiency or sloppiness," she says, "or being asked to do work that is meaningless busywork. The upshot of that is that when you work with me, you know I'm raising the standard."

The schedules and work habits of Autistic people challenge the prevailing neurotypical, one-size-fits-all conception of time. Like Sue, many of us are able to complete a great deal of work in a single hyperfocused burst, though typically we'll need much more rest and recovery in order to sustain such efforts. The sleep-wake cycles of Autistic adults also differ, on average, from the circadian rhythms of neurotypicals,[13] and many of us experience sleep disorders.[14] One reason that we may need more sleep than others is just how tiring it is for us to be in the world. Sensory overload, social overwhelm, and the pressures of masking all significantly drain our batteries. This means many of us are not well suited to a nine-to-five job, and keep other hours instead.

Of course, industrial-organizational research suggests that actually very few people thrive in a rigidly structured eight-hour work environment, regardless of disability status. Most workers are only capable of truly focusing and being "productive" for about four hours per day.[15] Long workdays and long commutes erode a person's life satisfaction,[16] job satisfaction,[17] and their physical and mental health.[18] In addition, many of the features of the neurotypical workplace are distracting and anxiety-provoking for allistics as well as Autistics. Allistics just tend to be better positioned to push through the discomfort of bright fluorescent lights or a coworker's pungent cologne. In this way, to acknowledge the needs of Autistic workers is to listen to the canaries in the coal mine: our sensitivities and needs help lay bare just how unfair many work expectations are, even for neurotypical people.

Many of the Autistic people I interviewed for this book are self-employed, independent contractors, or work in a field that allows for flexible scheduling. Autistic author and stripper Reese Piper tells me that her work schedule at the club varies based on her energy levels. Some weeks, she has it in her to work three ten-hour shifts; other weeks she only has the energy for one. When business is good, Reese can earn enough money to pay her monthly bills after just a couple of days of dancing, and she can take days or weeks off on relatively short notice. I know several other Autistic sex workers personally who got into the field because of the flexibility it allowed them. Plus, emotional labor and masking as friendly and interested is recognized as part of the work of sex work. Clients are often willing to pay a high price for an authentic-feeling social and emotional experience. For Autistic people who have been obliged to mask all their lives, it can be really empowering to be paid for that skill—and to be able to afford enough down time to recover from having to do it.

Sometimes, upending neurotypical approaches to time means pouring more energy into our passions, rather than less. Autistic sex educator and researcher Stevie Lang describes how intense focus on a special interest can itself be restorative:[19]

"When I am actively working on something, I turn my whole attention to it," he writes. "After this kind of focus, I need rest. Resting doesn't always look like relaxing baths or naps. It might look like immersing myself in work on as special interest, or zoning out in front of a screen."

Autistic people don't necessarily thrive in judiciously balanced days where rest, work, and play are parceled out in equal amounts. Some of us operate best on boom-and-bust cycles of intense hyperfocus followed by recuperation time. I've had periods of my life where I've spent upwards of thirty hours per week writing and blogging, in addition to my day job, and found that pace incredibly exciting. Other times I've spent every free moment deep-reading random subreddits and blogs until my eyes felt like they were going to melt out of my skull. I loved every minute of it, and craved doing it again. When I'm swept up in a special interest, I feel alive. The concepts of "work-life" balance and "burnout" just don't always translate to Autistic people's schedules in the ways neurotypicals might expect. I've gotten intense burnout from periods of my life where I worked relatively little but socialized a lot, for example.

Engaging our special interests is an important part of maintaining Autistic people's mental health; one study by clinical psychologist Melis Aday found that Autistic adults' participation in special interests was associated with stress management, and with having low levels of depression.[20] One interpretation of this data is that when an Autistic person has the energy to enjoy their special interests, doing so is a valuable anxiety-reduction technique. It's equally important that we make time for repetitive, self-stimulatory behavior as well, as research has repeatedly shown that improves our mental health and coping.[21] Neurotypical standards don't account for Autistic people's need for time to recharge, fidget, and hyperfocus on our favorite activities. This may mean we don't have the energy or time to keep up with other tasks at an abled person's pace.

Because Autistic people's motivation level, interests, and social and sensory requirements shift, Marta Rose suggests we can think of time as a spiral rather than a straight line.[22] Rather than being parceled out in detached chunks with predetermined purposes (lunch time, work time, sleep time), we can see time as flowing and even folding back on itself, an overlapping series of cycles, periods of dormancy intersecting with growth. She writes:

"Almost all of the standard measures of time that we now take for granted—the way our hours and days and weeks are structured—are based on a factory model of work. I call this Industrial Time. . . . There are other ways of thinking about time. Seasonal ways. Cyclical ways. Ancient ways."

Throughout much of human history, time was a relatively intuitive concept; the seasons and daylight cycles influenced people's activities and their expectations. This all changed with the invention of electricity, and industrialized work that took place in lightbulb-lit warehouses and offices. As digital work tools have expanded, the possibility of perpetual work has taken over our lives. There are no periods of dormancy, no dark nights, and no snow days. There is no escaping work (and productivity tools and apps), even when we are at home.

Under a capitalist, Industrial Time framework, any project that is abandoned or left unfinished is seen as a "failure"—time wasted because it didn't result in a clear end product. But when we look at time as a series of cycles or spirals with goals that are ever-shifting, we can recognize that the learning and reflection we put into an aborted project (or even into masking) often pays off, just not in the way we expected. Every disappointment or failure teaches us something about what we want, and what is best for us.

"Reframe failure as data," Marta writes, "and everything changes."

Marta encourages neurodiverse people to think of progress not as approaching a fixed point that lies ahead of us, but as movement and adaptation, slowing down and speeding up as our situation requires.

Because Autistic minds are all about understanding details and analyzing complex systems of information, it makes sense to think of our lives as fractal, forever expanding to new subjects and narrowing into precise focus at the same time. We're not single-minded Marios, running across a side-scrolling level to rescue Princess Peach. We're more like the protagonist of the video game Katamari Damacy, a freaky, colorful demigod who rolls an ever-growing ball of objects around, each step forward attracting more random items into his ball's expanding gravitational field until it engulfs the universe. We don't complete discrete projects. We build worlds.

On a practical level, how can an Autistic person learn to embrace spiral time? Marta Rose says it comes down to two points:

1. Expand the time frame you use to gauge productivity and success. Take the "long view" of your life. Don't be afraid to cycle back to old projects, or let a passion go when it's not serving you.
2. Slow down. Stillness helps neurodivergent minds process the huge quantities of data we take in.

It's very difficult for us to unhitch our self-images from neurotypical expectations, slow down, and build a life that really reflects the people we want to be. Almost every Autistic person I spoke to has found that in order to build a life that suits them, they've had to learn to let certain unfair expectations go, and withdraw from activities that don't matter to them. It's scary to allow ourselves to disappoint other people, but it can be radical and liberating, too. Admitting what we can't do means confronting the fact we have a disability, and therefore we occupy a marginalized position in society—but it also is an essential part of finally figuring out what assistance we need, and which ways of living are best for us. You have to be able to say no to certain unreasonable expectations in order to genuinely say "yes" to the things you care about.

Do Your Own Thing, Your Own Way

Rory is an ADHD and Autism self-advocate and researcher living in New Zealand. Like so many of us, they've developed Autism-friendly "life hacks" to make regular life manageable. These are compensation strategies in a sense, but their goal isn't to mask Rory's neurodiversity, so much as to make life easier and more bearable.

In the past Rory used to struggle to stay focused while doing chores. They'd get distracted and wander off to do something else. Now, when it's time to do the dishes, they put on a cute pink-and-cream colored apron, don some noise-blocking headphones, and place mirrors in front of exit points, so that if their mind (or body) wanders away from the sink, they see their reflection and remember to keep scrubbing.

"My dishes 'costume' helps me stay on track," they say. "Mirrors remind me what I am supposed to be doing."[23]

Autism and ADHD can make many household chores absolute hell to keep up with. Dirty dishes are smelly and slippery; scrubbing a sticky countertop or dirty toilet over and over is understimulating as well as physically unpleasant. Shifting between cleaning tasks is laborious, since most of us would much rather focus on just one thing at a time. We often have trouble dividing up complex activities into small steps, or putting those steps into a logical sequence. So a simple-sounding goal like "do the dishes" can quickly become a long list of exhausting steps: gather up the dirty glasses and bowls from around the house, soak the filthy pots and pans, make space on the dish rack, wash and dry everything, put everything away, all while coping with nauseatingly gross odors and wet shirtsleeves that make upsetting static travel up and down our arms.

Many neurodiverse people suffer from *Autistic inertia*.[24] The same heightened focus that makes us so good at studying our special interests for hours also makes it challenging for us to get off the couch and attend to the overflowing trash. To an external, neurotypical observer, it doesn't look like we're struggling. It just looks like we're being "lazy."

Almost every neurodiverse person I've spoken to has been deemed "lazy" numerous times by exasperated parents, teachers, and friends. People see us sitting frozen, incapable of taking action, and assume it's because we don't care or lack willpower.[25] Then they admonish us for being apathetic and unreliable, which leaves us feeling even more paralyzed by anxiety. Neurotypicals also tend to assume we know how to complete a chore or task without instructing us in exactly what it entails, not understanding that we can't intuit our way through unstated expectations. We may not recognize, for example, that a request to "clean the bathroom" includes scrubbing the shower, floor, sink, and mirrors, not just tidying up. Alternatively, we might not know what level of clean is acceptable, and get stuck meticulously stripping out every bit of detritus in the grout on the floor. When our best guesses at what neurotypicals want from us proves incorrect, we get reprimanded for going too slowly, doing too sloppy a job, or not taking the other person's perspective. Many of us get trapped in a feedback loop of learned helplessness, confusion, shame, and frozenness as a result.

Rory's "dishes costume" and mirror system is a brilliant solution to many of the problems that make chores difficult for Autistic people. The apron is cute and inviting, lending a bit of fun to a dull activity. Putting on a task-specific outfit helps Rory mentally shift into "cleaning mode." The headphones and mirrors help them mentally stay there. These tools allow Rory to take full responsibility for getting the dishes done, without relying on a non-Autistic person for guidance or prompting. (Sadly, we can't always rely on the people around us to be patient or understanding.)

Autistic people are constantly having to invent our own unique ways of getting things done. We use extensive research, digital tools, and a variety of little sneaks and cheats to brute-force our way through activities that NT people don't even think about. Rhi, an Autistic blogger based in the United Kingdom, explains that she uses online research to plan ahead any time she visits a new place.

"I need to know where the front door is. Where the parking is. Who I will have to interact with," she writes.[26] With tools like Google

Streetview and Yelp at her disposal, she says life is much easier than it used to be. Kaitlin, who is both Autistic and in recovery from an eating disorder, has also used online research to psychologically prepare for meals out with friends.

"I'll look at everything on the menu online," she says, "and figure out what I can eat that is not going to make my anorexia or sensory issues freak out. I'll also practice ordering it out loud, especially if the name for the dish is in another language, and I don't know how to pronounce it."

I don't know any neurotypical people who sit at home googling how to pronounce words like *bouillabaisse* or *injera* so they don't seem "weird" at a restaurant. But for Autistics, this level of scripting and pre-planning is normal.[27] It gives us a comforting sense of mastery and control. However, when neurotypical people figure out we've put this much time and thought into activities that are "basic" to them, they tend to find it very off-putting. So for masked Autistics, blending in isn't just a matter of figuring out the right hacks. We also learn to hide the fact we're relying on such hacks at all.

Kaitlin says that sometimes her friends "catch" her using social scripting at restaurants. Because of her eating disorder history, this level of effort and forethought reads as suspicious:

"My friend Amy figured out I was studying restaurant menus in advance, because I knew too much about the menu. She thought that meant I was counting calories and still active in my eating disorder. You have to walk this tightrope. Know enough, but not too much, or people find it very awkward."

Amy couldn't understand that Kaitlin studied the menu in order to manage and reduce anxiety related to her eating disorder. Instead, she assumed that her friend was worrying "too much" about the menu because she was restricting her diet again. For masked Autistic people, knowing "too much" or thinking about something too deeply is seen as suspect. People find it calculating or creepy for us to put more effort into something they never grant a passing thought.

In all of these ways, Autistic "life hacks" and the pressures of masking are quite often linked. But they don't have to be. Though neurotypical people expect us to hide the efforts we go to in order to fit in, not hiding our brushstrokes can be a revolutionary act. If something is difficult for us, we shouldn't have to pretend it's easy, or hide our exhaustion or stress. And if we need a lot of information in order to feel comfortable navigating an unfamiliar space, we shouldn't have to conceal that fact, either.

Though Kaitlin is not out as Autistic to everyone, she did decide to explain her "guilty" menu knowledge to Amy.

"When I was younger and even more insecure, it would have been an embarrassment to reveal oh yeah, actually I have been reading menus ahead of time. But Amy knows I have an Autistic brother, she knows how that affects his life. So I told her, *look, I'm like he is, and this is what we do.* It helps me to study new places and new foods."

Now that Amy understands Kaitlin's Autistic life hacks, the two have bonded over it. When they go out to eat, Amy asks Kaitlin about which ingredients are in a dish, or where a restaurant's bathrooms are located. Instead of needing to hide her prep work, Kaitlin gets to share it.

Many Autistic "life hacks" involve using subtle accessibility tools that don't mark us as disabled. We trade notes on which earplugs look the most subtle, which noise-canceling headphones are the most stylish, or how to use hobbies like crocheting or knitting to process social anxiety and avoid eye contact in classrooms. These are popular compensation methods because they work really well. But we don't always have to rely on subtle approaches that appeal to neurotypical sensibilities. We can proudly, visibly do our own things in our own ways, and share the shortcuts and systems that make our lives possible. We can stim with big, intense gestures, wear large, obvious ear defenders, and ask for help when we need it. The more honest we are about the challenges we're facing, the harder it will be for neurotypical people to ignore our voices, or the fact that most public spaces are still incredibly inaccessible. Being more radically visible is also an exercise in unlearning shame.

Be Radically Visible

Sky Cubacub is the founder of Rebirth Garments, a clothing and accessories company that centers on the needs of queer and disabled bodies. Sky's shop features a wide variety of colorful, comfortable items for people of all genders and sizes: bodysuits assembled from panels of fishnet and neon fabric, gender-affirming chest binders that aren't too restrictive or tight, and a large array of brightly patterned T-shirts, bandanas, and pins.

At the beginning of the COVID-19 pandemic, Rebirth Garments was one of the first shops to offer face masks with clear vinyl windows that make it possible to read the wearer's lips. For many disabled people (including Autistics), being able to read a person's lips makes it much easier to follow a conversation. With everyone wearing masks, I struggled to tell when someone was speaking to me, because I relied on the visual cue of their lips moving to tune my attention toward them.

The clear window masks were in such high demand Sky decided to give their design away for free. They're more than a fashion visionary; they're a political visionary, too, and that's evident in every aspect of how they run their business. Their entire body of work is driven by their philosophy of radical visibility, which they've discussed in workshops, a TEDx talk, and in their zine, *Radical Visibility: A Queercrip Dress Reform Movement Manifesto*.

What is radical visibility? It's an approach to LGBT and disabled acceptance that emphasizes and celebrates that which is usually obscured. It lays claim to words that have been used to dehumanize our communities—*queer, cripple, mad*—and wears them defiantly, as a source of pride. Radical visibility presents tools such as canes and prostheses as enviable fashion accessories. It renders our differences cool.

"Cultural norms don't encourage trans and disabled people to dress stylishly or loudly," Sky writes.[28] "Society wants us to 'blend in' and not draw attention to ourselves. But what if we were to resist society's desire to render us invisible? What if, through a dress reform, we collectively refuse to assimilate?"

Radical visibility, in other words, is absolutely antithetical to masking. Where masking conceals, radical visibility steps into the limelight. Where masking scans the environment constantly for signs of social threat, and reins in the unruly stims and tics of the Autistic body, radical visibility encourages it to simply be. A masker gets their needs met in private, through a serious of apologetic half measures and veiled coping mechanisms; a radically visible person openly declares who they are and what they require, because it's what they deserve.

Long before figuring out I was Autistic, I had noticed how visibly disabled people were encouraged to minimize their difference. In high school a close friend was looking to buy a wheelchair with an atomic green frame. It would have really suited her; she had a kind of emo-indie sense of style at the time and the bright green chair would have really worked with it. But my friend's mother discouraged her.

"You don't want your wheelchair to be the first thing people notice when they look at you," she said.

Having a black, nondescript wheelchair didn't really change the fact that disability was the first thing people saw when they looked at my friend. We were living in too ableist of a world for that. In public, strangers talked down to her, as if she were a child, or they acted as if she couldn't speak for herself. Ableism inclines us to zero in on the aspects of a person that strike us as unusual. The widespread social exclusion of disabled people contributes to this, too. The fewer people in wheelchairs you see, the more noteworthy a wheelchair seems. And the more strangers gawk and stare at wheelchair users, the less comfortable a physically disabled person feels entering the world. It's a self-perpetuating cycle of exclusion.

Having a bright green chair might have done more in the long term to normalize my friend's disability and make it unremarkable to people. It would have conveyed that wheelchairs are not something to hide, and that disability is not something to ignore or paper over with condescension or euphemism. And as the research on self-stigma that

I discussed earlier suggests, wearing one's identity with pride can reduce feelings of self-consciousness and alienation.

Autism isn't always as visually obvious as using a wheelchair, but research shows there are many subtle markers of our difference that neurotypical people do pick up on, though not always consciously. Sasson and colleagues (2017), for example, found that neurotypical people quickly and subconsciously identify that a stranger is Autistic, often within milliseconds of meeting them.[29] They don't realize that they've identified the person as Autistic, though; they just think the person is weird. Participants in the study were less interested in engaging in conversation with Autistic people and liked them less than non-Autistics, all based on a brief moment of social data. It's also important to point out that the Autistic people in this study didn't do anything "wrong"; their behavior was perfectly socially appropriate, as was the content of their speech. Though they tried their damnedest to present as neurotypical, their performance had some key tells, and was just slightly "off," and they were disliked because of it.

For all the effort that maskers put into hiding our neurodiversity, it often blows up in our faces. Inauthenticity and a forced-seeming social performance rubs neurotypicals the wrong way. In a landmark study into the psychology of perceived "creepiness," psychologists McAndrew and Koehnke (2016) asked 1,341 respondents to answer questions about which personal qualities and behaviors they associated with "creepy" people, and used statistical factor analysis to develop a measurable "creepiness" factor. The creepiness factor they developed included the following traits: a person having awkward, unpredictable behavior, an unnatural-looking smile, laughter that occurred at "unnatural" times, speaking for too long about a single topic, and not knowing when to end a conversation.[30] When Autistic people attempt to socialize and bond with others in an affable, enthusiastic way, these are often the very traits we embody. Even as we try to put the neurotypical people around us at ease by smiling, keeping the conversation moving, and staying present, we might be seen as scary or unsettling.

A series of experiments by social psychologists Leander, Chartrand, and Bargh (2012) found that when a person engages in social mirroring in an even slightly inappropriate way, it skeeves people out, and even makes them feel physically colder.[31] A little bit of mimicry is normal among friends. People mirror one another's postures and mannerisms as they get comfortable and fall into sync. But if you mirror someone too much, or at the wrong time, these studies show you can literally give other people the chills. Autistic maskers try really hard to mirror other people, but since we can't do it as fluently and effortlessly as neurotypicals do, we often unwittingly set off NT's creep-dars.

The solution, then, is to stop hiding and pretending to be something we're not. Instead of straining (and failing) to imitate NT people, we can become radically visible. Sasson's research found that when participants were told they were interacting with an Autistic person, their biases against us disappeared. Suddenly they liked their slightly awkward conversation partner, and expressed interest in getting to know them. Having an explanation for the Autistic person's oddness helped the creeped-out feeling go away. Follow-up research by Sasson and Morrison (2019) confirmed that when neurotypical people know that they're meeting an Autistic person, first impressions of them are far more positive, and after the interaction neurotypicals express more interest in learning about Autism.[32] Radical visibility has its rewards.

In Sky's work, to be radically visible is to embrace self-presentation as a form of protest. They write: "Radical Visibility is a call to action: to dress in order to not be ignored, to reject 'passing' and assimilation."

In person, Sky looks exactly as eye-catching and cool as they do in their photo shoots: they wear a silver-and-black headpiece made of metal scale mail and brightly patterned leggings and a crop top, with geometric crystal designs painted on their face. There's no ignoring them, no fear of the abled gaze causing them to hide how they naturally move, or what their body needs. Years ago, following the development of a stomach disorder, Sky had to stop wearing firm, structured pants (like jeans) in favor of bottoms made from stretchy materials. It's rare to see them wearing anything other than leggings or comfy bike shorts. In this respect, Sky's experiences are instructive to Autistics seeking to unmask. So many of us cram our bodies into uncomfortable, bland "professional" attire in order to blend in, though doing so can feel like the death of our individuality, or a sensory assault.

For masked Autistics who'd like to take a more radically visible approach to personal style, here are some ideas to get you started:

Radical Autism Visibility: Dressing to Unmask

- Identify which items of clothing put too much pressure on your body, or apply pressure in the "wrong" places. Replace too-tight pants with similar styles made from stretchy fabrics, for example, or swap out structured bras for bralettes. There are even neckties that come in soft, more flexible materials.

- Identify which types of clothing provide grounding or soothing sensory input. For example, some Autistic people enjoy the feeling of compression on their wrists, and tight watches or bracelets. Others enjoy heavy coats or vests.

- Find and remove other sources of sensory stress in your wardrobe: try cutting out all the tags in your clothing and placing inserts in uncomfortable shoes. Many Autistic people walk on the balls of their feet, so you may need extra support there.

- Figure out which patterns and styles really feel joyful to wear. Do you feel most "yourself" when you're all in black? Or do you prefer to be a bold rainbow?

- Incorporate special interests into your daily attire. Wear T-shirts with your favorite anime characters, or in more formal environments, get video-game-themed cuff links or lapel pins. "Closet cosplay" as your favorite characters in subtle ways.

- Stim in style: wear jewelry you can fidget with or chew on (chewelry), keep fidget toys in pockets, cover your phone case with colorful stickers or a pop-up stand you can fiddle with.

Many masked Autistic people are so divorced from their own bodies and self-presentation that it's hard to imagine how taking real ownership of it might feel. If your clothing has only ever been a neurotypical costume, you might not have any idea what authentic personal style would even look like. If that's the case, start small, and focus on alleviating your discomfort. Get rid of the clothing items that cause you pain or distress. Swap out uncomfortable items for more forgiving alternatives, and question ideas about respectability that might be holding you back. You might not need to wear the makeup, pantyhose, or rigid suit jackets a mentor or parent once taught you was compulsory. Maybe you can do the "big chop" and stop chemically straightening your hair,[33] or wear jewelry and textiles traditional to your home culture. Much of the professional world does place tight restrictions on how a person ought to dress and present themselves, but if you are among the majority of Autistics who work outside of a corporate environment, you may have more wiggle room than you think.

A growing number of Autistic creators are making wearable stim toys and accessibility tools. Carly Newman, a visual artist and jewelry designer, has made a line of earplug earrings for Autistic folks.[34] Instead of trying to hide the fact that I sometimes need earplugs when I'm in public, these earrings put my accessibility tools on display. Companies like Stimtastic and ARK Therapeutic specialize in stim jewelry, such as spinning rings and acupressure bracelets. Some Autistic creators have also made buttons, hats, and jewelry that do their communication for them: big badges in green that read *Come Say Hi!* or in yellow that say *Give Me Space*. At conventions that are well attended by Autistic people, these tools are invaluable, helping us socialize while also putting our boundaries on display. They aren't broadly normalized yet, but just like displaying one's pronouns on a pin or in an email signature, the more people adopt them, the more normalized thinking about them becomes.

Of course, wearing affirming clothing and accessories is just one means of embracing radical visibility. At its core, both unmasking and radical visibility are about dropping the façade of compliant neurotypicality, and learning to live openly and honestly as oneself. That is primarily a change in how we express ourselves and our needs to other people. To that end, here are a few tips for how to practice radical visibility in your daily life:

Everyday Unmasking: Daily Challenges for Being Radically Visible
Disappoint someone: Practice saying "no," "I'm not available to do that," "I'm uncomfortable with that," or "I have to go now" without any explanation or apology.
Express disagreement in a situation where you'd normally just nod along to keep the peace.
Notice when you feel pressured to do something you don't wish to do. Practice observing this aloud: "I'm not sure why you are pushing this, because I already said no."
Try to go an entire day without guessing or anticipating anyone's emotions.
Try to go an entire day without controlling what messages your facial expressions or body language is giving off.
Ask for something you usually feel too guilty to request.
Go through an entire conversation without faking any reactions or emotions.
Sing along to your favorite music while walking down the street.
Bring a stim toy with you to a social gathering or public space, and use it without shame.
Wear a fancy outfit or costume you absolutely love, instead of waiting for an event or an "excuse" to wear it.
When a friend asks you how you are doing, give them an honest answer.
Take action without running it past anyone else for approval.
Share big emotions with safe people: find someone you can cry with, or vent to a friend about something that fills you with rage.
Tell someone you trust about your neurodiversity, and what it means to you.

Radical visibility is self-advocacy, as well as self-expression. But for most masked Autistic people, it's downright terrifying to stand up for yourself. We tend to default to people pleasing, smiling, and laughing uncomfortably through social difficulty, and to do so in such a reflexive way that it's as if our true feelings and preferences disappear when other people are around. These reflexes exist to protect us, and there is no shame in having them. However, if we wish to live more freely, we need to cultivate relationships where we can communicate honestly and feel heard and respected. The next chapter is all about constructing Autistic relationships that help us to thrive. By this, I mean forming meaningful relationships and a sense of community with fellow Autistic people, as well as making our existing relationships with allistic people far more Autism-friendly.

CHAPTER 7

Cultivating Autistic Relationships

It's been years since he stopped working with Act Up and moved out of New York, but James Finn remains a highly engaged LGBTQ activist. From the small village in Michigan where he now lives, he regularly publishes articles about the latest legal and political attacks on LGBTQ rights happening throughout the world, and meets regularly with activist groups. He also helps manage one of the largest LGBTQ groups on Facebook. Sometimes, James's direct, very Autistic style of communicating rubs his fellow activists the wrong way. He once deeply offended a fellow organizer by asking her to slow down and explain her plans more clearly.

"I had to actually come out and say, listen I honestly don't understand you," James says, "I know that other people in this conversation probably do. But I'm Autistic and I have a lot of trouble reading between lines sometimes; can I ask you to just slow down?"

On paper, James had done everything right. He'd stood up for himself, asked for the relatively simple accommodation he needed, and even explained why he was finding it hard to keep up. He was unmasking flawlessly. Unfortunately, it didn't go over well—at least not at first.

"She said, I was gaslighting her and mansplaining," he says with a sigh. "I just made myself vulnerable and she became hostile."

Autistic people tend to love *infodumping* (sharing knowledge with other people as a means of bonding), we miss social cues that seem obvious to others, and we tend to speak in monotonous voices that are read as dry or sarcastic. A lot of us find the natural flow of conversation challenging, either interrupting people at the "wrong" times, or failing to jump in during a fast-paced exchange and being left out entirely. For these and other reasons, Autistic women (particularly women of color) are often viewed as cold or "bitchy," and Autistic men are often mistaken for being condescending "mansplainers." It's a very challenging social minefield to navigate, because of course most women have been mansplained to before, and have been gaslit, and are understandably on edge when facing behavior that resembles it. Abled people who are oppressed along one identity, such as gender, don't always understand they might wield a certain degree of power over disabled people who look very socially powerful to them.

The organizer was certain she was being mocked by James, or that he was asking her to re-explain her points in an attempt to derail her. No doubt men in activist meetings have used such tactics against her in the past. Luckily, there were other meeting attendees who were able to vouch for James's character.

"Fortunately, a couple other people in the room spoke up and said *no, he's not joking, he's pretty damn Autistic*," he says.

The other organizer wasn't willing to trust James when he spoke about his own disability (it's so rare that we are trusted and heard when we communicate our needs), but she did defer to the abled people who backed James up. The tension in the meeting was quickly disarmed. Without that support, James's honesty and self-advocacy might have been punished.

James's behavior is a perfect model of how to stand up for yourself as an Autistic person, and the response of his acquaintances are also a picture-perfect illustration of how to be an ally to Autistic people. Despite all of this, the interaction was still tense. I think it's important to show an example of nearly everyone acting correctly, or at least understandably, with a somewhat unsatisfying result. Unmasking isn't a universally positive experience; sometimes when we put ourselves first, we will frustrate and disappoint others, maybe even leave them feeling triggered or upset. It's vital we learn to navigate interactions marked by conflict, and practice standing firm in the face of negative reactions from others. As long as we haven't abused anyone or violated their rights, it's okay for our actions to make others unhappy. After all, neurotypical people step on conversational toes and continue breezily along all the time. Neurodivergent folks should, at the very least, be given the latitude to be flawed, fully present humans as well.

In many ways, masking is psychologically similar to codependency, a relational pattern of seeking to manage or control the reactions and emotions of other people that usually results from abuse.[1] Unmasking requires we stop relying on neurotypical people's acceptance in order to guide how we should act—and that means sometimes doing the "right" thing even when we know it will rub others the wrong way. Most masked Autistics need a lot of practice developing a strong sense of *discernment*, which is essentially using our own beliefs and perceptions to guide our behavior, rather than deferring to everyone else's fleeting reactions and impressions. Maskers tend to get very distressed when people are unhappy with us, because disapproval has been so dangerous and painful for us in the past. Many of us will do nearly anything to keep other people satisfied. Learning to tolerate the distress of upsetting someone is crucial to developing reliable self-advocacy skills.

Maskers are highly dependent on the opinions and feelings of other people. We bend over backward to make life easy for neurotypicals and the people we care about, we hide facets of ourselves that are distracting, weird, or inconvenient, and we become hypervigilant about tracking people for signs of disapproval. It's normal and healthy to be considerate toward other people, but masked Autistics tend to devote so much energy to people pleasing that we have almost no cognitive space left to think about (or listen to) ourselves. It also impedes us from connecting with people in a genuine way. You have to really recognize a person's emotions—good and bad—and respond to them honestly in order to forge a bond. Surface-level smiling and mimicry makes it harder to see and appreciate people in all their complexity.

Unmasking in public feels nearly impossible, because when we are around people, it's as if we have no thoughts or feelings of our own. I've been in that position myself, so profoundly inhibited I had no idea what my genuine preferences were, unable to recognize someone had crossed a boundary or made me uncomfortable until hours after the fact, when I was alone and had space to reflect. Though I wish I could present unmasking as a singularly positive experience where you unburden yourself of all anxiety and venture out into an accepting, enlightened world, I know for a fact this isn't the case. Often it will be nerve-racking and awkward. We have to choose to unmask because we recognize masking is hurting us, and that it is worth being subjected to neurotypical disapproval in order to claw our way out of that trap.

Sometimes unmasking means getting odd looks on the bus and working like hell to not let it keep you from stimming. Sometimes it means writing an email to a friend, days after an argument, to explain that you've just realized their words hurt your feelings. For Black and brown Autistics, unmasking is particularly fraught, as being visibly disabled in public can turn deadly. For many of us it will mean making hard decisions about where we feel most safe and accepted, and when and how we can unmask most effectively. There are a lot of competing forces at play when we bring our real selves to a social interaction, and a lot of risks that exist alongside the copious opportunities and benefits.

In order for unmasking to be sustainable and healthy for us, we have to put a lot of new coping strategies in our arsenal and have some truly supportive loved ones in our corner. We have to be able to manage conflict in our relationships and nourish the bonds we have with those who truly understand us. At times, unmasking means teaching our neurotypical friends and family to treat us better; in other situations, it may mean disengaging from those who aren't ever going to be worth the effort. This chapter is filled with exercises and research that are all about crafting relationships that serve your emotional and psychological needs as an Autistic person—and learning how to navigate the public spaces and social interactions that aren't as supportive and accepting as well.

Self-Disclose—When It Makes Sense To

When James explained that he couldn't follow what was being said because he is Autistic, he was *self-disclosing* his disabled status. Research is mixed on whether Autistic self-disclosure is beneficial. As I've already discussed, some experimental work does show that when a neurotypical person realizes they're speaking with an Autistic person, they exhibit less bias, and like the person more than if they hadn't known. Realizing that a person's awkwardness is actually just neurodivergence can make it seem more explicable and less "creepy." However, psychologists aren't sure this short-term benefit (observed in one-on-one conversations) translates to large groups or workplaces.

A recent study by Romualdez and colleagues asked Autistic adults about their experiences self-disclosing in professional settings.[2] The authors found that while most Autistics "came out" with the hope of getting workplace accommodations and being treated more patiently, 45 percent said the decision did not benefit them. Though relatively few people in this sample reported being mistreated after coming out as Autistic, many confessed that it didn't change anything about how they were treated, and only left them feeling more vulnerable. On the flip side, 40.4 percent of respondents said that coming out was a net positive, either because their supervisor was open to accommodating them or because coworkers were understanding and appreciative.

Additional research shows that the impact of Autistic self-disclosure really varies based on how knowledgeable a person is about the neurotype.[3] When someone's knowledge of Autism is shallow and stereotypical, they tend to react to self-disclosure in a highly stigmatizing, dehumanizing way. They may be startled to realize that Autism can even occur in adults, for example, and might blurt out the much-bemoaned, "but you don't look Autistic!" Sometimes an Autistic self-disclosure is met with infantilization (even literally being spoken to in a baby voice), or with a ton of condescending reassurance about how smart they are, and how good they are at seeming normal. When an Autistic person comes out at school or work, they may suddenly be given a very wide berth, because people are terrified of saying the wrong thing or offending them. However, meeting an Autistic adult and having a positive interaction with them often opens up neurotypical people's minds, and makes them more receptive to learning about Autism.

One avenue for practicing self-disclosure without risking IRL rejection is on social media. On social media platforms like TikTok and Instagram, Autistic teens and adults have gone viral with videos of themselves reacting to new music with their "masks" off. One such video depicting a nineteen-year-old Autistic woman stimming while wearing headphones became hyperpopular in July 2020; it's been viewed by more than 10 million people and shared far and wide.[4] Comments on the video are almost entirely supportive and curious, and the video's creator, Jay, has followed up with numerous other short clips educating her followers about Autism acceptance. Writer and Twitter power user Nicole Cliffe came out as Autistic in 2020,[5] after writing about her kids' Autism in a compassionate way for many years prior, and has frequently used her platform to educate her followers about masking and compensation. Her followers have been immensely supportive, and many have come forward to share their own neurodiverse experiences. After decades of widespread misinformation, fearmongering, and stereotyping, the public is finally taking an interest in how Autistic people describe our experiences, and we finally have the outlets to ensure we're being heard.

Of course, it's not always a positive experience to be openly Autistic online. When a Black Autistic dancer that I know posted videos of herself stimming along to music on Twitter, she was met with harassment and accusations of "faking" her disability for attention. I can't even cite her tweet anymore, because the deluge of harassment she received caused her to disable her account. It's noteworthy a Black woman was treated as suspicious for doing the exact same thing Jay, a white Autistic, received praise for: being openly, happily Autistic online in hopes of educating others.

The decision of when and how to self-disclose puts Autistic people in quite a double bind. In order to be known, we have to come out, but we're usually coming out in a harsh cultural landscape where it's likely that people won't actually understand us. By coming out, we help to counter ignorant images people have of our disability, but because those stereotypes are so pervasive and long-standing, it's impossible for a single counter-example to undo all the harm that's been done. Often, when a person from the majority group encounters information that runs against their stereotypes of an oppressed group, they respond by either *discounting* the information (for example, by saying "you're not really that Autistic!") or by *subgrouping* the people who deviate from stereotypes (for example, by telling them "you're not like those other Autistic people, the ones who are really impaired. You're one of the smart ones!").[6]

A lot of times, to self-disclose is to subject oneself to a deluge of invalidation and ignorance. The positive impact you make is not necessarily one you'll ever notice or benefit from directly. Crystal has struggled with this since the day she got diagnosed. Despite the fact that her mother and grandfather were the people who blocked her from being assessed as a kid, they reacted to her diagnosis as if it were completely baffling and shocking. They even said that her Autistic traits were better left ignored, that everyone struggles to fit in and keep up. This is unfortunately a common experience for the first person to come out as Autistic in their family. Relatives who share undiagnosed Autistic traits may defensively dismiss the newly identified person, saying that their struggles are just a normal part of life. Of course, this speaks to their own lifelong experiences of suffering in silence. Resistance and bitter reactions may reveal the resentment family members feel about having not gotten the help or recognition they deserved, either.

For Autistic self-disclosure to really have an impact on someone, you need a mutually respectful, trusting relationship. They need to be willing to keep learning and revise their understanding of what Autism is as they go along. Recently, Crystal started dating Aaqib, an elementary school teacher who told her he knew very little about Autism in adults. At first he said all the typical, oblivious things people usually say when you come out as Autistic to them: Crystal was too pretty and poised to be Autistic, and Autism wasn't a good enough "excuse" for her to forget dates they had planned. Crystal told Aaqib to step up and educate himself—and he did. He started watching videos by Autistic people, and bought some of the books Crystal recommended he read.

"I found one of the books I gave him dog-eared by the toilet at his house," she says. "Like he actually read it. Which shouldn't be a high bar, but my family never read any of the things about Autism that I sent to them."

Aaqib has proven himself to be worth the effort of self-disclosure and self-advocacy; Crystal's family has not.

I wish I could recommend that every Autistic person be loudly and visibly disabled in every area of their life. But I recognize how unrealistic and oversimplified such a statement would be. Though most of us are initially hesitant to self-disclose and sometimes have to overcome our anxiety and self-doubt, we also each know our own circumstances best. There are a lot of great reasons to self-disclose your disability to someone, and many equally valid reasons to avoid doing so. Here are some reflection questions to get you pondering how you'd like to navigate the issue:

1. Who do I want to "come out" as Autistic to?
2. Why do I want to come out? What do I hope will happen?
3. What do I wish people understood better about me?
4. How much energy am I willing to put into educating this person about what Autism "really" is?
5. Do I have a specific "ask" that I'd like to make, such as a request for an accommodation or different treatment?
6. Who "gets" me and can help advocate for me?

As these questions reveal, unmasking and coming out as Autistic are not one and the same, and neither decision is binary, either. You can be openly Autistic among friends and a select few trusted family members, for example, but not at large family gatherings or at work. You can choose to pour a lot of time into teaching people at your church about Autism if you think it will pay off—or you can just share the specific accommodations that you need, without delving into why. It's always helpful to have a trusted advocate at your side as well.

It isn't your responsibility to get everyone on the same page, or to subject yourself to judgment and stigma unnecessarily. For example, you may decide that it's easier to tell HR you get migraines, and that that's why you need a dimmer switch put on the lights. If saying you're too sick to go out is easier than telling your friends you're dealing with Autistic burnout, it's okay to use that as an "excuse" to cancel plans. It's also fine to come out slowly, first getting to know your unmasked self privately, then developing unmasked (or less-masked) relationships with the people who feel safest to you. A secure base of supportive people can help back you up when others doubt your disability, as James's activist friends did. They can step in and help you manage sensory overwhelm or remind you to check in with your body for signs of distress. It's much easier to believe that you deserve accommodation when you have people around you who act as though that is true. Here are a couple of affirmations to keep in mind when you are navigating the self-disclosure process:

- Autism is not something I need to apologize for.
- Other people don't need to understand me, or understand everything about Autism, in order to treat me with respect.
- I am [coming out/asking for accommodations] for me, not for anyone else.

It's vitally important that in addition to all the individual-level work we put into unmasking and demanding our needs get met, that we also find and cultivate supportive relationships with people who make it a lot easier to do so. That's what the next exercise is all about—breaking down any tendency to people-please, and developing deeper relationships with what Samuel Dylan Finch calls your "strawberry people."

Cultivating Unmasked Friendships— Find Your "Strawberry People"

In his writing about Autistic fawning and people pleasing, Samuel Dylan Finch describes how he used to push genuine friendships away. He associated loving a person with working hard to keep them happy. Conversely, if someone was consistently warm and giving, Samuel didn't trust it. He didn't think he could reciprocate real affection.

"I had this tendency to bail on [the] friends, partners, acquaintances, whoever, that were the most generous, warm, and emotionally-available," he writes.[7] "For people-pleasers, we're so used to working endlessly hard in relationships—it's disorienting when we aren't asked to."

Samuel felt more at home in insecure, hot-and-cold relationships. He dated abusive people, was exploited by professional contacts, and neglected new acquaintances that had the potential to become something more. After years of this, he recognized he needed to rewire his brain's social pathways. What felt familiar clearly was not good for him. So he sat down and made a list of the people who deserved his friendship.

"I made a Google doc of people who were 'too nice' to me," he writes. "In my phone contacts, I put emojis by their names. I put strawberries next to people who were super loving. I put seedling emojis by folks who taught me things that made me think or grow."

Samuel reached out to his "strawberry people" and told them that he wanted to prioritize his friendship with them. He admitted he'd discouraged their affection in the past because he'd been afraid of disappointing them. And from then on, whenever he got a notification on his phone and saw a strawberry or seedling symbol, he made sure to answer quickly, and enthusiastically. He didn't cancel plans with these friends anymore or create artificial distance. He centered them in his life.

By and large, Autistic people don't operate by social intuition the way neurotypicals do. Every notification we receive tends to be given equal weight, no matter how well we know a person or how we feel about them. This is particularly true for maskers, who can be so terrified of upsetting anyone that they seek to be equally friendly and responsive to everyone. It can be useful to outsource the social instincts that might come naturally to the average allistic person by labeling certain individuals as high priority, or turning off all notifications except for those from a specific group chat or app. Instead of having to make manual decisions about whom to respond to and in which order, the "strawberry people" system reinforces the idea that certain relationships are more important than others, because they help you cultivate a more solid sense of self.

Within a year of his making these changes in his life, many of Samuel's "strawberry people" had become members of his found family. They had his back as he worked through therapy for PTSD and eating disorder recovery. The strawberry people even became friends with one another—Samuel writes that they all talk in a single group chat.

Developmental psychology research has observed that Autistic people often have insecure attachments to other people, beginning from a very young age.[8] A person's attachment patterns are shaped by their early relationships, particularly the stability of their bond with their primary caregiver. The quality of a person's early attachments also tend to predict the quality of their later relationships, both romantic and otherwise, and their ability to accept comfort and emotional support from other people.

As developmental psychologists define it, a child with secure attachment uses their caregiver as a grounding, supportive "base" from which to explore the world. A securely attached toddler may venture around an unfamiliar playground a bit, fiddling with the playground equipment or trying to make new friends, for example, but they will return to their attachment figure periodically to check in and feel safe. When left alone, a securely attached child will experience sadness or distress, but they are quick to relax and feel soothed once their caregiver returns. As they grow up, securely attached children become adults who can bond with other people with relative ease, and who can handle conflicts and challenges in their relationship with a high degree of stability and trust.

There are several attachment patterns that developmental psychologists consider to be dysfunctional. For example, an anxiously attached child might be afraid to wander away from a caregiver for fear of being abandoned, and when left alone may experience extreme distress that they don't easily recover from. In contrast, an avoidantly attached child may fail to engage much with their caregivers. Autistics have been observed to exhibit what's called an anxious-ambivalent attachment style at rates that are elevated compared to the neurotypical population. People with an anxious-ambivalent attachment are difficult to soothe and reassure, and don't see close loved ones as a safe, "secure base" they can find comfort in when lost or threatened. As adults, people who are anxious-ambivalent tend to get into patterns of intense emotional dependency, combined with insecurity. They yearn to be accepted yet doubt that they can be. When other people try to connect with us, we rebuff them without even realizing it.

It bears mentioning here that developmental psychologists define what a secure attachment "looks like" based on how it presents in neurotypical children and adults. Neurotypical children who are securely attached check in with their parents in a very easy to recognize way, using eye contact and vocalizations that many Autistic children might find unnatural. Furthermore, many of the signs of having an insecure attachment style are difficult to distinguish from neurodivergence (and from being traumatized after living in a neurotypical world). Avoidant attachment, for example, is marked by a child turning their back to their caregiver and failing to seek them out for comfort when distressed. While these behaviors can indicate a child doesn't feel supported by their caregiver, it can also be a sign they're Autistic and averse to touch, eye contact, or verbal communication.

From an early age, many Autistic people experience rejection and lack of understanding from our primary caregivers. We also may be punished or neglected because we have failed to seek out comfort in neurotypical-approved ways. Our attempts at connection, such as playing next to another person but not making eye contact with them (sometimes called *parallel play*), may be mistaken as a lack of social interest. An intense Autistic meltdown may be mistaken for us being incapable of being soothed, and taken as a sign of an anxious attachment pattern. For these and a variety of other reasons, many Autistic people do wind up feeling very insecure in our attachments to other people, or having our heartfelt attempts at connection rebuffed or misconstrued. Neurotypical attachment "rules" essentially make it impossible for us to be viewed as suitable for regular, healthy bonds.

One way that an insecure attachment style sometimes manifests in Autistic adults is feeling discomfort when receiving praise or attention. You may not even recognize the positive attention you're getting is socially appropriate, because you're so used to being mocked or picked apart, or else being swallowed up in intense or abusive relationships. It can be beneficial to get an outsider's perspective to see if someone really is being "too nice" to you, as Samuel put it, or if you're just so accustomed to mistreatment that niceness strikes you as suspect.

Here are some questions to help you reflect on whether you push secure attachments away.

Are You Pushing Your "Strawberry People" Away?

1. When someone gives you a compliment, do you feel like you have to downplay it?
2. Are there people in your life who seem "too nice"? Who are they?
3. Are you afraid of trusting people because they might abandon you?
4. When someone gives you positive attention, do you feel creeped out?
5. Are you afraid that kind, loving people deserve "better" than to be friends with you?
6. When someone gets vulnerable with you, do you find ways to downplay it?
7. Do you have a hard time showing people that you like them?

These questions get to the heart of the protectiveness and self-doubt that lead many Autistic people to keep our emotional distance from others. Most of us have a slew of good reasons for fearing people. When I was younger, many of the people who took an interest in me were women who wanted to help "teach" me how to be better at womanhood. Sometimes classmates and coworkers would cozy up to me because they wanted my help with their classwork or writing. I started assuming that if someone took an interest in me, it was because they wanted to fix me for their own amusement, or because they thought I was useful. I figured every compliment I received was me being "negged"—a tactic where people highlight your difference or offer a backhanded compliment in order to make you feel insecure.

It's challenging for Autistic people to tell the difference between friends who genuinely like us, and superficial acquaintances who are responding favorably to our masks. One way to probe the difference, though, is to look at people who have stuck around when you haven't been perfect. You won't ever be able to relax around someone if their approval is conditional. Here are some questions I use to help distinguish between the people who are worthy of Samuel's strawberry emoji, and those who are only interested in the agreeable, "fawner" me.

1. Who do I feel comfortable expressing disagreement to?
2. Who helps me think about my opinions and choices in a nonjudgmental way?
3. Who tells me honestly when I've hurt them, and gives me a real opportunity to do better?
4. Who treats me with respect no matter what?
5. Who leaves me feeling rejuvenated or inspired?
6. Who brings out the wild, playful side of me?
7. Is there anyone I want to try being more open and unfiltered with?

When I think carefully about these questions, a handful of very thoughtful, reliable, nonjudgmental friends come to mind. Their affection is consistent, and it shows in small gestures, like remembering the details of stories I've shared. When we disagree, these friends try to understand my perspective, or reflect thoughtfully on why I might see things as I do. If I say something flippant and hurtful, they tell me for the sake of our friendship, but they don't relish me feeling ashamed. They share what they want from me, ask for help when they need it, and don't hold it against me when I fumble in my attempts to be there for them. These friends are also typically the people I can share messy emotions or half-formed opinions with, and who I feel comfortable being weird, petty, or silly around. Their support provides me a safe place to land when I'm angry, sad, or obsessing over some random thing a coworker said that I can't yet make sense of.

On the flip side, I've found that I can identify who is not destined to become a "strawberry person" for me by pondering these questions:

1. Who do I force myself to spend time with, out of a sense of obligation or guilt?

2. Who do I feel I have to earn the approval of?
3. Who makes me feel insecure and not good enough?
4. Who do I find exhausting to be around?
5. Who do I edit or censor myself around?

Often, the people who fall into this category are outgoing and do give me a lot of attention, but only in a surface-level way. They may show an interest in me, but their questions feel pointed, or like a test. Being around them doesn't help me relax and unmask; it puts me on edge. Some of them are people whom I really find funny or interesting, but whom I've witnessed ostracize or punish others for making a single social error or single choice they disagreed with. One person who came to mind was an incredibly charming friend whom I've noticed only ever tells me in a vague way that I've disappointed them, but refuses to actually explain what I've done, or why. Another friend who came to mind is an older writer I used to look up to, but who persistently lectured me about how I was too cold, too intellectual, and too "arrogant" every single time we hung out. Even if some of her observations are right, I have never felt accepted or even liked in her presence. She's not genuinely invested in my growth; she mostly seems to want to knock me down a peg.

The more time you spend with your "strawberry people," the more socially fluent you'll feel, and the less you'll associate human contact with having to put on a stressful, phony performance. Quality time with nonthreatening people can also help you develop social skills that carry over into other relationships, too. Neuroscientists have observed that Autistic brains continue to develop in areas associated with social skills for far longer than neurotypical brains are believed to.[9] One study, conducted by Bastiaansen and colleagues (2011), observed that though young Autistic people experienced far less activity than allistics in the inferior frontal gyrus (an area of the frontal lobe involved in interpreting facial expressions), by age thirty no differences between non-Autistics and Autistic people were evident. In other words, Autistic brains eventually "caught up" to neurotypical brains, in terms of how actively they processed and interpreted facial expressions as social data. Other studies have found that Autistic people over the age of fifty are comparable to allistic people, in terms of their ability to make sense of the motivations and emotions of others.[10]

Researchers aren't sure why these findings occur, only that they help to justify conceiving of Autism as a developmental disability or delay. For my part, I suspect that Autistic people get better at reading faces and understanding human behavior over time because we eventually develop our own systems and tricks for making sense of the world. We might have developed at the same pace as neurotypicals if we'd been given accessible tools earlier on. The social scripts and shortcuts that work for neurotypical people do not work for us, so we have to teach ourselves to develop social instincts.

Autistic people can get better at reading people's facial expressions as we age, and with the more social contact we have. But we also deserve to live in a world where neurotypicals try just as hard to understand us. When we spend time with people who do not terrify us or make us feel socially threatened, we may be get more comfortable with eye contact, initiating conversations, and being assertive.[11] As an Autistic person, you may never escape social anxiety entirely, and you might always be a bit reactive to the threat of abandonment. You also don't have to learn to express yourself or connect with others in a neurotypical-approved way. If eye contact is painful and overwhelming for you, unmasking by refusing to perform eye contact is more important than getting comfortable with it. By engaging with healthy, supportive people, you can learn to open up and express yourself effectively—in a way that works for you. As you get more comfortable in your own skin, you may find that people are less threatening and confusing as an added benefit.

Communicate Clearly and Honestly

Autistic people usually prefer explicit, clear messages that don't rely on tone or nonverbal cues. We like having specific expectations laid out for us, and being given many opportunities to ask questions and clarify meaning. When we share these needs with the allistic people around us, our relationships can open up, allowing for much greater depth and breadth of connection. When we accept the unique features and strengths of our communication style, we can also feel a lot less socially inept and disempowered.

Here's a table summarizing some common Autistic communication needs. You can share this table with neurotypical people in your life or organizations that are aiming to be more accessible, or simply request some of these specific adjustments for yourself.

Common Autistic Communication Needs	
Overall Need	**Some Accommodations You Might Request**
Clear Expectations	• Specific plans with details about time, place, and what is likely to happen • A clear "yes" or "no," no euphemisms like "I'll think about it" • Meeting agendas that are handed out in advance, and then adhered to • Reading materials, questions, and discussion topics being provided in advance of a panel, interview, or other high-stress public event • Step-by-step, detailed instructions on how to complete a task • Specific, measurable outcomes or goals.

Overall Need	Some Accommodations You Might Request
Explicit Messaging	• Not assuming people can use facial expression, tone of voice, posture, breathing, or tears as indicators of emotion • Giving direct explanations of feelings: "I am disappointed right now because . . ." • Recognition and respect of boundaries: "It doesn't sound like Sherry wants to talk about that right now." • Not punishing or judging people for failing to read between the lines. • Using clarifying questions: "What would you like me to do about this?"
Reduced Sensory/Social Load	• Having no expectation of eye contact during intense conversations • Giving space to talk about challenging topics while driving, taking a walk, or doing something with one's hands • Allowing people to express emotions and opinions via text, email, or handwritten note • Giving people time alone to reflect on their feelings and beliefs • Learning to recognize fawning, and signs of an upcoming meltdown • Providing frequent breaks from socializing, or quiet spaces people can retreat to

Just as we crave direct communication, we're equally good at dishing it out—sometimes too good, in fact. Throughout our lives, masked Autistics are punished for requesting clarity, being blunt, or saying directly the things others would rather imply. Over time we learn to filter our self-expression. However, as adults with more life experience and self-advocacy skills under our belts, we can begin to examine our communication style, and turn our conversational quirks into advantages.

More times than I can count, I've spoken up during a work meeting to ask what the actual point of the meeting is. In both academia and political organizing, it's quite common for people to call a meeting when they have a loose sense that something needs to be done, but aren't sure exactly what that something is yet, or how to accomplish it. My overly analytic Autistic brain yearns for structure, and my social anxiety and sensory issues mean I want most meetings to end as quickly as humanly possible. So, when the conversation seems to have lost the plot and people are talking in circles, I tend to jump into an unofficial facilitator role. If someone dances around expressing reservations, I try to understand their perspective and voice my own concerns explicitly. If someone behaves inappropriately or is offensive without realizing it, I redirect when I can. Many Autistic people can skillfully put their "little professor" and masking instincts to good use in situations like these, taking the tools they once used to placate and deescalate and putting them toward more prosocial ends.

Last winter, I was attending a Diversity & Inclusion committee meeting at my university. As a quick getting-to-know-you icebreaker, the meeting organizer asked us to introduce ourselves, and then share the thing we missed most about our pre-pandemic lives.

This is a very insensitive icebreaker question. At that point in time, many of us had been isolated for nearly a year, and were desperately craving social contact, physical touch, and events to look forward to. It was a miserably bleak, lonesome winter, capping off an absolutely horrific year filled with death. I'm sure that several people in the meeting had lost loved ones to COVID. Of course, during a work meeting you can't say that the thing you miss most about life pre-COVID is a beloved relative who died. You have to pick a sanitized, work-appropriate answer instead, like saying you miss eating at your favorite Peruvian restaurant. The dissonance made me feel ill. So when it came time to introduce myself to the group, I said this:

"Hi, everyone, I'm Devon, and I think I'll pass on that icebreaker.

If I get to talking about everything I miss from life before COVID, I'll start to cry!"

People laughed sympathetically at my remark, which I made sure to deliver in a lighthearted tone. I didn't want the meeting facilitator to feel criticized, but I felt it was important I highlight how uncomfortable his question had been. Masking and honesty weren't opposing forces in that moment—one helped facilitate the other.

After I spoke up, other meeting participants opted not to answer the icebreaker as well. One person privately messaged me, thanking me for saying what I did. Later in that same meeting, I shared my dismay that the committee wasn't considering a proposal, raised by many of Loyola's Black students, to have police taken off campus. I admitted I found much of the Diversity & Inclusion committee's goals (which involved things like counting the number of scholars of color listed on various course syllabi) somewhat insufficient, and thought we needed to do more to address police violence on our campus. As an Autistic, male-aligned white person who is valued for my directness, I knew I could get away with raising concerns others might not.

The first few times I asserted myself like this, I worried I'd come across as super rude. Instead, I've almost always been thanked. I have learned that many allistic people find clear communication to be a welcome relief. In the workplace, carefully dispensed Autistic candor can come in handy. Phrases like "No, I don't have time for that," "I'm uncomfortable with this," and "What's your budget?" cut through elaborate social performances and render vague matters far more concrete. I'm capable of being too blunt or saying the wrong thing at the absolute worst time, but for the most part I've figured out how to put my Autistic candor to work for me, after years of trying to hide it.

Though Autistic people have a reputation for being "bad" at communicating, the data shows that really isn't the case. A study by Crompton et al. published in 2019 found that when two Autistic people were paired together to work on a task, they were very efficient social communicators. They spread a lot of knowledge and nuance in a short span of time, completed the task quickly, and connected to one another easily.[12] However, when paired with non-Autistic conversation partners, Autistics were frequently misunderstood and not listened to. This study suggests that much of what researchers consider the "social deficits" of Autism aren't really deficits at all; they're just differences in our communication style that neurotypicals don't adjust to.

When neurodiverse people push for more explicit messaging, everybody benefits. Vague, symbolic communication is harder to parse if you're Deaf or hard of hearing, an immigrant from a different culture with different idioms, a nonnative English speaker, or a person with social anxiety. The more elaborate and symbolic a culture is, the more difficult people from outside the culture will find it to navigate. In some instances, this is done as a deliberate method of gatekeeping and exclusion. Academics are trained, for example, to write in a very dry, passive, and jargon-filled way, as a sign of our intellect and seriousness. Because it is hard to understand academic writing and it's only really taught within the academy, being able to follow it becomes a sign you "belong." But hard-to-understand writing is, by definition, less effective writing. Similarly, the business world relies on hyperspecific jargon and a variety of sports metaphors, which can leave those unfamiliar with its macho culture and communication style quite excluded. Tearing down barriers like these is essential to building a diverse, fluid community that is capable of evolution and growth.

I used to believe I was horribly inept for not being able to read between the lines of neurotypical speech. Now I realize most neurotypicals aren't all that good at it, either. Non-Autistic people process complex situations intuitively and efficiently, but make a lot of errors. Just think of how many times you've seen a really confident, outgoing person misread a situation, interrupt another person, or say something offensive without seeming to realize it, or to care. There are negative consequences to such actions, but usually the allistic person who made the error doesn't have to bear the brunt of them. It's everyone around them who has to scramble to pick up the pieces, clarify the misunderstanding, or smooth over hurt feelings. One of the most liberating realizations I've made as an out Autistic person is that it's not harmful for me to ask questions, interject when needed, or be honest about how I feel. When you tell people what you want and need, you actually stand a chance of getting it. You also free up other people to express their needs more openly, too.

Letting Go of Neurotypical Expectations

"Going into a new roommate situation I'll tell the person, I cannot always do the dishes," Reese says. "Like they're not going to be done, and you cannot expect that from me. If this is a problem, we cannot live together."

Before finding out she was Autistic in her mid-twenties, Autistic writer and stripper Reese Piper had a very difficult time holding her life together. She was extroverted and sociable, and had gotten good grades in school, but she couldn't seem to keep herself or her space clean or arrive places on time. Her clothing was often stained, and she got food on her face when she ate. She forgot to answer people's texts and could only maintain a couple of close friendships at a time. Finding out she was Autistic didn't fundamentally change any of that—but it did provide Reese with a context for why life had been so hard.

She says, "I have a disability and I've had a disability my whole life. Because it is a disability, I am entitled to some support, and admitting that is good."

Prior to accepting herself as Autistic, Reese tried to hide all the visible "tells" of her disabled status. At the strip club where she worked, she could come across as personable and glamorous, and charm clients into buying a lot of dances. She was good at learning the social scripts. But she kept potential friends and romantic partners at a distance. She didn't want them to see that her car was filled with trash, or that dishes were piling up in her sink. Keeping the world at bay was the most exhausting part of masking for her. Looking like a functional "adult" required a ton of concealment and panicked apologies. The most crucial part of her unmasking process has been openly admitting what she is and isn't capable of, and letting people deal with it.

"I would be really embarrassed to bring someone into my car right now, because it is like a dumpster," she says, "but if someone needs a ride, I'd say *fuck it, let them deal with it, it's not the end of the world. It's only mess.*"

For many Autistic people, including Reese, self-acceptance looks less like flawless and serene self-love and more like a "fuck it, let them deal with it" attitude that helps her shake off the desire to hide. She's willing to be honest about who she is—even if it scares off potential roommates who would have been a bad fit. Slowly, she's come to let go of neurotypical benchmarks for measuring her life.

Sometimes Autistic people believe that the end goal of unmasking is to overcome all internalized stigma and live completely free of shame. I don't think that's a realistic standard to hold ourselves to. Ableism is a pervasive social force, and one we can't entirely escape; what we can do, however, is learn to observe it as a cultural values system that exists outside of us, and that often runs counter to our personal values. The voice in my head that tells me it's pathetic that I don't cook is not my voice; it's society programming, speaking from within me, and I don't have to listen to it. Instead, I can call forth the side of myself that loves reading, writing, dance parties, and video games, and acknowledge that if eating a lot of snacks and fast food gives me more time to honor that person, it's a worthwhile trade. I can also take time to remind myself that I live in a world that exalts hyperindependence to a ridiculous, isolating degree. Throughout history and across many different cultures, most individuals did not cook for themselves.[13] Food was prepared communally, or by specialized workers, because it was a labor-intensive, time-intensive task. Fast food and street carts have existed since ancient times! Traditionally, most private residences did not even have dedicated kitchens, because people were less isolated and the responsibility of food prep was spread across the community. It's perfectly okay that I need help staying fed. If I were living in a time and place where individuals weren't held responsible for all their own food prep, my struggles with such things wouldn't be disabling at all.

Because we do live in such an individualistic world, many Autistic people have learned to make trade-offs and become comfortable with needing help. Most of us (neurotypical and neurodiverse alike) simply were not built to do everything on our own, and in order to lead fulfilling lives, we either need to enlist the help we need, or let some obligations go. This is highlighted in Autistic coach Heather Morgan's work: she challenges her clients (and herself) to compare and contrast their personal values with how they actually spend their day-to-day lives.

"I'm a married mom with two kids, and between the four of us there are a bucketload of disabilities and exceptionalities that both limit my energy and increase my workload," Heather writes on her blog.[14] "I face a litany of competing voices and priorities all scrambling for my time and attention."

Heather Morgan teaches, writes, coaches clients, and is completing a graduate degree in theology. She's incredibly busy, and because of her physical disabilities she has to get a lot done while resting in bed. There simply isn't enough time or energy available to attend to everything. But Heather has a finely honed sense of who she is and what matters most in her life, and that guides which tasks she prioritizes, what she says "yes" to, and what she lets drop.

Heather has taken herself through the Values-Based Integration exercise that she uses with clients, recalling core moments in her past that made her feel the most alive. She's really drilled down into those key memories to figure out what made them so powerful, and articulated the three values that unite them: honesty, connection, and transformation. Those are the three qualities she prioritizes most above all else. And she makes it a regular practice to contrast those values with the rhythms of her regular life. For Heather, examining whether her life currently lines up with her values comes down to asking four questions, which I've adapted and built out into a reflection exercise below. To complete this exercise, you'll want to have your own list of values from the previous Values-Based Integration exercises handy.

1. *What am I doing right now?*
Consider: How are you spending your time every day? Try to keep a detailed record of how you spend your days for at least a week.

2. *What matches my values and what brings me joy?*
Reflect: After you've kept a detailed journal of your activities for a week, look back and make a note of which activities line up with your values and which do not. You can assign each of your values a color, and use highlighters in those colors to mark which activities are values-consistent.

3. *What are the reoccurring themes?*
Notice: Are there patterns in which activities feel the best to complete, or things you consistently look forward to? What unites the activities that are values-consistent and the ones that are not?

4. *Let go of what isn't yours.*
Get help: As Heather puts it, "What are you doing that could be done by someone else? What are you doing that doesn't need to be done as regularly as you're doing it—if at all?"

Exercises like these can really highlight the ways in which we're "throwing" time away meeting the expectations of neurotypical people in our lives, or just trying to conform to a vague idea of what we think society wants from us. As soon as we're able to create a little distance between these implicit demands and our actual selves, saying "no" gets a lot easier.

On her blog, Heather tells the story of one client who completed this exercise and realized he was spending two hours per night vacuuming the house and cleaning the stove not because he enjoyed it (or appreciated the outcome), but because his mother had raised him to do so. He stopped doing it shortly thereafter.

My friend Cody is an Autistic person with a trauma history, and a big breakthrough for him involved realizing he'll never be able to get exercise the way society says an able-bodied person "should."

Anything that elevates Cody's heart rate reminds him too much of his abuse. In his childhood, breathing heavily only meant one thing: that he was trying to escape a dangerous situation. His body is a finely tuned instrument of self-protection, but it isn't well suited to any grueling physical activities. So he's decided to make peace with that fact, and only pursue physical activities that feel good, like gentle warm-ups, treading water, or getting a massage.

I know countless Autistic adults who have decided that in order to lead healthy lives, they've got to let certain things go. Many of us (including me) give up on cooking, for example, because it is such a time- and planning-intensive task. Timing out one's cooking and grocery-shopping schedules, prepping ingredients, remembering which ingredients you have, getting rid of leftovers in time, knowing days in advance which flavors and textures you'll be able to tolerate—it can be so much more effort than it's worth. Instead we let go of the burden entirely, and rely on ready-made snacks and fast food. Or enlist the help of a loved one to do all the meal planning and shopping. Staying fed and having time for what matters most to us in life is enough.

For many masked Autistics, learning in adulthood that you have been secretly nursing a disability all your life is quite the world-shattering experience. Adjusting your self-concept is a long process. It can involve mourning, rage, embarrassment, and dozens upon dozens of "wait, that was an Autism thing?" revelations. Though many of us come to see Autistic identity as a net positive in our lives, accepting our limitations is an equally important part of the journey. The clearer we are with ourselves about where we excel and where we need help, the more likely we are to eke out an existence that's richly interdependent, sustainable, and meaningful.

A final (and I believe crucial) piece of this puzzle is resetting your expectations about what a normal or healthy Autistic life looks like. The best way to normalize your neurotype is surrounding yourself with other Autistic and disabled people, taking in the rich diversity of our community and learning to appreciate the many unique ways that we live.

Finding (and Making) Your Community

"What most normal, kind of vanilla people don't understand," Tisa says, "is that the kink world is just full of Autistic nerds. People think it's this scary, intense weird thing and it's like . . . just a bunch of nerds learning about different kinds of rope and stimming by getting flogged and shit."

Tisa organizes an annual BDSM convention in a midwestern suburb. She looks the way you might expect someone in that scene to look: long purple braids that go down to her waist, lots of black clothing, a bunch of piercings. She's also a totally Autistic nerd. When she's not busy worrying about the logistics of setting up a dungeon in a hotel conference center, she plays board games with friends and paints miniature figurines. Tisa says her nerdy social circles and her kinky ones overlap massively. Both groups are filled with neurodivergent people.

"Autistic people love to get lost into a Dungeons and Dragons campaign for five hours, and some of us also love you know, the sensory experience of getting tied up. Both those communities are for outsiders."

Autistic people have built many niche communities from the ground up—both out of necessity and because our interests and modes of being are, well, weird. If you walk into any furry convention, anime club, BDSM dungeon, anarchist squat, or competitive video-game-playing circuit, I can pretty much guarantee you're going to see dozens of Autistic people there, many of them in essential leadership or organizing positions.

Autistic people created the concept of fandom. In his book *Neuro-Tribes*, Steve Silberman describes how Autistic nerds in the early 1900s traveled across the country by car, on foot, and even by hopping trains in order to meet people who shared their niche interests.[16] In the early days of science fiction, Autistic adults maintained the first fan magazines and traded fan fiction with one another by mail and radio.[17] Autistic people helped to plan the first science fiction conventions, and were among the early Trekkies and fan fiction writers. Long before the internet existed, Autistic nerds found one another through personal ads in the back of magazines. Once the internet was up and running, Autistic people filled it with forums, chat rooms, massively multiplayer online games, and other social networks that helped them find community and organize.[18]

It's not just that Autistics tend to be obsessive about hyperspecific subjects, and have the technical skills necessary to build these networks.[19] In fact, many masked Autistics focus instead on the social and practical aspects of connecting online and in person. They are often the ones to schedule the tabletop gaming sessions, tweak the forum settings until the site is easy on the eyes, and write the meeting rules that keep members from fighting.

"I am not the math-minded type of Autistic," Tisa says. "I am the kind who thinks about people obsessively. What kind of venue will be the most comfortable for folks? What chairs are good for fat bodies? How can I keep this one person from having to interact with that other person they hate? That is the kind of stuff I make charts about in my head."

When Autistic people are at the reins of event planning, we can craft environments that are tailored to our sensory and social needs, In small, mask-free subcultures that are created and maintained by Autistic people, we get a glimpse of what a society that truly accepts neurodiversity might look like. It turns out, an Autism-accepting world is broadly accessible to a wide array of people, not just Autistics. They're often far more comfortable for everyone.

I used to shy away from nerdy communities, or from socializing with anybody who couldn't hide their awkwardness as well as I could. I was trying my damnedest to seem as normal and neurotypical as possible and feared that if I even stood near someone who violated society's rules, I'd be outed as the freak I secretly was.

I have met some particularly self-hating transgender people who exhibited the same attitude about befriending anyone they think makes our community look bad. They may resent very visibly trans people who put zero effort into "passing" as cisgender, for example, or claim that people who don't experience debilitating gender dysphoria are only faking being trans for attention. It's a horribly self-defeating attitude to have; it keeps us atomized, distant from, and resentful toward one another. Instead of building up the networks of support and organizing power we desperately need, our self-loathing drives us apart.

Though I recognize how destructive this attitude is for trans people, I used to feel that way about joining forces with fellow Autistics. It was the exact attitude I exhibited toward visible Autistics like my former classmate Chris. Around my peers, I made fun of him like everyone else did, and internally I obsessed over his mannerisms and movements. It's only now, looking back with the benefit of hindsight, that I realize I liked Chris and was drawn to him. He was smart and interesting, and his body moved freely the way that it needed to. It captivated me, but I resented and feared those feelings. Internalized stigma curdled inside me, poisoned my feelings, and made me into a self-hating bigot.

In my late twenties and early thirties, as I finally began to accept my Autistic identity and meet other Autistic people, my misplaced hatred slowly dropped away. The first step was joining a local discussion group for genderqueer people. I didn't intend to meet Autistics there, but I had recently discovered I was neurodiverse and quickly recognized some of my own traits in the other people present. Everyone was a bit shy and emotionally distant, yet they'd perk up at the mention of their favorite manga or philosophy texts. People were experimenting with unique styles and gender presentations, yet no one was criticized for looking "wrong" or failing to perform gender norms correctly.

The genderqueer group's rules and procedures also seemed to be tailor-made for Autistic people and our communication needs.

Unmasking Autism

Moderators provided a specific discussion topic each week and articulated specific rules about how to know when to speak, how to respect other people's boundaries, and what to do and say if someone accidentally said something offensive. Adults my own age came to the meetings with stuffed animals and other comfort items and participated without ever looking up or making eye contact. Some people arrived silently, curled up in cuddly heaps on the floor, and rarely said anything at all. Every few weeks the group had a "blanket fort day," where we all worked together to transform the fluorescently lit meeting space into a cozy, fairy-light-decorated den lined with pillows and comforters. Even a few years prior, I would've been ashamed to bring myself to such a touchy-feely space, but I was in desperate need of more trans friends, and in the genderqueer group I felt at ease.

After a few months of attending this genderqueer group, the topic of Autism came up. I outed myself to everyone, and found out that many of the attendees were themselves neurodivergent, too. I learned from the organizers that the group's policies and structure were created with the needs of neurodiverse people in mind. Throughout the many years the group had run, much of its leadership had been Autistic, or later discovered they were Autistic. No wonder it was the first public space I'd truly felt at ease in as an adult. I started hanging out with group members outside of the group itself, and found I wasn't ashamed to be a visibly identifiable member of a "weird" crowd anymore. Instead, I felt accepted.

These experiences made me want to branch out, to meet other weird and neurodivergent adults who lived openly as themselves and wouldn't look down on me. So I started attending Autistic self-advocacy group meetings at the Chicago Public Library. There, too, I felt instantly at ease. We all sat in staggered positions pointing in various directions, chatting while looking down at our shoes or into our phones. I felt no need to sit up straight, put my feet on the floor, and fake smiles and nods in order to keep the conversation moving. It was bliss.

The Autistic self-advocacy group I had attended was Autistics

Against Curing Autism Chicago, which had begun as a chapter of the national Autistic Self Advocacy Network. Both versions of the group had been put together and run by Timotheus Gordon Jr., the Autistic researcher, self-advocate, and lover of football and Pokémon that I spoke with in Chapter 1. Much of Timotheus's unmasking journey has been defined by his talent for finding and creating community spaces that allow him to be himself—and which free up other Autistics to be ourselves, too.

After a childhood and adolescence of presenting as a football-loving cool guy, Timotheus went away to college at the University of Minnesota. He joined a fraternity and made new friends there. He also began participating in slam poetry and meeting other nerdy people. Slowly he began to broaden how he saw himself, and find like-minded folks who could appreciate every side of him.

"My self in Chicago was the person wearing the mask," he explains. "I had to be the student athlete who is basically the belle of the ball or whatever you want to call it. The person who is into everything that society has to offer. I had to be the cool guy. But I found out in Minnesota that I could be myself and still get a lot of attention."

When he moved back to Chicago a few years later (after living in Atlanta for a bit, and connecting with the Autistic self-advocacy community there), Timotheus found he was able to deepen his existing friendships, as well as forge new ones. Now that he knew his full, openly Autistic self was loved and appreciated, he could actually build bonds he was fully present for. He was a talented writer and performer. A cool guy who could light up the room with an affable smile. An advocate for justice who knew how to organize and develop resources for fellow disabled people. And he was a nerd who could sit at home playing games and recharging for a day or two. He brought this same spirit of easygoing yet radical acceptance to the organizing he did for the Autistic community. He centered Black and brown Autistics in his work, and ensured that the spaces he created were actively, warmly welcoming toward LGBTQ people. With the help of other organizers, he helped push for CESSA, the Community Emergency Services and Support Act. This Illinois bill will establish a mental health response team to address mental-health-related 911 calls, instead of sending police or law enforcement.[20] In his work, as in his social life, Timotheus has found a way to fully embody his values, and fight to make the city of Chicago a space where Black Autistic personhood is actually respected and cherished.

Around the time that I discovered the Autistic self-advocacy meetings Timotheus organized, I decided to make up for the childhood and adolescence I had denied myself and began attending anime and comic book conventions. There I found Autistic bliss all over again. Everyone was dressed in comfortable, eye-catching clothing. You could start a conversation with someone based on their costume, or a video-game-themed pin they were wearing. Panels were filled with interesting people who looked down at their hands while over-analyzing the plots of decades-old books that almost no one has read. Their unabashed passion stoked the fires of my own self-love.

It wasn't just that these various groups were filled with weird people like me. They were designed to be comfortable for us. Anti-harassment policies made it clear how you were supposed to engage with other people, and what you were supposed to do if you witnessed violence, sexual harassment, or bigotry. At many cons, there were apps you could use to report a problem or harassment, so even if you were frozen in the midst of an Autistic shutdown, you could ask for help. Volunteers were posted at every corner, helping people navigate the space, explaining where to stand and what to do. There were sensory-friendly rooms, where anyone who was feeling overwhelmed could relax among dim lights, soft music, and snacks.

I couldn't get enough of con culture, so I started attending even more events: Midwest FurFest, Anime Central, International Mr. Leather. That's when I met Tisa, the Autistic BDSM organizer, and learned that neurodiverse organizers were at the heart of many of these spaces.

"People say that the internet is a world for Autistics, built by Autistic people," she says. "But most IRL nerdy and kinky subcultures

are, too. It takes an Autistic level of passion to put these things together. And a resolve to let one's freak flag fly."

It's true that Autistic people are a driving force in many of these
communities. At Midwest FurFest, there are multiple panels each year
about Autism within the furry community, because the two identities
overlap so much. The Brony (*My Little Pony* fan) community is famously dominated by Autistic children and adults. Netflix's documen-
tary about the subculture made a point of highlighting that fact,[21] as
have research papers on the therapeutic benefits of nerdy fandoms for
Autistic adults and kids alike.[22] The worlds of anime, manga, and
comics are also heavily populated with neurodiverse people of all ages.

Disabled adults help curate the panels and build spaces around
people's sensory needs; they provide much of the programming, staff
the booths, lovingly handcraft the goods for sale in the Dealer's Dens.
It's hard to get a good estimate of just how numerous Autistic people
are within these subcultures, but it's clear that we have helped construct them from the ground up, both because we're desperately in
need of places to find belonging, and because geeky subcultures provide a great outlet for our hyperfocus and a means to express our difference without getting too vulnerable.[23]

Research shows that when we are around fellow neurodiverse people, Autistics feel far more socially at ease.[24] We also crave friendship
and belonging to the same degree that allistics do.[25] Though non-
Autistic people mistakenly get the impression that we aren't interested
in socializing, most of us are fighting to find acceptance every day of
our lives. When we spend time with one another, it's far easier for us
to get those social needs met in a way that feels genuine and easy.

As Reese Piper put it, "It's neurotypicals who categorized autism
as a social disorder." Autistic people don't actually lack communication
skills, or a drive to connect. We aren't doomed to forever feel lonely
and broken. We can step out of the soul-crushing cycle of reaching for
neurotypical acceptance and being rejected despite our best efforts.
Instead, we can support and uplift one another, and create our own
neurodiverse world where everyone—including neurotypicals—is

welcome. In the final chapter of the book, we'll discuss what such a world might look like. But before we discuss reshaping the world to make it more accommodating of us, here are some tips for finding community with fellow Autistics and other neurodiverse people:

Self-Advocacy Organizations

- If you are in the United States, Canada, or Australia, you can look to see if your area has a local affiliate chapter of the Autistic Self Advocacy Network by visiting this site: https://autisticadvocacy.org /get-involved/affiliate-groups/
- In the United Kingdom, you can join the Neurodiverse Self Advocacy group: https://ndsa.uk/
- Consider joining the Autism National Committee (https://www .autcom.org/) and attending their annual conference either physically or virtually.
- Look for groups that describe themselves as self-advocacy groups or disability justice groups, and are run by Autistic people, for Autistic people.
- If a group is focused on serving the allistic family members of Autistic people first and foremost, or supports searching for a "cure," it's most likely an unsupportive environment.
- Avoid Autism Speaks, and any organization that has partnered with Autism Speaks.[26]
- Trustworthy organizations will be run by Autistics, and allow for a variety of different methods of participation, so that nonverbal Autistics and those with physical disabilities are centered.

Online Groups

- On social media sites, peruse tags such as #ActuallyAutistic, #AutisticAdult, #AutisticJoy, #Neurodivergent, #AutisticSelfAdvocacy, and #Neurodivergence.
- Though Facebook is a less active social media platform than it once was, I also recommend doing a cursory search for Autistic self-advocacy groups there, particularly ones local to your area, or for

specific communities (Black Autistics, transgender Autistics, Autistics in eating disorder recovery, etc.). Private Facebook groups can allow for more in-depth conversations than some other social media sites.

- On reddit, the group r/AutismTranslated is a great place for in-depth discussions, resource sharing, and exploring an Autistic identity. I also enjoy r/Aspergers and r/AspieMemes, and r/AutisticPride is very active.

- Wrong Planet (https://wrongplanet.net/) is a long-standing forum for Autistic people, ADHDers, and other neurodivergent people. It's an old-fashioned forum in its setup, making it great for slow, in-depth conversations.

- As you search through tags and find accounts to follow, look for communities that center Black and brown Autistic voices, transgender Autistics, nonverbal Autistics, and that encourage healthy conflict and dissent.

- Avoid groups and pages that are for non-Autistic parents of Autistic kids, accounts that infantilize Autistics or oversimplify our experiences, and accounts where individuals overgeneralize their experiences as representative of all Autistic people.

Special Interest Meetups

- A great way to meet like-minded neurodivergent people is by joining communities devoted to a special interest you both share. Search online to find local comic book groups, D&D groups seeking new players, anime or cosplay clubs, foraging groups, hiking groups, or clubs devoted to anything that interests you.

- If a cursory online search doesn't turn up any groups you're interested in, look for events and clubs run by your local library, bookstore, comic book shop, queer community center, gay bar, BDSM dungeon, park district, café, or collectible shop.

- Though both platforms are less active than they once were, Facebook and Meetup.com are still useful places for finding groups that share common interests with you, as well as gatherings for those with social anxiety or who aren't confident in their social skills.

- Look for conventions related to your special interests that visit your area, and join online communities related to them. Often there is a robust local community that holds smaller meetups and events throughout the year.
- Since groups devoted to shared interests aren't explicitly for Autistic people, try to gather information on their accessibility policies. Though there are many Autistic anime nerds, for example, there is also a contingent of the community that is ableist, racist, and has alt-right leanings. This is true of almost any broad community; it may take some digging to find out which spaces are safe for you and align with your values.

General Tips and Things to Look Out For

- It's pretty common to feel awkward or out of place the first time you meet someone new or attend an event. Unless a serious red flag occurs, I recommend giving a new space three visits before you conclude it's a bad fit.
- Pay attention to who is encouraged to attend an event or access a space, and who is overlooked or discouraged. Are meetings in a neighborhood that's easier for wealthy white people to access? Is the location accessible to people in wheelchairs?
- While there is no such thing as a fully accessible group (because some people have incompatible or competing access needs), groups should do their best to accommodate both current and potential attendees. Are there nonverbal and asynchronous (that is, not live) ways to participate? Are the sensory needs of attendees anticipated (for example, with policies banning strong fragrances)?
- As you get better acquainted with a group, take note of how conflict and critique are handled. Does leadership welcome critique and take it seriously? Are members able to handle heathy conflict and

treat it as a source of growth, or is there a lot of pressure to "smooth things over" as quickly as possible? Does it feel like a space where you are free to change your mind on something or be wrong?

- If you have been masked all your life, you probably will experience some anxiety in Autistic-centered spaces. You might even find yourself judging other people's behavior. Remember that this is completely normal. Society has drilled very particular, often cruel rules into your head, and it can be jarring at first to see people violating some of them. Over time, you will get more comfortable with visibly neurodivergent behavior—and this will make it easier for you to open up, too.

CHAPTER 8

Creating a Neurodiverse World

Most countries' legal systems, health care systems, and educational institutions approach disability using what is called the *medical model of disability*. The medical model understands disability as a condition that exists inside an individual person's body or mind. If you're disabled, you personally have a problem that must be identified, diagnosed, and then either treated or cured. The purpose of medicine and psychiatry is to identify what is wrong with people and prescribe some kind of intervention that will make the symptoms of that wrongness go away. It is because of this belief system that we have organizations such as Autism Speaks, which presents Autism as a terrible affliction that steals children away from their parents and which desperately needs a cure,[1] and therapeutic methods such as ABA therapy, which does not improve Autistic kids' happiness or comfort, but does render them obedient and less of a barrier to their parents living busy, productive lives.

The medical model of disability has given many of us (and most of our doctors and therapists) the idea that human suffering is best understood as a problem to be fixed through individual changes. And for many illnesses and disabilities, medical care and a medical lens is undeniably appropriate. If you're someone who is in excruciating, daily pain due to nerve damage, medical treatment and medication can help you. If you have a degenerative condition that progressively gets worse, such as multiple sclerosis, you have every reason to support medical research in pursuit of a cure.

Where the medical model of disability fails is in making sense of disabilities that come from social exclusion or oppression. Sometimes what society (and the psychiatric establishment) considers to be an individual defect is in fact a perfectly benign difference that needs accommodation and acceptance instead. Though being gay was once classed as a mental illness, it never actually was one. Trying to "cure" gayness never worked, and only caused more psychological damage. In fact, categorizing gay people as sick created the illusion that they actually were mentally ill, because ostracism and shame does frequently contribute to depression, anxiety, substance use, and self-harming behaviors, among other psychological issues.

Enter the *social model of disability*, originally coined in the 1980s by disabled academic Mike Oliver.[2] In his writing, Oliver described disability as a political status, one that is created by the systems that surround us, not our minds and bodies. A clear-cut example of this is how most educational institutions exclude Deaf students. There are entire school systems and communities run by Deaf people, for Deaf people, where everyone uses sign language and access to audio captioning and other resources are provided as a matter of course. In this context, being Deaf is not a disability. In fact, a hearing person who doesn't know sign language is the one who would be marginalized, if they were living in a Deaf-centered world.

However, most people live in a world where Deafness and sign language use have mostly been seen as undesirable, and an indication a person is defective. The word *dumb* is an insult specifically because nonspeaking Deaf people were seen as less competent and less fully human than their speaking, hearing peers. Due to this attitude, most public spaces don't provide Deaf people with the resources they need.[3] It is in this way that most schools (and other institutions) actively *disable* Deaf people. The same can be said for Blind people, who are frequently excluded from public education and denied Braille materials and screen-reading software. It's also true of fat people, whose bodies are not accommodated on public transit, in classrooms, or in medical equipment, and who are frequently excluded from medical research.[4]

The social model of disability applies to many of the struggles Autistic people experience. Each of us has been repeatedly overlooked and excluded because society views our differences as shameful defects rather than basic human realities to accept. Often, we are dis-abled for completely arbitrary reasons, just as Deaf people are. A world where everyone uses sign language is possible, but because hearing people have greater numbers and more social power than Deaf people do, spoken language gets prioritized. Similarly, a world where eye contact is not required is entirely possible (and in fact, there are many cultures where avoiding eye contact is considered polite).[5] However, in cultures where eye contact is expected, the Autistic people who find it painful are dis-abled both socially and professionally. And it isn't just Autistics who are penalized by this norm: people who find eye contact difficult because of social anxiety, trauma, or because their home culture discourages it are also harmed by this social norm.

Having a social disability goes hand in hand with the obligation to mask. If stimming in public will get you assaulted or arrested, you are both socially *dis-abled* and forced to mask. If you struggle at work because you can't play by elaborate, unstated social rules, and you wind up unemployed as a result, you have been socially disabled and severely punished for your failure to mask correctly. This is why unmasking at a personal level has its limits. An individual solution cannot fix a far-reaching system of oppression. As long as Autistic people exist in a culture and a political system that constantly creates and re-creates our disabled status, we aren't fully free to unmask ourselves and live with authenticity and ease.

At present, the Autistic people (or anyone who is neurodiverse) who have the greatest freedom to unmask are the ones who otherwise have the most powerful social position. I have a PhD and a cushy job as a professor; that means I get to set my own schedule many days, can dress in a comfortable, quirky way that doesn't give me gender dysphoria or sensory overwhelm, and block out alone time on my calendar when I feel a meltdown coming on. My Autistic friends who work in grocery stores, restaurants, bars, and day care centers have no such options. Their daily schedules, attire, and even emotional displays are all tightly controlled when they are at work. All too often, they must plaster a smile on their face, swallow their pain, and incur significant psychological damage in order to stay employed. As a small, "non-threatening" white person, I can flap my hands in public and scrunch my face into all kinds of grumpy expressions without much consequence. In contrast, if a Black Autistic person or a tall Autistic trans woman fails to act perfectly poised in public, they may be harassed, have the cops called on them, or worse.

On paper, many of these exploited and marginalized Autistics might look less medically "well" than I do. They might suffer from depressive episodes, anxiety attacks, migraines, stomachaches, and more. In order to cope with the extreme stress of their lives, they're more likely to smoke, drink, and use drugs than I am. They don't get as much sleep as I do, and don't feel as at ease in their bodies. But their disabilities aren't more medically severe than my own. They're just more socially disabled than I am, with less social power and freedom, and that takes a real toll.

The only way that all Autistic people will be able to unmask is if society changes dramatically. A world with more flexible norms and less stigma is a more accessible world, with fewer disabilities and far less human suffering. It's also a world that's more welcoming to people with mental illnesses, immigrants and diasporic people, and anyone who has suffered because they're not the perfect, cookie-cutter worker bee. As the psychiatric anthropologist Roy Richard Grinker writes in his titular book, *Nobody's Normal,* our current definition of mental health is tied to the state and employers' desire for productive, inoffensive conformity.[6] Emotions that are too large, passions that are too childish and not profitable, habits that are too repetitive, and bodies and minds that require daily assistance all challenge this incredibly narrow definition of health. It is only by expanding our definition of what is acceptable human behavior and working to meet other people's manifold needs that we can move forward.

Many people who are categorized today as disabled or mentally ill might have functioned just fine outside of an industrialized capitalist economy. Someone who might thrive as a hunter, midwife, storyteller, or seamstress in a more interdependent society may appear dysfunctional if trapped in an office. In fact, some genomic evidence suggests that when humans moved away from hunter-gatherer-based societies and toward agrarian (and later, industrial) ones, alleles that predict neurodivergence became a disadvantage.[7] For example, in societies where daily life offered less stimulation and novelty than a life of hunting and gathering did, ADHD traits turned disadvantageous. Some researchers have theorized that the same is true of Autism, but much of the research on the subject is quite poorly done, because it assumes Autism must have always been a pathology and an impairment to reproductive success.[8] We don't really have good reason to believe that is true across all societies and all periods of time, though. Our ways of living and of caring for each other are so numerous, and haven't always been as atomized as they are today.

Many neurotypes simply are not suited to long workdays, lengthy commutes, nuclear families, and isolated "independence." Arguably, none of us are well suited for that—the nine-to-five workday is not evidence-based—but some of us suffer more visibly and pervasively than others. By tearing down our current, constricting definition of mental health, and celebrating different ways of thinking, feeling, and behaving, we can improve countless lives. By reworking society to make it more flexible and accommodating of difference, we can improve the mental and physical health of all people. In this way, unmasking is a political goal. It requires we place value on all human life, no matter a person's abilities or needs, and view society as a social system that exists to care for all people—not an apparatus to make everyone as productive as possible.

So how do we go about creating a world where neurodiversity is accommodated, difference isn't pathology, and everyone is free to be their true selves? It's a lofty project, but here are some concrete policies that most Autistic self-advocacy organizations advocate for and are supported by the available social science, and which I believe would make a real difference:

Expanded Legal Protections for Disabled People

In the United States, the Americans with Disabilities Act (the ADA) dramatically improved life for disabled people, and expanded their ability to participate in public life. The law targeted two major policy areas: first, it required that buildings and public transit become more physically accessible (for example, by requiring accessible parking spots and wheelchair ramps); second, it banned discrimination against disabled people in housing, hiring, promotion, and compensation.[9] Throughout the world, similar disabilities rights acts have been passed that aim to create greater access for disabled people by granting fair access to shelter, work, education, and public resources and spaces.[10]

Unfortunately, for all its strengths, the ADA and many similar laws did not go anywhere near far enough. Though the law led to thousands of elevators and wheelchair ramps being built, and countless Braille signs being installed outside public restrooms, it also provided numerous exceptions to older and historical buildings. Many small businesses are still woefully inaccessible to wheelchairs and other assistive devices now, more than thirty years after the law passed. In some cases, recalcitrant cities and businesses exploited legal loopholes that allowed them to ignore ADA dictates, such as the grandfathering in of old structures and infrastructure.

Throughout the 1980s, the Chicago Transit Authority refused to purchase buses with wheelchair lifts, despite repeated promises to the disabled community that all new equipment would be accessible. It took a years-long series of well-organized, disruptive protests[11] in which physically disabled activists blocked street traffic with their wheelchairs for hours at a time[12] before the city finally budged and agreed to acquire accessible transportation options.[13] Even after the ADA was codified into law, this same resistance to include disabled people persisted. To this day, about a third of CTA train stations lack elevators for wheelchair users, for example.[14] Whenever a station is remodeled to include an elevator and wheelchair ramps, local business owners and residents express outrage at the inconvenience and costliness of the improvements.

Enforcement of ADA building requirements varies widely from state to state, and even those buildings that are perfectly compliant are really only accessible in a handful of ways. The ADA does not require that public events be captioned or sign language interpreted, for example, or that remote options be provided for those who can't leave their homes. The law has nothing to say about bright lights, intense smells, loud music, or any of the other sensory torments that make many public spaces inaccessible to Autistic people. Often, buildings that are technically ADA-compliant remain practically inaccessible. For example, my friend Angel uses a wheelchair and requires help using the toilet. Many ADA-compliant bathroom stalls are large enough to accommodate Angel's wheelchair, but not large enough to accommodate both his wheelchair and his caregiver. Most buildings are also too noisy and crowded for Angel to handle, so his exclusion from public life is many layered.

If Autistic people are to be fully included in public life, we must vastly expand accessibility requirements to cover the sensory needs of Autistic people and regulate the accessibility of events as well as buildings. It's not just architecture that can be hostile to disabled bodies and minds. As this book has repeatedly shown, many of the ways that disabled people are excluded are far more subtle, and social, than a clear-cut lack of ramps or Braille signage. Today, some grocery stores and retail shops offer weekly "sensory friendly" hours for Autistic shoppers and their families, where the lights are dimmed, the crowds are reduced, and the music and PA systems are turned off.[15] This is currently done on a completely voluntary basis, by only a small number of shops around the world, but it provides a helpful blueprint for what sensory accessibility guidelines might look like. The Autistic Self Advocacy Network also has a toolkit on best practices for creating sensory-friendly spaces, which highlights the following:[16]

Building Sensory-Friendly Public Spaces
Advice from the Autistic Self Advocacy Network

Visual

- Make lights dimmable
- Use diffused light sources rather than overhead or fluorescent lights
- Restrict use of flash photography
- Use clear, contrasting colors for presentation slides
- Make signage and handouts easy to read and simple
- Limit "visual noise": remove distracting graphics, posters, etc.

Auditory

- Remind people to silence phone notifications
- Replace applause with "sparkle fingers" or another quieter alternative
- Ensure speakers use microphones consistently—yelling is much harder to understand than speaking evenly into a mic is
- Equip spaces with materials that absorb and dampen echo, when possible. Even a large rug can make a big difference!

Tactile

- Make elbow bumping or waving the default greeting, not handshakes or hugs
- Adopt a relaxed dress code, so people can dress comfortably
- Normalize the use of stress balls, fidget spinners, doodling, etc.
- Fight the idea that makeup, uncomfortable formalwear, high heels, or bras make a person more "professional"
- Space out chairs, provide semiprivate seating near corners or barriers

---

Unmasking Autism

Olfactory and Gustatory

- Ban the use of strong perfumes or colognes at events
- Use physical distance, barriers, or fans to keep kitchen and bathroom smells out of other areas
- Use sensory-friendly, green cleaning supplies
- For catered events, tell attendees the exact menu beforehand
- Provide "bland" foods as a backup

In addition to ensuring that public spaces are accessible on a sensory level, the ADA (and similar laws throughout the world) should expand the accessibility of public events. Captioning, sign language interpretation, and virtual participation options should be provided for large-scale public events as a matter of course, rather than by advance request only (as they currently are). In many cases, expanding the accessibility of public events would require providing sufficient funds and resources, including education on what accessibility means and why it matters. This approach would facilitate change (and reshape public attitudes toward disability) far better than a more punitive, fine-based approach, at least when it comes to public events.

When it comes to enforcing building accessibility requirements and preventing discrimination in housing and employment, the ADA could be reworked to grant disabled people more power to self-advocate. The state of California is one of the most ADA-compliant states in the United States, in part because any disabled person who encounters an inaccessible business in that state is free to sue the business for a minimum of $4,000 in damages, plus legal fees.[17] This approach gives disabled people the legal power to challenge inaccessibility when they encounter it, and the financial means to do so, rather than simply hope that an inaccessible building is eventually inspected by the state. In most of the country, it's incredibly difficult for a disabled person to prove they have been discriminated against or excluded. If the California model were expanded to the entire country, and modified to apply to employment and housing discrimination cases, disabled people would have far more recourse for discriminatory treatment.

Ending most states' *at-will employment* status would also improve life considerably for disabled adults. At present, it's easy for managers to fire an Autistic person (or a person with depression, schizophrenia, or Tourette's) once they discover we are disabled, so long as they lie and say they're terminating us for some reason other than our disabilities. Since anyone can be fired at any time for nearly any reason, there's almost always an acceptable shield for ableism.

Expanding worker protections and making it harder to arbitrarily fire someone with no notice would help prevent this from happening, and would improve the financial and job security of countless people. Autistic individuals benefit from having clear, measurable work outcomes, and a move away from at-will employment would force companies to actually articulate their expectations in a documented way. Legal protections that expand access to short- and long-term disability leave at work would also improve quality of life for many disabled people, including Autistics who are at an elevated risk of extreme burnout. It would mean we'd experience less pressure to mask any pain or despair we are experiencing. Legally requiring employers to provide flextime and remote work options without proof of disability would also immensely benefit Autistic employees (both diagnosed and self-realized), and make work more accessible to parents, people with elder care responsibilities, and many others. In these and many other ways, accommodating the needs of Autistics would create a more forgiving world for everyone, in addition to freeing us from the obligation to mask.

Broadened Social Norms

Expanding public accessibility and worker protections in the ways I outlined above would have a massive impact on public attitudes toward disability and neurodivergence. The simple act of welcoming more Autistic people into the social world is not only a powerful symbolic gesture of support, it would also be a massive step forward in normalizing neurodiverse mannerisms, behaviors, and communication styles. If Angel could use public restrooms easily and move through the public library or grocery store without experiencing a sensory meltdown, far more members of his community would get to meet him, interact with him, and witness him stimming and communicating using his iPad. At first, Angel would be met with far more stares and questions than ever before. But over time, neurotypical people in his community would find his differences mundane, and come to recognize that nonspeaking people who need caregiver support are complex, fully realized humans to be listened to and included.

Historically, people with mental illnesses and disabilities were institutionalized and locked away because they were viewed as unsightly and a threat to public order. Throughout European history, asylums were places for anyone who flouted societal rules, including debtors who refused to work, criminals who had violated the ethical and moral rules of the age, and people who either looked unusual, or acted unusually, even in completely benign ways. Something as simple as a harmless physical disfigurement could be grounds to exclude someone from a free, public existence.[18] We still live with the legacy of these views today. Even in the twentieth century, until deinstitutionalization took hold in the 1980s, it was considered normal and appropriate to keep intellectually disabled and visibly Autistic relatives hidden from society, and even from their family members. Locking disabled and neurodivergent people in institutions creates a feedback loop of stigma and social repression: individuals who diverge from the norm even slightly are unthinkable, and unseeable, and so society shapes itself around an increasingly narrow realm of existence, which in turn makes life harder for the next generation of people who deviate. It's only by resisting this downward spiral of rejection and dehumanization, and opening society back up, that we can undo the massive harm that's been done and build institutions and communities that welcome all people.

Social psychological research shows that contact with marginalized groups does help reduce public prejudice toward those groups.

However, only specific forms of contact are beneficial. After all, white enslavers in the American South had regular, daily contact with the people they had stolen the freedom of, but that contact did not make them any less inclined toward white supremacy. The power structures surrounding the relationship and the financial incentives of exploiting enslaved Black people made it impossible for contact to change the social order. This same problem is evoked when Black activists state today that they don't just want a "seat at the table" in white institutions. The table was not made for them, it was constructed to keep them out, and thus it needs to be upended entirely so that we can all gather around something new. Similar principles are often at work when we contemplate meaningfully including disabled people.

Merely observing a disabled person as an outsider or a pitiable curiosity won't do much to reduce neurotypical people's biases. Instead, research suggests that collaborative,[19] extended[20] contact shared between *equals* is what's necessary to really change attitudes.[21] It's not enough for Autistic people to be tolerated at stores and restaurants. We need to be given equal footing (relative to neurotypical people) in volunteer positions, in the workplace, and in our churches, community centers, and gyms. Those centers of public life must be radically reorganized to suit the needs, work styles, and communication methods of everyone. Only when neurotypicals are required to work and collaborate with us as their peers will the social script be flipped, replacing the pressure to mask with the obligation to accommodate. Notably, getting to this place requires justice be attained for all marginalized people—it's not enough for white Autistic people to be treated as equal to white neurotypical coworkers; Black people, women, trans people, immigrants, and other oppressed groups must be at equal footing as well.

Expanded Public and Professional Education on Neurodiversity

Though collaborative contact is a powerful force of prejudice reduction, it also places a heavy burden on the Autistic people who lead the change. Being visible as a marginalized person is a double-edged sword, as any out transgender person will tell you. Public awareness can put a target on your back just as easily as it can liberate. In a truly just world, I wouldn't have to educate neurotypical people about how I think and process information, and I wouldn't have to slowly warm people up to tolerating me, worrying the entire time that I might be mocked or attacked if I challenge neurotypical expectations too dramatically.

So, while making the world more accessible does benefit Autistic people, it's insufficient on its own. A robust program of educating the public on neurodiversity would have to accompany the policy changes I've recommended up to this point. Public schools should include units on mental health stigma and neurodiversity in health and social science classes, starting from a very young age. As I've outlined in this book, ableism and masking hits Autistic people when we are incredibly young, and so interventions need to begin early as well. When we teach children about racism, sexism, and imperialism throughout history, we should highlight how the oppressed were often branded as hysterical, paranoid, and insane. It's important that all people—neurodiverse and neurotypical alike—come to realize how narrow definitions of sanity and "functioning" are used to harm and dehumanize. And since mental health concerns are so common (in any given year, roughly 20 percent of the population will experience some mental illness),[22] it would benefit all people to have a strong psychoeducation starting from childhood.

Targeted trainings on neurodiversity should be provided to doctors, teachers, and mental health professionals as well. Educators should be aware that some of their well-behaved yet withdrawn students may be masked Autistics in need of assistance, and that their acting-out "problem" kids similarly might be neurodiverse. Therapists and counselors need far more robust training in serving the needs of Autistic patients, and modifying or replacing treatments that rarely work for us (such as cognitive behavioral therapy) with those better suited to our needs. Of course, this also requires that more research be conducted on how to treat things like eating disorders, depression, social anxiety, and substance use in our populations.

Autistic and otherwise neurodiverse scientists should be prioritized when funding such efforts. Much of the work published in the journal *Autism in Adulthood* illustrates how much the scientific literature can improve and deepen when those affected by an issue are the ones that study it. Even when I was in graduate school in the early 2010s, professionals looked down on "me-search," as they called it, and implied that if you were studying something you had a personal stake in, you couldn't be trusted to be objective about it. Slowly these attitudes are changing, but the stigma against being a researcher with mental health diagnoses or disabilities is still severe. Grant funding that actively encourages disabled and neurodiverse researchers would do a great deal to counter that bias.

As I've mentioned throughout this book, most professionals know very little about Autism, particularly in adults and those who mask, and almost all approach the disability from a medical disability lens. I've offered workshops on neurodiversity to medical professionals, and I have taught clinical psychologists, and I was initially gobsmacked to discover most had never even *heard* of the social model of disability. For a lot of care providers, the belief in disability as a medical defect to be cured is absolute and unflinching. Because they have been trained to approach difference through a medical lens, and have never learned about alternatives, they routinely pathologize completely neutral, harmless Autistic traits and behaviors. Our caring professionals and educators must be made aware that alternate understandings of disability exist, and that their prejudicial attitudes often create disability where none might otherwise be there.

Below are some common Autistic behaviors that teachers,

therapists, and doctors tend to flag as signs of dysfunction, but which are completely harmless and ought to be understood and normalized:

Common, Healthy Autistic Behaviors
Intense studying of a new favorite topic
Not noticing sounds or social signals when focusing on an engrossing task
Needing to know exactly what to expect before entering an unfamiliar situation
Sticking to a very rigid schedule, and rejecting deviations to that schedule
Taking a long time to think before responding to a complex question
Spending hours or days alone sleeping and recharging after a socially demanding event or stressful project
Needing "all the information" before coming to a decision
Not knowing how they feel, or needing a few days to figure out how they feel about something
Needing a rule or instruction to "make sense" before they can follow it
Not putting energy toward expectations that seem unfair or arbitrary, such as wearing makeup or elaborate grooming

The more educated professionals and the public become about Autism, the less Autistic people will have to mask. We won't have to languish, unseen and unaccepted for years, feeling alienated but unable to name why. In the first chapter of this book, I likened being a masked Autistic to being a closeted gay person. Gay people are forced into the closet at birth, because society assumes everyone is heterosexual, and is set up only to meet the needs of heterosexuals. At some point remaining closeted becomes a process we put effort into, but it's a status that is forced on us, not a free choice. In much the same way, all Autistic people are expected at birth to behave like neurotypicals. If we aren't diagnosed and treated with respect as children, we have no choice but to continue on wearing a neurotypical mask for years. But as acceptance of neurodiverse people expands, the assumption that all people must think, act, and feel the same way will gradually erode. If neurodiverse people and our allies continue our push for just treatment, we can eventually reach a place where society is not constantly disabling so many of us, all while withholding from us the knowledge that we're disabled.

Universal Health Care and Basic Income

Many Autistics wind up having to mask because they never were identified as disabled when they were young. Ignorance among teachers and care providers about the varied ways that Autism can present is a huge part of this, but in countries like the United States, a lack of health care coverage plays a huge role. According to 2020 survey data from the organization Mental Health America, over 57 percent of Americans who experienced mental health struggles that year did not receive treatment.[23] For those who desired treatment but could not access it, lack of insurance and lack of adequate insurance were among the most common barriers.[24] Considering how costly an Autism assessment is, and how difficult it is for masked Autistics to locate competent care, it's clear that mental health care access in the United States is in need of dramatic extension. At least half of all Autistics in the country are currently undiagnosed, and the diagnosis rate is likely far lower for women, trans people, people of color, and those in poverty. If we are to normalize the Autistic experience and build robust social systems that support Autistics and our needs, we'll need to properly care for the mental health of all people.

Autistics, like most disabled people, are unemployed and underemployed at far higher rates than the neurotypical population. Even those of us who can mask and present as "professional" occupy a very perilous spot. One awkward moment or verbal misstep at work can get us fired, particularly if we are visibly disabled or already out about our neurodiverse status. Autistic job seekers struggle to find work, because job interviews are ambiguous, high-stress performance situations. Interview questions are rarely provided in advance, and job seekers are expected to provide socially acceptable responses and reactions without appearing to "try too hard" to do so.

At present, Autistic people must either mask ourselves in order to get and maintain a job, or apply for disability benefits that are too meager to live on, and which come with a variety of caveats and strings attached.[25] If you are on disability, you can't get married to someone with an income (including their own disability benefits) without having your payments reduced.[26] You also can't put more than two thousand dollars in savings, or own any assets, lest you be disqualified and cease getting payments as soon as the very next month.[27] And that's if you are able to qualify for benefits in the first place. Undiagnosed Autistics are not able to apply for disability, and recipients must have their eligibility reevaluated on a regular basis (between every six to eighteen months).[28]

Processing and investigating disability benefit cases is incredibly costly. It is for this reason that writer and anthropologist David Graeber suggested in the book *Bullshit Jobs* that it would be far less expensive and far more socially just to simply provide a baseline, universal basic income to all people, with no strings attached. While replacing *all* social welfare programs with universal basic income is probably not a wise move, based on the available data,[29] a less restrictive, more generous approach to providing disability benefits would clearly improve disabled people's quality of life. Rather than forcing Autistic people (and others) to prove and re-prove that we truly are disabled, and truly cannot work, universal basic income would be doled out to everyone, symbolically and practically asserting that all humans deserve to have enough money to live, no matter what.

Abolition of Carceral Systems

There is no getting rid of ableism without eradicating the oppressive, dehumanizing social structures that created it. As anthropologist Roy Grinker writes in *Nobody's Normal* and psychiatrist Andrew Scull details in *Madness in Civilization*, throughout most of European history mentally ill people, disabled people, and people who broke the law were all locked up in the exact same facilities. There wasn't a clear legal separation between being arrested for acting strangely, and being arrested for physically assaulting someone or stealing. Both "criminals" and "lunatics" were often regarded as disposable problems, not human beings. Eventually, though, European legal systems saw fit to distinguish between those who behaved "badly" because they were sick, and those who behaved badly because they were criminal or evil. At this point, asylums and prisons were separated, though both groups of incarcerated persons were denied legal rights. In the twentieth century, the separation between the "evil" and the "ill" reversed somewhat, as forensic psychologists began to explain law-breaking behavior as being caused by mental illnesses such as antisocial personality disorder, schizophrenia, and Autism.[30] Evil was no longer understood as a moral state, but a psychological state of incurable brokenness, essentially. Functionally though, that outlook on human nature isn't really any better. To this day, many Autistic children of color are put on the school-to-prison pipeline as early as elementary school,[31] being severely punished for small misbehaviors, and even having the cops called on them when they disobey their teachers or have meltdowns. This reaction is predicated in part on the belief that some people are just "bad," and that it's best to remove them from society, not extend them compassion.

The criminal justice system and mental health system are deeply interwoven, and they both serve to perpetuate ableism. As I described earlier in the book, disabled people are at extremely high risk of being shot by police. Black and brown Autistic people are, in particular, at an elevated risk of police violence and incarceration. Defunding the police and prisons and working to abolish these oppressive institutions will help liberate Black Autistic people, as well as others with disabilities and mental illnesses. Many people who oppose racist police violence argue that cops be replaced with social workers or therapists, and that a state-run mental health force should be dispatched when emergency calls are made. The law Timotheus Gordon Jr. and his fellow activists have helped pass in Illinois, CESSA, would do exactly that. Such a policy change would no doubt save numerous lives per year, particularly Black and brown neurodivergent lives. However, if we oppose the state-sanctioned racist violence of the police, it is equally important that we examine how mental health professionals forcibly institutionalize people of color and disabled people, take away their children, declare them legally incompetent, and otherwise further the exact same societal evils that cops do. In the summer of 2021, the world was shocked to learn that Britney Spears had been forcibly inserted with a contraceptive IUD as part of her legal conservatorship,[32] and that her father had control not only of her finances, but her performance schedule, access to her children, and ability to visit with her boyfriend. These are just some of the rights that are routinely stripped from people with mental illnesses and disabilities, and for those who lack the public visibility and privilege of someone like Spears, there is almost no recourse.

Though culturally competent, compassionate mental health services can be life-changing, psychiatry and psychology have also done immense structural harm to the very people they purport to serve. From the Tuskegee Syphilis Study, to Hans Asperger's research on "high functioning" Autistics, to the forced lobotomies performed on gay people and communists, immense violence has been done in the name of science and "protecting" the public. When looked at through a medical, individual lens, a push for greater mental health can quickly warp into demanding compliance. So if we are to create a world where all Autistic people of all backgrounds are able to unmask, we have to remove the systems of power that might violently punish those who fail or refuse to conform.

Unmasking Is for Everyone

About eight years ago, my friend Wendy quit her job as an attorney very abruptly. I assumed that like many people in that field, she had gotten burnt out. In the years that followed, Wendy slowly pivoted to a new career as a legal writer. It seemed to suit her much better: she got to work from home, spend more time with her children, and go weeks without wearing anything but sweatpants.

After I came out as Autistic, Wendy reached out to me privately about that time in her life.

"My daughter is on the spectrum," she told me. "She was having a really rough time a few years ago, lots of meltdowns and no friends, and we couldn't figure out why. That's the real reason I left my old job."

I had suspected Wendy was Autistic herself. She was private and introverted, with little patience for phoniness. She was unpretentious, with long, free-flowing hair and no makeup. Sensitive and artistic, she had never seemed like a good fit for the image-conscious, intense legal world. But as it turned out, Autism was not the explanation:

"I really looked into it, but it turns out I'm not Autistic," she said. "Was I depressed and anxious at that time, because my job was horrible and my kid was suffering? Yes, absolutely. But from raising my daughter I've learned I'm very *not* Autistic. I just happen to love an Autistic lifestyle."

Wendy's life changed dramatically following her daughter's diagnosis. She pulled back on her career so she could attend family therapy and homeschool her kid. They joined groups for Autistic kids and their families, and her daughter started slowly making friends. Their family moved from the city to a small house in the countryside, and they all started spending a lot more time outside. As Wendy's family began to live at a slower, more Autism-friendly pace, Wendy felt her own depression abating. She was more relaxed and fulfilled. She found time to write poetry and make music, and to care for her older relatives when they got sick.

Wendy says, "Getting to know who my daughter really is, and getting to shape our lives around that has been the best thing that's happened to our family. So it pisses me off so much when I hear other 'Autism mommies' on the internet talking about how it's this curse. It was a lifesaver for us!"

When Wendy discovered that she had an Autistic child, her life was radically transformed for the better. Circumstances forced her to get off the hamster wheel of conformity and productivity and constantly doing too much, and take a step back to reevaluate what mattered most in her life. She had radically unmasked herself, even though she's not Autistic: stripped free of the expectations of a job that didn't match her needs, she eked out a living in a messy, cozy home filled with craft projects and clutter, and no longer felt the pressure to present as a put-together, corporate success who could "have it all."

Of course, all these big changes were only possible because Wendy had the financial and community support to make them possible. Her spouse was excited about the move to the country. The cost of living in the rural area they relocated to was cheap enough for Wendy to transition to part-time work. Through her husband's job, both Wendy and their daughter maintained their health insurance. It was access to that health insurance that had made her daughter's diagnosis possible in the first place. The family had community support that made child care and tutoring possible. When Wendy's mother said ignorant things about Autism, Wendy was able to sit down with her in therapy and work through their past issues, and recorrect her mother's ignorance.

Many Autistic people and our loved ones lack such advantages. Without access to shelter, health care, and a supportive network of loving people who are willing to grow with us, none of us are free to become our true, unmasked selves. This is why it is vital for the project of unmasking to be more than just a personal one. All the self-affirmations and radical visibility practices in the world cannot overcome economic injustice, racism, transphobia, or profound social exclusion. We have to fight to create a more just, accepting, and supportive world for all people if we wish for everyone to be free to unmask.

I know so many Autistic people for whom their diagnosis or self-realization was a clarifying and affirming moment. After the initial shock and shame passes, coming into a neurodiverse identity can prompt you to reexamine your entire life, and all your old values, allowing you to build something slower, more peaceful, and more beautiful. But it's not only Autistics who benefit from embracing neurodiversity in that way. We all deserve to take a step back and ask whether our lives line up with our values, whether the work we do and the face we show to others reflects our genuine self, and if not, what we might want to change.

When we accept individuals as they are, instead of warring with their unique needs and challenges, life can move at a more relaxed, accepting pace. A world that allows all Autistics to safely unmask is a world where anyone with strange interests, passionate emotions, environmental sensitivities, social quirks, or other differences is still seen as worthy and whole. Creating that world will require a lot of tireless political work as well as Autistic self-advocacy. But for the neurodivergent and the neurotypical alike, it will be worth it.

CONCLUSION

Integration

Before I knew I was Autistic, I was profoundly alienated in every possible sense. I was at odds with myself, unable to understand why normal life felt so perplexing and imprisoning to me. I was detached from the world, with no trust in others or in my own potential to connect and be understood. Because I was so alone, my identity was also completely unmoored. I had no community to anchor myself within. I had no idea I was transgender, no idea I was disabled, and couldn't articulate what I wanted out of life. Internally, I was fractured, a series of faked personalities and protective shields that kept people at a distance. I could only drop the shield when I was alone, but even in my solitude I was miserable and confused. I was all defense mechanisms, with nothing left inside worth defending.

When a masked Autistic person lacks self-knowledge or any kind of broad social acceptance, they are often forced to conceive of themselves as compartmentalized, inconsistent parts. *Here is the person I have to be at work, and the person I must be at home. These are the things I fantasize about doing but can't tell anybody about. Here are the drugs that keep my energy levels up, and the lies I tell to be entertaining at parties. These are the tension-defusing distractions I'll deploy when someone begins to suspect there's something off about me.* We don't get the chance to come together into a unified whole that we can name or understand, or that others can see and love. Some sides of us go unacknowledged entirely, because they don't serve our broader goal of remaining as inoffensive and safe as possible.

In the transgender community, we have a term for the fragile, confused state many of us inhabit before we recognize our gender identity and decide to come out: it's called being in "egg mode." An *egg* is a trans person who is either too isolated from the trans community or too enveloped in denial to be able to acknowledge who they are. When you're in egg mode, you feel ill at ease and out of place, without any clue why. You avoid considering certain painful desires that lurk inside you, because confronting them would shatter the fake cisgender identity you built in order to survive. When I was in egg mode, I wore a lot of flowing dresses and low-cut tops because I believed I was too "womanly" to ever look good in the androgynous clothing I actually wanted to wear. I thought my body had doomed me to forever be a curvaceous woman. Everywhere I went people repeatedly told me I was incredibly womanly and talked a lot about how "fertile" I looked. Family, friends, and even complete strangers did their damnedest to convince me I owed society my womanhood. My self-hatred and society's rejection completely distorted the way I saw myself. Once I finally broke through that resistance and started dressing the way I liked and speaking in a lower tone of voice, I realized I had been lied to. I actually looked and felt great as an androgynous trans person. I hadn't lost anything by giving up the façade. I was just free.

In my experience, being a masked Autistic is eerily similar to being in the closet about being gay or trans. It's a painful state of self-loathing and denial that warps your inner experience. Though it often feels like being "crazy," it's not actually an internal neurosis. It's caused by society's repeated, often violent insistence you are not who you say you are, and that any evidence to the contrary is shameful.

Before I knew I was Autistic, I imposed a lot of rules on myself, to help me "pass" as neurotypical. One of them was that I could never buy a piece of furniture I couldn't move by myself. Self-sufficiency meant I could pack up and leave at any time. To ask for help or to lead a richly interdependent life would be akin to painting the words *weak* and *pathetic* on my body in bright crimson letters. I lived in such a way that no help was required.

I slept on an air mattress. I made a "dresser" for myself out of milk crates I'd stolen from behind the grocery store by my house. I kept my small TV on the floor. These measures also fulfilled another rule I'd set for myself: that I should spend as little money as possible, and sacrifice comfort in the name of frugality. The more money I socked away, the more self-sufficient I was, and the less disastrous it would be if I got fired due to awkwardness or burnout. This same logic fed into my eating disorder and social isolation. Life as a person who didn't eat, drink, or ever leave the house very much was cheap and low-risk. I would survive by making myself smaller and smaller. I wondered why I was so unhappy and uncomfortable all the time, why I stomped around the house sobbing for hours, but could not recognize that my compulsive self-denial was contributing to my misery.

Masking also alienated me from everyone I loved. I never allowed myself to become vulnerable with anybody, to share any of the anger, frustration, dysphoria, or obsessive yearning that roiled inside me. When safe people made overtures to connect with me, I swatted them away and iced them out. Friends asked me how I was doing, and I responded with hostility. They tried to show me physical affection and I froze up. When I was breaking down physical and mentally, I did all I could to continue seeming stony and strong. Even my most accepting loved ones had no choice but to love a half version of me. I had almost no sense of who I was, either. When I had free time, I just sat alone in my room and stared at the wall or mindlessly scrolled online.

All of this also slowly began to change the day I sat down in a hot tub with my cousin at an amusement park, and heard his theory that everyone in our family was Autistic. I wasn't ready for the information at first. But the moment I heard the word applied to my relatives, I couldn't stop attaching it to myself. All my life I'd been a jumble of disconnected parts, but now an image of myself, and a name for what I was experiencing, was finally coming together.

The opposite of alienation is *integration*, a psychological sense of connection and wholeness.[1] People whose identities are integrated can see a through-line connecting the many selves they have been across various times and places. Every human being changes over time, of course, and alters their behavior depending on the situation or setting they're in. There is no static "true self" that stops adapting and changing. To a masked Autistic person, this fact can be really disturbing, because we may lack a consistent "story" to tell ourselves about who we really are. Our personalities are just means to an end, externally motivated rather than driven by some internal force or desire. Someone with an integrated identity isn't disturbed by change and variance, though, because they see a connection that endures across the many people they have been: core values that persist across their life span, and a narrative of personal growth that explains how they moved from the person they once were, to who they are today.[2]

Research (particularly decades of work by psychologists Dan McAdams and Jonathan Adler) has found that people who have integrated self-concepts are generally quite adaptable, resilient, and self-forgiving. They are able to develop new skills and pivot when life becomes challenging. They see themselves as the protagonists of their life story. They're also more likely to experience *post-traumatic growth*, understanding painful past experiences as something that helped make them into a resilient person who can help others, rather than viewing it as a terrible "contamination" that ruined their lives or weakened them.[3] In particular, McAdams and colleagues have observed that as people develop in maturity or recover from trauma, they tend to craft a *redemptive* narrative about themselves. A redemptive view of the self tends to highlight a few key qualities:

Key Qualities of the Redemptive Self[4]	
Generative	Works to improve the world, or benefit future generations
Sensitive	Cares about the needs of others, and is concerned by social injustice
Committed to Values	Develops their own set of core beliefs and values, which guide their behavior throughout their lifetime
Balances Independence with Connection	Has a strong sense of one's own agency and power, but also connects meaningfully with other people and recognizes we are all interdependent

It's striking to me how compatible the redemptive self is with the process of unmasking. The redemptive self essentially is an unmasked Autistic self: unashamed of one's sensitivity, profoundly committed to one's values, passionately driven by the causes ones cares about, strong enough to self-advocate, and vulnerable enough to seek connection and aid. A person with an integrated, redemptive sense of self knows who they are, and isn't ashamed of it. They're able to resolve life's tensions in an authentic way that honors their feelings and personal ethics.

In McAdams and Adler's work (and related work by others), there is no one path a person must take to develop an integrated or redemptive sense of who they are. Narrative therapy has been found to be beneficial for those who want to reexamine the stories they tell themselves about their lives and their past, and cast them in a new light.[5] And some initial evidence suggests narrative therapy can be beneficial for Autistic people struggling with social anxiety or communication challenges.[6] However, the redemptive self also can arise organically, as a person comes to understand themselves and to forge healthy, supportive bonds. In my own life, I know that meeting other Autistic people and learning to understand what Autism is naturally led to me writing a new "story" about my past and who I was.

The final stage of Heather Morgan's values-based integration exercise is to sum up your core values in about three to five words, and contemplate how each of those values connects to one another to create a cohesive whole. To this end, Heather frequently encourages clients to draw how their values interlock with one another, using whatever visual metaphor suits them best.[7] One client of Heather's drew each of their five values (Openness, Acceptance, Achievement, Leveling Up, and Captivation) as separate strings on a guitar. Each could be activated and "played" on its own, but it's only when each of the values join together in a resonant harmony that they make the best music. Another person listed their values (Compassion, Community, Creativity, Integrity, Intrinsic Worth, and Justice) as distinct colors in a rainbow. Another saw their values each as separate spokes on a bicycle wheel, all supporting one another and making forward movement possible. These metaphors reflect how Heather's clients see their principles connecting to one another, and aids them in contemplating their life as a whole greater than its underlying parts.

Here is some space for you to explore how your own values relate to one another. To complete this exercise, you'll want to revisit the Values-Based Integration exercises from the Introduction, Chapter 5, and Chapter 7.

Values-Based Integration
Putting Your Values Together

---

1. Reexamine the Key Moments of your life that you described in the introduction to this book, and the 3 to 5 core values you identified as essential to those moments back in Chapter 5.

   List those values here. Ideally, you want to aim to identify three to five distinct values:

2. In the space below, write down a definition for each of your values. This should be a personal definition, not a dictionary definition. You want to identify specifically what each value means to you.

Value:
What this value means to me:

Value:
What this value means to me:

Value:
What this value means to me:

Value:
What this value means to me:

Value:
What this value means to me:

3. Finally, draw an image that represents your values and how they connect with one another. This image might represent a hobby or an experience that is important to you, or it might evoke one of the key moments where you felt particularly alive. The goal is to create an image that connects all of your values together, and helps you envision and remember all of them.

A person's values don't all have to be equally weighted as they are in these example metaphors. You could draw one particularly important value (say, Love) as a pillar on which the others rest, or draw one value as a wide umbrella that covers and protects the rest. One client of Heather's drew three of their values as spokes on an anchor, with their fourth value as the hook connecting the anchor to the "boat" of their life.

I took several months to guide myself through Heather Morgan's values-based integration process, as I was working on an early draft of this book. I considered carefully what the key moments were in my past that had made me feel truly alive. The interviews I conducted with other Autistic people and the research I did helped guide my self-reflection. Ultimately, I recalled a wide array of powerful moments in my past where I felt fully alive and realized as a person, and those moments made it clear to me what my core values were. I thought it might be worthwhile to share them here as an example:

Value #1: Candor

What this value means to me: Honestly sharing how I feel and the way I see things. Sharing observations that might not be convenient, but which are true and important to hear. Being honest with myself about who I am, who I enjoy spending time with, and what I want out of life. Speaking out when I see someone being mistreated.

Value #2: Courage

What this value means to me: Trusting my intuition and being willing to take risks. Standing up for my beliefs even when they are unpopular. Enthusiastically, passionately saying "yes" to the things that I want, instead of searching for excuses to say "no." Letting my emotions be loud and bold. Taking up space, and taking a huge, hungry bite out of life.

Value #3: Inspiration

What this value means to me: Observing the world around me, filling myself up with ideas, and sharing my thoughts and passions with the world. Listening to my own creative drive and bursts of insight. Being a light that can guide others, by empowering people to do what is best for themselves.

Value #4: Passion

What this value means to me: Giving myself the space to feel things deeply. Making time to be sad, angry, resentful, or joyous. No longer filtering emotions based on how others might receive them. Being unashamed of who I am, pursuing the things I desire that feel good, and letting myself leave the situations that distress me.

Stepping back and taking a look at my key memories and core values, I can see that I'm a dynamic, powerful, clear-headed person who is always growing, and who has risen up to defend the people and ideas that matter to me many times. I am so different from the inept, powerless, clueless, needy figure that I have always worried abled people might see me as. I'm also nothing like the frigid, passive intellectual I've often masked myself as.

This exercise also made it painfully clear just how much my old, masked life blocked me and kept me dissatisfied. Alone in my apartment, socializing with no one, I had no room to inspire others or to express myself. I was so afraid of upsetting other people that I didn't risk standing up for what I believed in and didn't indulge in anything that gave me pleasure. It was my attempt at a neurotypical persona that failed me—the real me was a beautiful person who deserved so much more.

The ideal result of this exercise is to help an Autistic person trust themselves more. And looking back, I can't think of a single time when I've regretted a decision guided by candor, confidence, inspiration, or passion. Every time I've cut through polite bullshit, quit an unfulfilling job, said yes to a random invitation, spoken out, or suddenly gotten an impulse tattoo, it's felt incredible. Like coming up after a lifetime underwater, finally able to take fortifying gasps of fresh air. On the flip side, I can recall countless bad and regrettable decisions I've made that were motivated by fear, inhibition, or a desire to be polite. Every single time I've apologized for an outburst, downplayed a need, said yes to a job that wasn't a good fit for me, or tolerated a friendship that wasn't respectful, it's left me feeling soul-sick and anxious. It's never helped me sustain a meaningful connection. All it's done is waste my time and fill me with resentment. It's always been better to be myself, no matter the cost.

When I think of how my four values integrate into a larger whole, I picture a shield. When I transitioned, I chose the name Devon in part because it means *defender*. When I was in the closet (about both my transness and my Autism) I used to be shrinking and defensive.

My whole existence was an apology for who I really was. Now I draw strength from who I truly am, and I aim to be a shield for others: a steadfast, brave presence that confronts the world head-on, and tries to shelter those who need it. My values protect me and the people I care about. I used to believe that my mask protected me, but really it just weighed me down. Honoring my values does the exact opposite. It places my most Autistic traits front and center and lets them lead me into battle, rather than hiding them away. I am thankful now for the person I am, and I know others are thankful to know that person, too. And in the course of coming into an Autistic identity, I have met so many people who have gone along a similar path toward self-acceptance and openness, finally feeling free, integrated, and attuned to their values after years of a false, fear-driven performance. I want the same things for you.

I don't want to pretend that life as an out Autistic person is effort-less. Ableism is a powerful force of oppression. There are plenty of Autistics who are never fully able to unmask. Some of us are in such perilous positions that opening up is too dangerous. Some Autistics conclude it is better to find small pockets of acceptance where they can get it, and maintain their mask everywhere else, rather than risk homelessness, police violence, relational abuse, or forced institutional-ization by taking their mask off. For them, systemic social change is needed, as is a significant improvement of life circumstances.

A majority of Autistic people are underemployed and suffer from exploitation, isolation, and poverty. For masked Autistics who are women, transgender, Black, in poverty, or multiply marginalized, it's especially dangerous to think about dropping the mask. Even for those of us who have the freedom to radically unmask ourselves, there is still a lot of social judgment and the pain of past trauma to wrestle with. A single person asserting their self-worth isn't enough to overcome these forces. A world that embraces neurodiversity would, by definition, be a place where all people, cultures, and ways of being receive the same level of dignity, autonomy, and respect. However, for Autistics seeking to achieve widespread acceptance and justice, unmasking represents both an essential step forward, and a way to stay sane while the world remains unjust. I've witnessed firsthand how much an Autistic person can socially and psychologically blossom once they escape an unsafe situation and find an accepting community. I've gone through that exact process myself. We will never be able to build a more neurodiverse society if we do not name our common struggles, form community ties with one another, and loudly declare that our way of functioning isn't broken or bad. Much of the neurotypical world still wants to "cure" us of our difference, using genetic therapies and screening tools that would prevent more of us from being born, and abusive therapeutic methods that train us, like dogs, to become more compliant. Even those of us who have not been forced through formal Autism treatment are still manipulated and pressured, day by day, into becoming smaller, softer, more agreeable versions of ourselves.

To unmask is to lay bare a proud face of noncompliance, to refuse to buckle under the weight of neurotypical demands. It's an act of bold activism as well as a declaration of self-worth. To unmask is to refuse to be silenced, to stop being compartmentalized and hidden away, and to stand powerfully in our wholeness alongside other disabled and marginalized folks. Together we can stand strong and free, shielded by the powerful, radical acceptance that comes only when we know who we are, and with the recognition that we never had anything to hide.

ACKNOWLEDGMENTS

Thank you to my agent Jenny Herrera for seeing the potential in my writing, and giving me the confidence to pursue a life as an author I'd never had the courage to embark on myself. I've said it before, and I'll say it again: you have truly changed my life. To my editor Michele Eniclerico: thank you so much for your interest in and support of this book, for your astute questions, your insightful restructuring suggestions, and your trust in my judgement. I'm so grateful that you encouraged me to make this a book that speaks to Autistics specifically, rather than appeal to a neurotypical gaze. Chapter eight is now the part of the book I'm proudest about having written, and it wouldn't even be here without your suggestions. Thank you Jeanne Widen at Loyola's School of Continuing and Professional Studies for always supporting my writerly work and viewing it as a worthwhile part of my scholarly identity. You've always treated me with such warmth and trust, and I'm incredibly grateful. Thank you to the entire team at Harmony for making this book look beautiful and helping me bring it to the world.

So many Autistic and otherwise neurodivergent writers and thinkers have played an integral role in shaping this book: Heather Morgan, James Finn, Jesse Meadows, Marta Rose, Keillan Cruickshank, Timotheus Gordon Jr., Jersey Noah, and Jess White, thank you for every conversation we have shared, all the resources you have created for the community, and all the feedback you have given me. Amythest Schaber, Rabbi Ruti Reagan, Jen White-Johnson, Sky Cubacub, Samuel Dylan Finch, ChrisTiana ObeySumner, Rian Phin, Tiffany Hammond, Anand Prahlad, and everyone else I quoted in this book: thank you for everything you have created. Thank you to everyone who allowed me to interview you for this book, as well as the hundreds of Autistic people online who responded to polls and requests for your thoughts and feedback on my ideas. I tried to take in as many Autistic perspectives as possible while writing this book, and I hope that I've honored all the stories you have shared with me and treated your generosity with the respect and gratitude it deserves.

Thank you to everyone who has helped me feel less broken over the years, particularly every friend who has extended me grace when I didn't understand myself or how to relate to other people. I've done so much to turn myself away from those who love me, because I was so consumed with doubt and fear, but your love and honesty have been my touchstones. Thank you to every Autistic and neurodivergent friend who has come out to me since I started writing about my own disability, giving us both a wonderful opportunity to trade life hacks and commiserate. Thanks to my family for always allowing me to be my own person, and to speak from my own experience without ever trying to stifle my voice. To all my friends on the Dump Truck Discord server, thank you for keeping me feeling relatively stable and truly connected during the pandemic. Finally, thank you to Nick for dimming the lights, giving me excuses to leave busy functions, constructing a sensory overwhelm panic room under the bed, and plugging in your headphones when the chess.com sound effects get too painfully loud. A lot of the time, I still hate myself for being so irritable and needy, and can't fathom how anybody could love me as I am. I promise someday I will be able to recognize your unconditional acceptance and love as a thing that I (and you! And all people!) deserve.

NOTES

1. Thomas, P., Zahorodny, W., Peng, B., Kim, S., Jani, N., Halperin, W., & Brimacombe, M. (2012). The association of autism diagnosis with socioeconomic status. *Autism*, *16*(2), 201–213.

2. Hull, L., Petrides, K. V., & Mandy, W. (2020). The female autism phenotype and camouflaging: A narrative review. *Review Journal of Autism and Developmental Disorders*, 1–12.

3. "Interview with Temple Grandin." January 2, 2006. Retrieved April 14, 2019.

4. Petrou, A. M., Parr, J. R., & McConachie, H. (2018). Gender differences in parent-reported age at diagnosis of children with autism spectrum disorder. *Research in Autism Spectrum Disorders*, *50*, 32–42.

5. Livingston, L. A., Shah, P., & Happé, F. (2019). Compensatory strategies below the behavioural surface in autism: A qualitative study. *The Lancet Psychiatry*, *6*(9), 766–777.

6. https://www.cdc.gov/mmwr/volumes/69/ss/ss6904a1.htm?s_cid=ss6904a1_w.

7. Cage, E., Troxell-Whitman, Z. (2019). Understanding the Reasons, Contexts and Costs of Camouflaging for Autistic Adults. *Journal of Autism and Developmental Disorders* 49, 1899–1911, https://doi.org/10.1007/s10803-018-03878-x.

8. Livingston, L. A., Shah, P., & Happé, F. (2019). Compensatory strategies below the behavioural surface in autism: A qualitative study. *The Lancet Psychiatry*, *6*(9), 766–777.

9. Cassidy, S. A., Gould, K., Townsend, E., Pelton, M., Robertson, A. E., & Rodgers, J. (2020). Is camouflaging autistic traits associated with suicidal thoughts and behaviours? Expanding the interpersonal psychological theory of suicide in an undergraduate student sample. *Journal of Autism and Developmental Disorders*, *50*(10), 3638–3648.

Chapter 1

1. Corrigan P. W. (2016). Lessons learned from unintended consequences about erasing the stigma of mental illness. *World Psychiatry, 15*(1), 67–73. https://doi.org/10.1002/wps.20295.

2. Ben-Zeev, D., Young, M. A., & Corrigan, P. W. (2010). DSM-V and the stigma of mental illness. *Journal of Mental Health, 19*(4), 318–327.

3. Ysasi, N., Becton, A., & Chen, R. (2018). Stigmatizing effects of visible versus invisible disabilities. *Journal of Disability Studies, 4*(1), 22–29.

4. Mazumder, R., & Thompson-Hodgetts, S. (2019). Stigmatization of Children and Adolescents with Autism Spectrum Disorders and their Families: A Scoping Study. *Review of Journal of Autism and Developmental Disorders* 6, 96–107. https://doi.org/10.1007/s40489-018-00156-5.

5. Raymaker, D. M., Teo, A. R., Steckler, N. A., Lentz, B., Scharer, M., Delos Santos, A., . . . & Nicolaidis, C. (2020). "Having All of Your Internal Resources Exhausted Beyond Measure and Being Left with No Clean-Up Crew": Defining Autistic Burnout. *Autism in Adulthood, 2*(2), 132–143.

6. Buckle, K. L., Leadbitter, K., Poliakoff, E., & Gowen, E. (2020). "No way out except from external intervention": First-hand accounts of autistic inertia.

7. Demetriou, E. A., Lampit, A., Quintana, D. S., Naismith, S. L., Song, Y. J. C., Pye, J. E., . . . & Guastella, A. J. (2018). Autism spectrum disorders: meta-analysis of executive function. *Molecular Psychiatry, 23*(5), 1198–1204.

8. Some people who otherwise exhibit Autism spectrum traits and report Autistic cognitive challenges do not exhibit social or behavioral signs, due to camoflauging of symptoms: L. A. Livingston, B. Carr, & P. Shah. (2019). Recent advances and new directions in measuring theory of mind in autistic adults. *Journal of Autism and Developmental Disorders,* 49, 1738–1744.

9. Thapar, A., & Rutter, M. (2020). Genetic advances in autism. *Journal of Autism and Developmental Disorders,* 1–12.

10. Gernsbacher, M. A., Dawson, M., & Mottron, L. (2006). Autism: Common, heritable, but not harmful. *Behavioral and Brain Sciences, 29*(4), 413.

11. Rylaarsdam, L., & Guemez-Gamboa, A. (2019). Genetic causes and modifiers of autism spectrum disorder. *Frontiers in Cellular Neuroscience, 13*, 385.

12. Hahamy, A., Behrmann, M. & Malach, R. (2015). The idiosyncratic brain: Distortion of spontaneous connectivity patterns in autism spectrum disorder. *Nature Neuroscience 18*, 302–309. https://doi.org/10.1038/nn.3919.

13. Autistic people of all genders continue to develop in their social skills and communication abilities throughout the life span. See: Rynkiewicz, A., Schuller, B., Marchi, E. et al., (2016). An investigation of the "female camouflage effect" in autism using a computerized ADOS-2 and a test of sex/gender differences. *Molecular Autism 7*, 10. https://doi.org/10.1186/s13229-016-0073-0.

14. Zhou, Y., Shi, L., Cui, X., Wang, S., & Luo, X. (2016). Functional Connectivity of the Caudal Anterior Cingulate Cortex Is Decreased in Autism. *PloS One, 11*(3), e0151879. https://doi.org/10.1371/journal.pone.0151879.

15. Allman, J. M., Watson, K. K., Tetreault, N. A., & Hakeem, A. Y. (2005).

Intuition and autism: A possible role for Von Economo neurons. *Trends in Cognitive Sciences, 9*(8), 367–373.

16. Rosenberg, A., Patterson, J. S., & Angelaki, D. E. (2015). A computational perspective on autism. *Proceedings of the National Academy of Sciences, 112*(30), 9158–9165.

17. Hahamy, A., Behrmann, M., & Malach, R. (2015). The idiosyncratic brain: Distortion of spontaneous connectivity patterns in autism spectrum disorder. *Nature Neuroscience* 18, 302–309. https://doi.org/10.1038/nn.3919; Dinstein, I., Heeger, D. J., & Behrmann, M. (2015). Neural variability: Friend or foe? *Trends in Cognitive Sciences, 19*(6), 322–328.

18. See this press release from the Weizmann Institute: https://www.eurekalert.org/pub_releases/2015-01/wios-abg-012115.php.

19. Koldewyn, K., Jiang, Y. V., Weigelt, S., & Kanwisher, N. (2013). Global/local processing in autism: Not a disability, but a disinclination. *Journal of Autism and Developmental Disorders, 43*(10), 2329–2340. https://doi.org/10.1007/s10803-013-1777-z.

20. L. Mottron, S. Belleville, E. Ménard. (1999). Local bias in autistic subjects as evidenced by graphic tasks: Perceptual hierarchization or working memory deficit? *Journal of Child Psychology and Psychiatry, 40,* 743–755.

21. D. Hubl, S. Bolte, S. Feineis-Matthews, H. Lanfermann, A. Federspiel, W. Strik, et al. (2003). Functional imbalance of visual pathways indicates alternative face processing strategies in autism. *Neurology, 61,* 1232–1237.

22. Minio-Paluello, I., Porciello, G., Pascual-Leone, A., & Baron-Cohen, S. (2020). Face individual identity recognition: A potential endophenotype in autism. *Molecular Autism, 11*(1), 1–16.

23. Longdon, E., & Read, J. (2017). 'People with Problems, Not Patients with Illnesses': Using psychosocial frameworks to reduce the stigma of psychosis. *Israel Journal of Psychiatry and Related Sciences, 54*(1), 24–30.

24. https://www.wired.com/story/how-earnest-research-into-gay-genetics-went-wrong/.

25. Guiraud, J. A.; Kushnerenko, E.; Tomalski, P.; Davies, K.; Ribeiro, H.; & Johnson, M. H. (2011). Differential habituation to repeated sounds in infants at high risk for autism. *Neuroreport, 22,* 845–849.

26. Brosnan, M., Lewton, M., & Ashwin, C. (2016). Reasoning on the autism spectrum: A dual process theory account. *Journal of Autism and Developmental Disorders, 46*(6), 2115–2125.

27. Brosnan, M., Ashwin, C., & Lewton, M. (2017). Brief report: Intuitive and reflective reasoning in autism spectrum disorder. *Journal of Autism and Developmental Disorders, 47*(8), 2595–2601.

28. Seltzer, M. M., Krauss, M. W., Shattuck, P. T., Orsmond, G., Swe, A., & Lord, C. (2003). The symptoms of autism spectrum disorders in adolescence and adulthood. *Journal of Autism and Developmental Disorders, 33*(6), 565–581.

29. Hazen, E. P., Stornelli, J. L., O'Rourke, J. A., Koesterer, K., & McDougle, C. J. (2014). Sensory symptoms in autism spectrum disorders. *Harvard Review of Psychiatry, 22*(2), 112–124.

30. Jordan, C. J., & Caldwell-Harris, C. L. (2012). Understanding differences in neurotypical and autism spectrum special interests through internet forums. *Intellectual and Developmental Disabilities*, *50*(5), 391–402.

31. Kapp, S. K., Steward, R., Crane, L., Elliott, D., Elphick, C., Pellicano, E., & Russell, G. (2019). 'People should be allowed to do what they like': Autistic adults' views and experiences of stimming. *Autism*, *23*(7), 1782–1792.

32. Tchanturia, K., Smith, K., Glennon, D., & Burhouse, A. (2020). Towards an improved understanding of the Anorexia Nervosa and Autism spectrum comorbidity: PEACE pathway implementation. *Frontiers in Psychiatry*, *11*, 640.

33. Wijngaarden-Cremers, P. J. M., Brink, W. V., & Gaag, R. J. (2014). Addiction and autism: A remarkable comorbidity. *Journal of Alcoholism and Drug Dependence*, *2*(4), 170.

34. McKenzie, R., & Dallos, R. (2017). Autism and attachment difficulties: Overlap of symptoms, implications and innovative solutions. *Clinical Child Psychology and Psychiatry*, *22*(4), 632–648.

35. McElhanon, B. O., McCracken, C., Karpen, S., & Sharp, W. G. (2014). Gastrointestinal symptoms in autism spectrum disorder: A meta-analysis. *Pediatrics*, *133*(5), 872–883.

36. Baeza-Velasco, C., Cohen, D., Hamonet, C., Vlamynck, E., Diaz, L., Cravero, C., . . . & Guinchat, V. (2018). Autism, joint hypermobility–related disorders and pain. *Frontiers in Psychiatry*, *9*, 656.

37. Bolton, P. F., Carcani-Rathwell, I., Hutton, J., Goode, S., Howlin, P., & Rutter, M. (2011). Epilepsy in autism: Features and correlates. *British Journal of Psychiatry*, *198*(4), 289–294.

38. Antshel, K. M., Zhang-James, Y., & Faraone, S. V. (2013). The comorbidity of ADHD and autism spectrum disorder. *Expert Review of Neurotherapeutics*, *13*(10), 1117–1128.

39. Russell, G., & Pavelka, Z. (2013). Co-occurrence of developmental disorders: Children who share symptoms of autism, dyslexia and attention deficit hyperactivity disorder (pp. 361–386). *InTech*.

40. Hull, L., Levy, L., Lai, M. C., Petrides, K. V., Baron-Cohen, S., Allison, C., . . . & Mandy, W. (2021). Is social camouflaging associated with anxiety and depression in autistic adults? *Molecular Autism*, *12*(1), 1–13.

41. https://leader.pubs.asha.org/doi/10.1044/leader.FTR2.25042020.58.

42. This essay by Damian Milton sums it up well: ". . . there is no neuro-typical to deviate from other than an idealised fantastical construction of Galtonian inspired psychological measurement." (Francis Galton is the inventor of eugenics. Thanks to Jesse Meadows for sharing this piece with me.)

   http://www.larry-arnold.net/Autonomy/index.php/autonomy/article/view/AR10/html.

43. Singer, Judy. (1999). "Why can't you be normal for once in your life?" From a "problem with no name" to the emergence of a new category of difference. In Corker, Mairian, & French, Sally (eds.). *Disability Discourse*. McGraw-Hill Education (UK). p. 61.

44. Takarae, Y., & Sweeney, J. (2017). Neural hyperexcitability in autism spectrum disorders. *Brain Sciences*, *7*(10), 129.

45. Stewart, L. P., & White, P. M. (2008). Sensory filtering phenomenology in PTSD. *Depression and Anxiety*, *25*(1), 38–45.

46. Though of course sensory overwhelm can also contribute to anxiety. It's likely a bidirectional relationship; see: Green, S. A., & Ben-Sasson, A. (2010). Anxiety disorders and sensory over-responsivity in children with autism spectrum disorders: Is there a causal relationship? *Journal of Autism and Developmental Disorders*, *40*(12), 1495–1504.

47. Bora, E., Aydın, A., Saraç, T., Kadak, M. T., & Köse, S. (2017). Heterogeneity of subclinical autistic traits among parents of children with autism spectrum disorder: Identifying the broader autism phenotype with a data-driven method. *Autism Research*, *10*(2), 321–326.

48. https://www.cdc.gov/mmwr/volumes/67/ss/pdfs/ss6706a1-H.pdf.

49. Mandell, D. S., et al. (2009). Racial/ethnic disparities in the identification of children with autism spectrum disorders. *American Journal of Public Health*, *99*(3), 493–498. https://doi.org/10.2105/AJPH.2007.131243.

50. https://www.cdc.gov/ncbddd/autism/addm-community-report/differences-in -children.html.

51. Stevens, K. (2019). Lived Experience of Shutdowns in Adults with Autism Spectrum Disorder.

52. Endendijk, J. J., Groeneveld, M. G., van der Pol, L. D., van Berkel, S. R., Hallers-Haalboom, E. T., Bakermans-Kranenburg, M. J., & Mesman, J. (2017). Gender differences in child aggression: Relations with gender-differentiated parenting and parents' gender-role stereotypes. *Child Development*, *88*(1), 299–316.

53. Cage, E., & Troxell-Whitman, Z. (2019). Understanding the Reasons, Contexts and Costs of Camouflaging for Autistic Adults. *Journal of Autism and Developmental Disorders*, *49*(5), 1899–1911. https://doi.org/10.1007/s10803 -018-03878-x.

54. Andersson, G. W., Gillberg, C., & Miniscalco, C. (2013). Pre-school children with suspected autism spectrum disorders: Do girls and boys have the same profiles? *Research in Developmental Disabilities*, *34*(1), 413–422.

55. Silberman, S. (2015). *NeuroTribes: The Legacy of Autism and the Future of Neurodiversity*. New York: Penguin. Chapter 5: "Fascinating Peculiarities."

56. https://www.nature.com/articles/d41586-018-05112-1.

57. Burch, S., & Patterson, L. (2013). Not Just Any Body: Disability, Gender, and History. *Journal of Women's History*, *25*(4), 122–137.

58. https://nsadvocate.org/2018/07/11/treating-autism-as-a-problem-the -connection-between-gay-conversion-therapy-and-aba/.

59. Hillier, A., Gallop, N., Mendes, E., Tellez, D., Buckingham, A., Nizami, A., & OToole, D. (2019). LGBTQ+ and autism spectrum disorder: Experiences and challenges. *International Journal of Transgender Health*, *21*(1), 98–110. https:// doi.org/10.1080/15532739.2019.1594484.

60. https://www.spectrumnews.org/news/extreme-male-brain-explained/.

61. Evans, S. C., Boan, A. D., Bradley, C., & Carpenter, L. A. (2019). Sex/gender differences in screening for autism spectrum disorder: Implications for evidence-based assessment. *Journal of Clinical Child & Adolescent Psychology, 48*(6), 840–854.

62. Metzl, J. M. (2010). *The Protest Psychosis: How Schizophrenia Became a Black Disease.* Boston: Beacon Press.

63. Halladay, A. K., Bishop, S., Constantino, J. N., Daniels, A. M., Koenig, K., Palmer, K., Messinger, D., Pelphrey, K., Sanders, S. J., Singer, A. T., Taylor, J. L., & Szatmari, P. (2015). Sex and gender differences in autism spectrum disorder: Summarizing evidence gaps and identifying emerging areas of priority. *Molecular Autism, 6,* 36. https://doi.org/10.1186/s13229-015-0019-y.

64. Becerra, T. A., von Ehrenstein, O. S., Heck, J. E., Olsen, J., Arah, O. A., Jeste, S. S., . . . & Ritz, B. (2014). Autism spectrum disorders and race, ethnicity, and nativity: A population-based study. *Pediatrics, 134*(1), e63–e71.

65. Though fans have long suspected that Rick was Autistic (much like his creator Dan Harmon), this wasn't officially confirmed until the finale of season three, "The Rickchurian Mortydate," where during a brief exchange, Rick acknowledges this fact to Morty.

66. https://autismsciencefoundation.org/what-is-autism/how-common-is-autism /#:~:text=In%20the%201980s%20autism%20prevalence,and%20later%201 %20in%201000.

67. https://www.nami.org/Support-Education/Publications-Reports/Public-Policy -Reports/The-Doctor-is-Out#:~:text=800%2D950%2DNAMI&text=Each %20year%20millions%20of%20Americans,States%20go%20without%20any %20treatment.

68. Bora, E., Aydin, A., Saraç, T., Kadak, M. T., & Köse, S. (2017). Heterogeneity of subclinical autistic traits among parents of children with autism spectrum disorder: Identifying the broader autism phenotype with a data-driven method. *Autism Research, 10*(2), 321–326.

69. For a state-by-state breakdown of what is covered, see here: https://www.ncsl .org/research/health/autism-and-insurance-coverage-state-laws.aspx.

70. https://www.clarifiasd.com/autism-diagnostic-testing/#:~:text=There%20is %20a%20cost%20associated,more%20than%20doubles%20the%20cost.

71. https://www.quora.com/How-much-does-it-typically-cost-to-get-a-formal -diagnosis-of-an-autism-spectrum-disorder.

72. https://www.wpspublish.com/ados-2-autism-diagnostic-observation-schedule -second-edition.

73. https://devonprice.medium.com/from-self-diagnosis-to-self-realization -852e3a069451.

74. https://www.bgsu.edu/content/dam/BGSU/equity-diversity/documents /university-policies/evidence-prove-discrimination.pdf.

75. For a good primer on the social and medical models of disability, and their interplay, see Goering S. (2015). Rethinking disability: The social model of disability and chronic disease. *Current Reviews in Musculoskeletal Medicine, 8*(2), 134–138. https://doi.org/10.1007/s12178-015-9273-z.

76. https://www.phrases.org.uk/meanings/differently-abled.html.

77. Longmore, P. K. (1985). A Note on Language and the Social Identity of Disabled People. *American Behavioral Scientist, 28*(3), 419–423. https://doi.org /10.1177/000276485028003009.

78. https://journals.sagepub.com/doi/abs/10.1177/000276485028003009 ?journalCode=absb.

79. https://www.nature.com/articles/d41586-018-05112-1.

80. Significant Gay Events Timeline (PDF). Gay Police Association Scotland. Archived from the original (PDF) on March 15, 2014. Retrieved March 15, 2014.

Chapter 2

1. Ashley, F. (2020). A critical commentary on "rapid-onset gender dysphoria." *Sociological Review, 68*(4), 779–799. https://doi.org/10.1177/003802612 0934693.

2. https://www.washingtonpost.com/lifestyle/2020/03/03/you-dont-look-autistic -reality-high-functioning-autism/.

3. Bargiela, S., Steward, R., & Mandy, W. (2016). The experiences of late-diagnosed women with autism spectrum conditions: An investigation of the female autism phenotype. *Journal of Autism and Developmental Disorders, 46*(10), 3281–3294.

4. Mandy, W., Chilvers, R., Chowdhury, U., Salter, G., Seigal, A., & Skuse, D. (2012). Sex differences in autism spectrum disorder: Evidence from a large sample of children and adolescents. *Journal of Autism and Development Disorders, 42*: 1304–13. doi:10.1007/s10803-011-1356-0.

5. Meier, M. H., Slutske, W. S., Heath, A. C., & Martin, N. G. (2009). The role of harsh discipline in explaining sex differences in conduct disorder: A study of opposite-sex twin pairs. *Journal of Abnormal Child Psychology, 37*(5), 653–664. https://doi.org/10.1007/s10802-009-9309-1.

6. Aznar, A., & Tenenbaum, H. R. (2015). Gender and age differences in parent–child emotion talk. *British Journal of Developmental Psychology, 33*(1), 148–155.

7. Fung, W. K., & Cheng, R. W. Y. (2017). Effect of school pretend play on preschoolers' social competence in peer interactions: Gender as a potential moderator. *Early Childhood Education Journal, 45*(1), 35–42.

8. Goin-Kochel, R. P., Mackintosh, V. H., & Myers, B. J. (2006). How many doctors does it take to make an autism spectrum diagnosis? *Autism,10*: 439–51. doi:10.1177/1362361306066601.

9. http://www.myspectrumsuite.com/meet-rudy-simone-autistic-bestselling -author-advocate-director-worldwide-aspergirl-society/.

10. Full checklist archived at https://mostlyanything19.tumblr.com/post /163630697943/atypical-autism-traits; original site Help4Aspergers.com is now down.

11. https://www.psychologytoday.com/us/blog/women-autism-spectrum-disorder /202104/10-signs-autism-in-women.

12. https://www.aane.org/women-asperger-profiles/.

13. https://slate.com/human-interest/2018/03/why-are-a-disproportionate-number-of-autistic-youth-transgender.html.

14. https://www.wesa.fm/post/some-autism-furry-culture-offers-comfort-and-acceptance#stream/0.

15. Huijnen, C., Lexis, M., Jansens, R., & de Witte, L. P. (2016). Mapping Robots to Therapy and Educational Objectives for Children with Autism Spectrum Disorder. *Journal of Autism and Developmental Disorders*, *46*(6), 2100–2114. https://doi.org/10.1007/s10803-016-2740-6.

16. https://www.psychologytoday.com/us/blog/the-imprinted-brain/201512/the-aliens-have-landed.

17. Warrier, V., Greenberg, D. M., Weir, E., Buckingham, C., Smith, P., Lai, M. C., . . . & Baron-Cohen, S. (2020). Elevated rates of autism, other neurodevelopmental and psychiatric diagnoses, and autistic traits in transgender and gender-diverse individuals. *Nature Communications*, *11*(1), 1–12.

18. https://www.queerundefined.com/search/autigender.

19. van der Miesen, A. I. R., Cohen-Kettenis, P. T., & de Vries, A. L. C. (2018). Is there a link between gender dysphoria and autism spectrum disorder? *Journal of the American Academy of Child & Adolescent Psychiatry*, *57*(11), 884–885. https://doi.org/10.1016/j.jaac.2018.04.022.

20. Neely Jr., B. H. (2016). To disclose or not to disclose: Investigating the stigma and stereotypes of autism in the workplace. Master's thesis in psychology, submitted for partial fulfilment of degree requirements at Pennsylvania State University.

21. https://www.jkrowling.com/opinions/j-k-rowling-writes-about-her-reasons-for-speaking-out-on-sex-and-gender-issues/.

22. Dale, L. K. (2019). *Uncomfortable Labels: My Life as a Gay Autistic Trans Woman*. London: Jessica Kingsley.

23. Dale, L. K. (2019). *Uncomfortable Labels: My Life as a Gay Autistic Trans Woman*. London: Jessica Kingsley, 26.

24. https://www.nature.com/articles/d41586-020-01126-w.

25. Fernando, S. (2017). *Institutional Racism in Psychiatry and Clinical Psychology*. London: Palgrave Macmillan.

26. For a great review of how mental illness and disability's definitions have shifted over time, see Scull, A. (2015). *Madness in Civilization: A Cultural History of Insanity from the Bible to Freud, from the Madhouse to Modern Medicine*. Princeton Univ. Press.

27. Dababnah, S., Shaia, W. E., Campion, K., & Nichols, H. M. (2018). "We Had to Keep Pushing": Caregivers' Perspectives on Autism Screening and Referral Practices of Black Children in Primary Care. *Intellectual and Developmental Disabilities*, *56*(5), 321–336.

28. Begeer, S., El Bouk, S., Boussaid, W., Terwogt, M. M., & Koot, H. M. (2009). Underdiagnosis and referral bias of autism in ethnic minorities. *Journal of Autism and Developmental Disorders*, *39*(1), 142.

29. Bhui, K., Warfa, N., Edonya, P., McKenzie, K., & Bhugra, D. (2007). Cultural competence in mental health care: A review of model evaluations. *BMC Health Services Research*, *7*(1), 1–10.

30. https://www.apa.org/monitor/2018/02/datapoint#:~:text=In%202015%2C%2086%20percent%20of,from%20other%20racial%2Fethnic%20groups.

31. https://www.npr.org/sections/health-shots/2020/06/25/877549715/bear-our-pain-the-plea-for-more-black-mental-health-workers.

32. https://www.hollywoodreporter.com/features/this-is-the-best-part-ive-ever-had-how-chris-rocks-extensive-therapy-helped-prepare-him-for-fargo.

33. https://www.spectrumnews.org/news/race-class-contribute-disparities-autism-diagnoses/.

34. Mandell, D. S., Listerud, J., Levy, S. E., & Pinto-Martin, J. A. (2002). Race differences in the age at diagnosis among Medicaid-eligible children with autism. *Journal of the American Academy of Child & Adolescent Psychiatry, 41*(12), 1447–1453.

35. Dyches, T. T., Wilder, L. K., Sudweeks, R. R., Obiakor, F. E., & Algozzine, B. (2004). Multicultural issues in autism. *Journal of Autism and Developmental Disorders, 34*(2), 211–222.

36. Mandell, D. S., Ittenbach, R. F., Levy, S. E., & Pinto-Martin, J. A. (2007). Disparities in diagnoses received prior to a diagnosis of autism spectrum disorder. *Journal of Autism and Developmental Disorders, 37*(9), 1795–1802. https://doi.org/10.1007/s10803-006-0314-8.

37. https://www.spectrumnews.org/opinion/viewpoint/autistic-while-black-how-autism-amplifies-stereotypes/.

38. Sometimes referred to as African American Vernacular English or AAVE, though this is technically incorrect. AAE refers to a whole spectrum of communication styles and contexts, not just a vernacular. See Di Paolo, M., & Spears, A. K. *Languages and Dialects in the U.S.: Focus on Diversity and Linguistics.* New York: Routledge, 102.

39. DeBose, C. E. (1992). Codeswitching: Black English and standard English in the African-American linguistic repertoire. *Journal of Multilingual & Multicultural Development, 13*(1-2), 157–167.

40. Walton, G. M., Murphy, M. C., & Ryan, A. M. (2015). Stereotype threat in organizations: Implications for equity and performance. *Annual Review of Organizational Psychology and Organizational Behavior, 2*, 523–550. https://doi.org/10.1146/annurev-orgpsych-032414-111322.

41. Molinsky, A. (2007). Cross-cultural code-switching: The psychological challenges of adapting behavior in foreign cultural interactions. *Academy of Management Review, 32*(2), 622–640.

42. https://hbr.org/2019/11/the-costs-of-codeswitching.

43. Molinsky, A. (2007). Cross-cultural code-switching: The psychological challenges of adapting behavior in foreign cultural interactions. *Academy of Management Review, 32*(2), 622–640.

44. https://www.spectrumnews.org/features/deep-dive/the-missing-generation/.

45. https://apnews.com/b76e462b44964af7b431a735fb0a2c75.

46. https://www.forbes.com/sites/gusalexiou/2020/06/14/police-killing-and-criminal-exploitation-dual-threats-to-the-disabled/#39d86f6e4f0f.

47. https://www.chicagotribune.com/opinion/commentary/ct-opinion-adam
-toledo-little-village-20210415-yfuxq4fz7jgtnl54bwn5w4ztw4-story.html.

48. https://namiillinois.org/half-people-killed-police-disability-report/.

49. https://www.forbes.com/sites/gusalexiou/2020/06/14/police-killing-and
-criminal-exploitation-dual-threats-to-the-disabled/#c4b478c4f0fa.

50. Prahlad, A. (2017). *The Secret Life of a Black Aspie: A Memoir*. Fairbanks:
University of Alaska Press, 69.

51. This Twitter thread by Marco Rogers is a great, approachable primer on racial
and cultural differences in approaches to "real talk." https://twitter.com/polotek
/status/1353902811868618758?lang=en.

52. Deep, S., Salleh, B. M., & Othman, H. (2017). Exploring the role of culture in
communication conflicts: A qualitative study. *Qualitative Report*, *22*(4), 1186.

53. https://www.webmd.com/brain/autism/what-does-autism-mean.

54. From the Greek "allo," or other.

55. https://www.vulture.com/2018/05/the-st-elsewhere-finale-at-30.html#:~:text
=Today%20is%20the%2030th%20anniversary,gazes%20at%20all%20day
%20long.

56. The movie has been widely criticized by Autistics, and by critics in general. See,
for example: https://www.indiewire.com/2021/02/music-review-sia-autism
-movie-maddie-ziegler-1234615917/; https://www.rollingstone.com/movies
/movie-features/sia-music-movie-review-controversy-1125125/; https://www
.nytimes.com/2021/02/11/movies/sia-music-autism-backlash.html.

57. For a quick rundown of some of the issues with Music, including how it
misrepresents augmentic communication, see: https://www.bitchmedia.org
/article/sia-film-music-ableism-autistic-representation-film.

58. Wakabayashi, A., Baron-Cohen, S., & Wheelwright, S. (2006). Are autistic
traits an independent personality dimension? A study of the Autism-Spectrum
Quotient (AQ) and the NEO-PI-R. *Personality and Individual Differences*,
41(5), 873–883.

59. Nader-Grosbois, N., & Mazzone, S. (2014). Emotion regulation, personality
and social adjustment in children with autism spectrum disorders. *Psychology*,
5(15), 1750.

60. Morgan, M., & Hills, P. J. (2019). Correlations between holistic processing,
Autism quotient, extraversion, and experience and the own-gender bias in face
recognition. *PloS One*, *14*(7), e0209530.

61. Extraverted people high in Autism spectrum traits are less likely to camouflage
themselves in as intense a way as introverted Autistics do; see Robinson, E.,
Hull, L., & Petrides, K. V. (2020). Big Five model and trait emotional
intelligence in camouflaging behaviours in autism. *Personality and Individual
Differences*, *152*, 109565.

62. Fournier, K. A., Hass, C. J., Naik, S. K., Lodha, N., & Cauraugh, J. H. (2010).
Motor coordination in autism spectrum disorders: A synthesis and meta-
analysis. *Journal of Autism and Developmental Disorders*, *40*(10), 1227–1240.

63. Lane, A. E., Dennis, S. J., & Geraghty, M. E. (2011). Brief report: Further
evidence of sensory subtypes in autism. *Journal of Autism and Developmental
Disorders*, *41*(6), 826–831.

64. Liu, Y., Cherkassky, V. L., Minshew, N. J., & Just, M. A. (2011). Autonomy of lower-level perception from global processing in autism: Evidence from brain activation and functional connectivity. *Neuropsychologia, 49*(7), 2105–2111. https://doi.org/10.1016/j.neuropsychologia.2011.04.005.

65. See thread by the Autisticats that summarizes this research well: https://twitter .com/autisticats/status/1343996974337564674. It is also archived permanently here: https://threadreaderapp.com/thread/1343993141146378241.html.

66. Mottron, L., Dawson, M., Soulieres, I., Hubert, B., & Burack, J. (2006). Enhanced perceptual functioning in autism: An update, and eight principles of autistic perception. *Journal of Autism and Developmental Disorders, 36*(1), 27–43.

67. https://www.queervengeance.com/post/autistic-people-party-too.

68. https://www.wcpo.com/news/insider/logan-joiner-addresses-his-fears-and -those-of-others-on-the-autism-spectrum-by-riding-and-reviewing-roller -coasters#:~:text=Facebook-,Roller%20coaster%20conqueror%20Logan %20Joiner%2C%20on%20the%20autism%20spectrum,helps%20others%20 overcome%20their%20fears&text=Since%20then%2C%20he's%20gone %20from,reviewer%20with%20a%20YouTube%20following.

69. Gargaro, B. A., Rinehart, N. J., Bradshaw, J. L., Tonge, B. J., & Sheppard, D. M. (2011). Autism and ADHD: How far have we come in the comorbidity debate? *Neuroscience & Biobehavioral Reviews, 35*(5), 1081–1088.

70. Möller, H. J., Bandelow, B., Volz, H. P., Barnikol, U. B., Seifritz, E., & Kasper, S. (2016). The relevance of "mixed anxiety and depression" as a diagnostic category in clinical practice. *European Archives of Psychiatry and Clinical Neuroscience, 266*(8), 725–736. https://doi.org/10.1007/s00406-016-0684-7.

71. https://www.sciencemag.org/news/2018/05/cold-parenting-childhood -schizophrenia-how-diagnosis-autism-has-evolved-over-time.

72. Moree, B. N., & Davis III, T. E. (2010). Cognitive-behavioral therapy for anxiety in children diagnosed with autism spectrum disorders: Modification trends. *Research in Autism Spectrum Disorders, 4*(3), 346–354.

73. https://medium.com/@KristenHovet/opinion-highly-sensitive-person-hsp -and-high-functioning-autism-are-the-same-in-some-cases-842821a4eb73.

74. https://kristenhovet.medium.com/opinion-highly-sensitive-person-hsp-and -high-functioning-autism-are-the-same-in-some-cases-842821a4eb73.

75. https://www.autismresearchtrust.org/news/borderline-personality-disorder-or -autism.

76. Knaak, S., Szeto, A. C., Fitch, K., Modgill, G., & Patten, S. (2015). Stigma towards borderline personality disorder: Effectiveness and generalizability of an anti-stigma program for healthcare providers using a pre-post randomized design. *Borderline Personality Disorder and Emotion Dysregulation, 2*(1), 1–8.

77. King, G. (2014). Staff attitudes towards people with borderline personality disorder. *Mental Health Practice, 17*(5).

78. Agrawal, H. R., Gunderson, J., Holmes, B. M., & Lyons-Ruth, K. (2004). Attachment studies with borderline patients: A review. *Harvard Review of Psychiatry, 12*(2), 94–104. https://doi.org/10.1080/10673220490447218.

79. Scott, L. N., Kim, Y., Nolf, K. A., Hallquist, M. N., Wright, A. G., Stepp, S. D.,

Morse, J. Q., & Pilkonis, P. A. (2013). Preoccupied attachment and emotional dysregulation: Specific aspects of borderline personality disorder or general dimensions of personality pathology? *Journal of Personality Disorders, 27*(4), 473–495. https://doi.org/10.1521/pedi_2013_27_099.

80. Lai, M. C., & Baron-Cohen, S. (2015). Identifying the lost generation of adults with autism spectrum conditions. *Lancet Psychiatry, 2*(11):1013–27. doi:10.1016/S2215-0366(15)00277-1. PMID:26544750.

81. Baron-Cohen S. The extreme male brain theory of autism. Trends Cogn Sci. 2002 Jun 1;6(6):248–254. doi: 10.1016/s1364-6613(02)01904-6. PMID: 12039606.

82. Sheehan, L., Nieweglowski, K., & Corrigan, P. (2016). The stigma of personality disorders. *Current Psychiatry Reports, 18*(1), 11.

83. https://www.nytimes.com/2021/05/24/style/adhd-online-creators-diagnosis.html.

84. Lau-Zhu, A., Fritz, A., & McLoughlin, G. (2019). Overlaps and distinctions between attention deficit/hyperactivity disorder and autism spectrum disorder in young adulthood: Systematic review and guiding framework for EEG-imaging research. *Neuroscience and Biobehavioral Reviews, 96*, 93–115. https://doi.org/10.1016/j.neubiorev.2018.10.009.

85. Many ADHDers do benefit from using stimulant medications. For a nuanced view of this topic, Jesse Meadow's essay on Critical ADHD Studies offers an excellent primer: https://jessemeadows.medium.com/we-need-critical-adhd-studies-now-52d4267edd54.

86. Again, Jesse Meadows has a fabulous essay on the link between Autism and ADHD: https://www.queervengeance.com/post/what-s-the-difference-between-adhd-and-autism

87. Velasco, C. B., Hamonet, C., Baghdadli, A., & Brissot, R. (2016). Autism Spectrum Disorders and Ehlers-Danlos Syndrome hypermobility-type: Similarities in clinical presentation. *Cuadernos de medicina psicosomática y psiquiatria de enlace*, (118), 49–58.

88. Black, C., Kaye, J. A., & Jick, H. (2002). Relation of childhood gastrointestinal disorders to autism: Nested case-control study using data from the UK General Practice Research Database. *BMJ, 325*(7361), 419–421.

89. Bolton, P. F., Carcani-Rathwell, I., Hutton, J., Goode, S., Howlin, P., & Rutter, M. (2011). Epilepsy in autism: Features and correlates. *British Journal of Psychiatry, 198*(4), 289–294.

90. https://www.youtube.com/watch?v=GCGlhS5CF08.

91. https://www.instagram.com/myautisticpartner/.

92. https://autisticadvocacy.org/2012/10/october-2012-newsletter/.

93. https://www.iidc.indiana.edu/irca/articles/social-communication-and-language-characteristics.html. See also: Foley-Nicpon, M., Assouline, S. G., & Stinson, R. D. (2012). Cognitive and academic distinctions between gifted students with autism and Asperger syndrome. *Gifted Child Quarterly, 56*(2), 77–89.

94. For more on this, see Price, D. (2021). *Laziness Does Not Exist*. New York: Atria Books.

Chapter 3

1. Hume, K. (2008). *Transition Time: Helping Individuals on the Autism Spectrum Move Successfully from One Activity to Another.* The Reporter 13(2), 6-10.

2. Raymaker, Dora M., et al. (2020). "Having All of Your Internal Resources Exhausted Beyond Measure and Being Left with No Clean-Up Crew": Defining Autistic Burnout. *Autism in Adulthood,* 132–143. http://doi.org/10.1089/aut.2019.0079.

3. The idea that the lives, feelings, opinions, and experiences of minors have less value than those of adults is called adultism; for more on what adultism is and how it shapes the mistreatment of minors, see Fletcher, A. (2015). *Facing Adultism.* Olympia, WA: CommonAction.

4. Livingston, L. A., Shah, P., & Happé, F. (2019). Compensatory strategies below the behavioural surface in autism: A qualitative study. *Lancet Psychiatry,* 6(9), 766–777.

5. J Parish-Morris, J., MY Lieberman, M. Y., Cieri, C., et al. (2017). Linguistic camouflage in girls with autism spectrum disorder. *Molecular Autism, 8,* 48.

6. Livingston, L. A., Colvert, E., Social Relationships Study Team, Bolton, P., & Happé, F. (2019). Good social skills despite poor theory of mind: Exploring compensation in autism spectrum disorder. *Journal of Child Psychology and Psychiatry,* 60, 102.

7. Cage, E., & Troxell-Whitman, Z. (2019). Understanding the reasons, contexts and costs of camouflaging for autistic adults. *Journal of Autism and Developmental Disorders, 49,* 1899–1911.

8. Lai, M.-C., Lombardo, M. V., Ruigrok, A. N. V., et al. (2017). Quantifying and exploring camouflaging in men and women with autism. *Autism, 21,* 690–702

9. Zablotsky, B., Bramlett, M., & Blumberg, S. J. (2015). Factors associated with parental ratings of condition severity for children with autism spectrum disorder. *Disability and Health Journal,* 8(4), 626–634. https://doi.org/10.1016/j.dhjo.2015.03.006.

10. https://sociallyanxiousadvocate.wordpress.com/2015/05/22/why-i-left-aba/.

11. https://autisticadvocacy.org/2019/05/association-for-behavior-analysis-international-endorses-torture/.

12. https://www.nbcnews.com/health/health-care/decades-long-fight-over-electric-shock-treatment-led-fda-ban-n1265546.

13. https://www.nbcnews.com/health/health-care/decades-long-fight-over-electric-shock-treatment-led-fda-ban-n1265546

14. https://newsone.com/1844825/lillian-gomez-puts-hot-sauce-on-crayons/.

15. Lovaas, O. Ivar. *Teaching Developmentally Disabled Children: The Me Book Paperback.* April 1, 1981, p. 50, "Hugs."

16. https://neurodiversityconnects.com/wp-content/uploads/2018/06/PTSD.ABA_.pdf.

17. https://madasbirdsblog.wordpress.com/2017/04/03/i-abused-children-for-a-living/?iframe=true&theme_preview=true.

18. https://southseattleemerald.com/2018/12/05/intersectionality-what-it-means-to-be-autistic-femme-and-black/.

19. Chris's name and some details have been changed to preserve his anonymity.

20. https://truthout.org/articles/as-an-autistic-femme-i-love-greta-thunbergs-resting-autism-face/.

21. Woods, R. (2017). Exploring how the social model of disability can be reinvigorated for autism: In response to Jonathan Levitt. *Disability & Society, 32*(7), 1090–1095.

Chapter 4

1. Bellini, S. (2006). The development of social anxiety in adolescents with autism spectrum disorders. *Focus on Autism and Other Developmental Disabilities, 21*(3), 138-145.

2. Lawson, R. P., Aylward, J., White, S., & Rees, G. (2015). A striking reduction of simple loudness adaptation in autism. *Scientific Reports, 5*(1), 1–7.

3. Takarae, Y., & Sweeney, J. (2017). Neural hyperexcitability in autism spectrum disorders. *Brain Sciences, 7*(10), 129.

4. Samson, F.; Mottron, L.; Soulieres, I.; & Zeffiro, T. A. (2012). Enhanced visual functioning in autism: An ALE meta-analysis. *Human Brain Mapping, 33,* 1553–1581.

5. Takahashi, H.; Nakahachi, T.; Komatsu, S.; Ogino, K.; Iida, Y.; & Kamio, Y. (2014). Hyperreactivity to weak acoustic stimuli and prolonged acoustic startle latency in children with autism spectrum disorders. *Molecular Autism, 5,* 23.

6. Jones, R. S., Quigney, C., & Huws, J. C. (2003). First-hand accounts of sensory perceptual experiences in autism: A qualitative analysis. *Journal of Intellectual & Developmental Disability, 28*(2), 112–121.

7. Rothwell, P. E. (2016). Autism spectrum disorders and drug addiction: Common pathways, common molecules, distinct disorders? *Frontiers in Neuroscience, 10,* 20.

8. https://www.theatlantic.com/health/archive/2017/03/autism-and-addiction/518289/.

9. Rothwell, P. E. (2016). Autism spectrum disorders and drug addiction: Common pathways, common molecules, distinct disorders? *Frontiers in Neuroscience, 10,* 20.

10. https://devonprice.medium.com/the-queens-gambit-and-the-beautifully-messy-future-of-autism-on-tv-36a438f63878.

11. Brosnan, M., & Adams, S. (2020). The Expectancies and Motivations for Heavy Episodic Drinking of Alcohol in Autistic Adults. *Autism in Adulthood, 2*(4), 317–324.

12. Flanagan, J. C., Korte, K. J., Killeen, T. K., & Back, S. E. (2016). Concurrent Treatment of Substance Use and PTSD. *Current Psychiatry Reports, 18*(8), 70. https://doi.org/10.1007/s11920-016-0709-y.

13. Sze, K. M., & Wood, J. J. (2008). Enhancing CBT for the treatment of autism spectrum disorders and concurrent anxiety. *Behavioural and Cognitive Psychotherapy, 36*(4), 403.

14. Helverschou, S. B., Brunvold, A. R., & Arnevik, E. A. (2019). Treating patients with co-occurring autism spectrum disorder and substance use disorder: A clinical explorative study. *Substance Abuse: Research and Treatment, 13*, 1178221819843291. For more on modifications to CBT (though this research is very limited, in that it's based on a child sample and reflects a lot of ableist assumptions about the socia skills of Autistics) see J. J. Wood, A. Drahota, K. Sze, K. Har, A. Chiu, & Langer, D. A. (2009). Cognitive behavioral therapy for anxiety in children with autism spectrum disorders: A randomized, controlled trial. *Journal of Child Psychology and Psychiatry, 50*: 224–234.

15. https://jessemeadows.medium.com/alcohol-an-autistic-masking-tool -8aff572ca520.

16. Dorian identifies as an Aspie, not an Autistic person, because the diagnosis they received at age twenty-four was of Asperger's Syndrome, not Autism Spectrum Disorder.

17. https://www.youtube.com/watch?v=q8J59KXog1M.

18. Assouline, S. G., Nicpon, M. F., & Doobay, A. (2009). Profoundly gifted girls and autism spectrum disorder: A psychometric case study comparison. *Gifted Child Quarterly, 53*(2), 89–105.

19. https://www.youtube.com/watch?v=zZb0taGNLmU.

20. Hobson, H., Westwood, H., Conway, J., McEwen, F. S., Colvert, E., Catmur, C., . . . & Happe, F. (2020). Alexithymia and autism diagnostic assessments: Evidence from twins at genetic risk of autism and adults with anorexia nervosa. *Research in Autism Spectrum Disorders, 73*, 101531.

21. Wiskerke, J., Stern, H., & Igelström, K. (2018). Camouflaging of repetitive movements in autistic female and transgender adults. *BioRxiv*, 412619.

22. Coombs, E., Brosnan, M., Bryant-Waugh, R., & Skevington, S. M. (2011). An investigation into the relationship between eating disorder psychopathology and autistic symptomatology in a non-clinical sample. *British Journal of Clinical Psychology, 50*(3), 326–338.

23. Huke, V., Turk, J., Saeidi, S., Kent, A., & Morgan, J. F. (2013). Autism spectrum disorders in eating disorder populations: A systematic review. *European Eating Disorders Review, 21*(5), 345–351.

24. Tchanturia, K., Dandil, Y., Li, Z., Smith, K., Leslie, M., & Byford, S. (2020). A novel approach for autism spectrum condition patients with eating disorders: Analysis of treatment cost-savings. *European Eating Disorders Review*.

25. Tchanturia, K., Adamson, J., Leppanen, J., & Westwood, H. (2019). Characteristics of autism spectrum disorder in anorexia nervosa: A naturalistic study in an inpatient treatment programme. *Autism, 23*(1), 123–130. https://doi .org/10.1177/1362361317722431.

26. Tchanturia, K., Dandil, Y., Li, Z., Smith, K., Leslie, M., & Byford, S. (2020). A novel approach for autism spectrum condition patients with eating disorders: Analysis of treatment cost-savings. *European Eating Disorders Review*.

27. Li, Z., Dandil, Y., Toloza, C., Carr, A., Oyeleye, O., Kinnaird, E., & Tchanturia, K. (2020). Measuring Clinical Efficacy Through the Lens of Audit Data in Different Adult Eating Disorder Treatment Programmes. *Frontiers in Psychiatry, 11*, 599945. https://doi.org/10.3389/fpsyt.2020.599945.

28. https://www.youtube.com/watch?v=6Her9P4LEEQ.

29. Zalla, T., & Sperduti, M. (2015). The sense of agency in autism spectrum disorders: A dissociation between prospective and retrospective mechanisms? *Frontiers in Psychology*, 6, 1278.

30. Zalla, T., Miele, D., Leboyer, M., & Metcalfe, J. (2015). Metacognition of agency and theory of mind in adults with high functioning autism. *Consciousness and Cognition*, 31, 126–138. doi:10.1016/j.concog.2014.11.001.

31. Schauder, K. B., Mash, L. E., Bryant, L. K., & Cascio, C. J. (2015). Interoceptive ability and body awareness in autism spectrum disorder. *Journal of Experimental Child Psychology*, *131*, 193–200. https://doi.org/10.1016/j.jecp .2014.11.002.

32. Schauder, K. B., Mash, L. E., Bryant, L. K., & Cascio, C. J. (2015). Interoceptive ability and body awareness in autism spectrum disorder. *Journal of Experimental Child Psychology*, *131*, 193–200.

33. https://www.spectrumnews.org/features/deep-dive/unseen-agony-dismantling -autisms-house-of-pain/.

34. https://www.spectrumnews.org/news/people-alexithymia-emotions -mystery/#:~:text=In%20a%20series%20of%20studies,to%20alexithymia%2C %20not%20to%20autism.

35. Poquérusse, J., Pastore, L., Dellantonio, S., & Esposito, G. (2018). Alexithymia and Autism Spectrum Disorder: A Complex Relationship. *Frontiers in Psychology*, *9*, 1196. https://doi.org/10.3389/fpsyg.2018.01196.

36. https://www.marketwatch.com/story/most-college-grads-with-autism-cant -find-jobs-this-group-is-fixing-that-2017-04-10-5881421#:~:text=There %20will%20be%20500%2C000%20adults,national%20unemployment%20rate %20of%204.5%25.

37. Ohl, A., Grice Sheff, M., Small, S., Nguyen, J., Paskor, K., & Zanjirian, A. (2017). Predictors of employment status among adults with Autism Spectrum Disorder. *Work* 56(2): 345–355. doi:10.3233/WOR-172492. PMID: 28211841.

38. Romualdez, A. M., Heasman, B., Walker, Z., Davies, J., & Remington, A. (2021). "People Might Understand Me Better": Diagnostic Disclosure Experiences of Autistic Individuals in the Workplace. *Autism in Adulthood*.

39. Baldwin, S., Costley, D., & Warren, A. (2014). Employment activities and experiences of adults with high-functioning autism and Asperger's disorder. *Journal of Autism and Developmental Disorders*, *44*(10), 2440–2449.

40. Romano, M., Truzoli, R., Osborne, L. A., & Reed, P. (2014). The relationship between autism quotient, anxiety, and internet addiction. *Research in Autism Spectrum Disorders*, *8*(11), 1521–1526.

41. Mazurek, M. O., Engelhardt, C. R., & Clark, K. E. (2015). Video games from the perspective of adults with autism spectrum disorder. *Computers in Human Behavior*, *51*, 122–130.

42. Mazurek, M. O., & Engelhardt, C. R. (2013). Video game use and problem behaviors in boys with autism spectrum disorders. *Research in Autism Spectrum Disorders*, *7*(2), 316–324.

43. Griffiths, S., Allison, C., Kenny, R., Holt, R., Smith, P., & Baron-Cohen, S. (2019). The vulnerability experiences quotient (VEQ): A study of vulnerability,

mental health and life satisfaction in autistic adults. *Autism Research, 12*(10), 1516–1528.

44. Halperin, D. A. (1982). Group processes in cult affiliation and recruitment. *Group, 6*(2), 13–24.

45. https://www.spectrumnews.org/features/deep-dive/radical-online-communities-and-their-toxic-allure-for-autistic-men/.

46. https://medium.com/an-injustice/detransition-as-conversion-therapy-a-survivor-speaks-out-7abd4a9782fa; https://kyschevers.medium.com/tell-amazon-to-stop-selling-pecs-anti-trans-conversion-therapy-book-7a22c308c84d.

47. Lifton, R. J. (2012). Dr. Robert J. Lifton's eight criteria for thought reform. Originally published in *Thought Reform and the Psychology of Totalism,* Chapter 22 (2nd ed., Chapel Hill: University of North Carolina Press, 1989) and Chapter 15 (New York, 1987).

48. Deikman, A. J. (1990). *The Wrong Way Home: Uncovering the Patterns of Cult Behavior in American Society.* Boston: Beacon Press.

49. Dawson, L. L. (2006). *Comprehending Cults: The Sociology of New Religious Movements.* Vol. 71. Oxford: Oxford University Press.

50. https://www.huffpost.com/entry/multilevel-marketing-companies-mlms-cults-similarities_l_5d49f8c2e4b09e72973df3d3.

51. See Karen Kelskey's TedX Talk "Academia Is a Cult" for a description of abusive patterns in academic programs, particularly graduate programs that exploit students' labor: https://www.youtube.com/watch?v=ghAhEBH3MDw.

52. Wood, C., & Freeth, M. (2016). Students' Stereotypes of Autism. *Journal of Educational Issues, 2*(2), 131–140.

53. Walker, P. (2013). Complex PTSD: From surviving to thriving: A guide and map for recovering from childhood trauma. Createspace.

54. http://pete-walker.com/fourFs_TraumaTypologyComplexPTSD.htm?utm_source=yahoo&utm_medium=referral&utm_campaign=in-text-link.

55. Raymaker, D. M., et al. (2020). *Autism in Adulthood,* 2(2): 132–143. http://doi.org/10.1089/aut.2019.0079.

56. https://letsqueerthingsup.com/2019/06/01/fawning-trauma-response/.

57. https://www.healthline.com/health/mental-health/7-subtle-signs-your-trauma-response-is-people-pleasing.

58. https://www.autism-society.org/wp-content/uploads/2014/04/Domestic_Violence___Sexual_Assult_Counselors.pdf.

59. Kulesza, W. M., Cisłak, A., Vallacher, R. R., Nowak, A., Czekiel, M., & Bedynska, S. (2015). The face of the chameleon: The experience of facial mimicry for the mimicker and the mimickee. *Journal of Social Psychology, 155*(6), 590–604.

60. https://www.instagram.com/p/B_6IPryBG7k/.

Chapter 5

1. https://www.spectrumnews.org/opinion/viewpoint/stimming-therapeutic
-autistic-people-deserves-acceptance/.

2. Ming, X. Brimacombe, M., & Wagner, G. (2007). Prevalence of motor impairment in autism spectrum disorders. *Brain Development, 29*, 565–570.

3. Kurcinka, M. S. (2015). *Raising Your Spirited Child: A Guide for Parents Whose Child Is More Intense, Sensitive, Perceptive, Persistent, and Energetic.* New York: William Morrow.

4. Waltz, M. (2009). From changelings to crystal children: An examination of 'New Age' ideas about autism. *Journal of Religion, Disability & Health, 13*(2), 114–128.

5. Freedman, B. H., Kalb, L. G., Zablotsky, B., & Stuart, E. A. (2012). Relationship status among parents of children with autism spectrum disorders: A population-based study. *Journal of Autism and Developmental Disorders, 42*(4), 539–548.

6. https://www.washingtonpost.com/outlook/toxic-parenting-myths-make-life
-harder-for-people-with-autism-that-must-change/2019/02/25/24bd60f6
-2f1b-11e9-813a-0ab2f17e305b_story.html.

7. https://www.realsocialskills.org/blog/orders-for-the-noncompliance-is-a-social
-skill. Retrieved January 2021.

8. Corrigan, P. W., Rafacz, J., & Rüsch, N. (2011). Examining a progressive model of self-stigma and its impact on people with serious mental illness. *Psychiatry Research, 189*(3), 339–343.

9. See Liao, X., Lei, X., & Li, Y. (2019). Stigma among parents of children with autism: A literature review. *Asian Journal of Psychiatry, 45*, 88–94. I have conducted a thorough literature review and found numerous studies on self-stigma reduction for people who are not actually Autistic, but merely related to someone Autistic, and the above review lists some of the most seminal papers. At the time of this writing I can find no papers on self-stigma reduction for the actual members of the stigmatized group—Autistic people ourselves.

10. Corrigan, P. W., Kosyluk, K. A., & Rüsch, N. (2013). Reducing self-stigma by coming out proud. *American Journal of Public Health, 103*(5), 794–800.

11. Martínez-Hidalgo, M. N., Lorenzo-Sánchez, E., García, J. J. L., & Regadera, J. J. (2018). Social contact as a strategy for self-stigma reduction in young adults and adolescents with mental health problems. *Psychiatry Research, 260*, 443–450.

12. There is some research that suggests that Autistic people make for good whistle-blowers: effective whistle-blowers tend to be comfortable with being disliked, and have a firm sense of morality that isn't influenced by social pressure. See for example Anvari, F., Wenzel, M., Woodyatt, L., & Haslam, S. A. (2019). The social psychology of whistleblowing: An integrated model. *Organizational Psychology Review, 9*(1), 41–67.

13. Grove, R., Hoekstra, R. A., Wierda, M., & Begeer, S. (2018). Special interests and subjective wellbeing in autistic adults. *Autism Research, 11*(5), 766–775.

14. Dawson, M. The Misbehaviour of the Behaviourists: Ethical Challenges to the Autism-ABA Industry. https://www.sentex.ca/~nexus23/naa_aba.html.

15. Grove, R., Hoekstra, R. A., Wierda, M., & Begeer, S. (2018). Special interests and subjective wellbeing in autistic adults. *Autism Research, 11*(5), 766–775.

16. Teti, M., Cheak-Zamora, N., Lolli, B., & Maurer-Batjer, A. (2016). Reframing autism: Young adults with autism share their strengths through photo-stories. *Journal of Pediatric Nursing, 31*, 619–629.

17. Jordan, C. J., & Caldwell-Harris, C. L. (2012). Understanding differences in neurotypical and autism spectrum special interests through internet forums. *Intellectual and Developmental Disabilities, 50*(5), 391–402.

18. Special Interest Week concept and #AutieJoy tag by Jersey Noah, prompts developed by Jersey, myself, and many other Autistic self-advocates, table instructions by me.

19. https://poweredbylove.ca/2020/05/08/unmasking/.

20. Table and activity adapted from Heather Morgan's Values-Based Integration exercise.

21. Haruvi-Lamdan, N., Horesh, D., Zohar, S., Kraus, M., & Golan, O. (2020). Autism spectrum disorder and post-traumatic stress disorder: An unexplored co-occurrence of conditions. *Autism, 24*(4), 884–898.

22. Fisher, J. (2017). *Healing the Fragmented Selves of Trauma Survivors: Overcoming Internal Self-Alienation.* New York: Taylor & Francis.

Chapter 6

1. Rose, M. Principles of Divergent Design, 1A. https://www.instagram.com/p/CKzZOnrh_Te/.

2. Van de Cruys, S., Van der Hallen, R., & Wagemans, J. (2017). Disentangling signal and noise in autism spectrum disorder. *Brain and Cognition, 112*, 78–83.

3. Zazzi, H., & Faragher, R. (2018). "Visual clutter" in the classroom: Voices of students with Autism Spectrum Disorder. *International Journal of Developmental Disabilities, 64*(3), 212–224.

4. If you can afford it – see this critique about how minimalism is often a class status symbol https://forge.medium.com/minimalism-is-a-luxury-good-4488693708e5.

5. Rose, M. Principles of Divergent Design, Part 2A. https://www.instagram.com/p/CK4BHVjhmiR/.

6. White, R. C., & Remington, A. (2019). Object personification in autism: This paper will be very sad if you don't read it. *Autism, 23*(4), 1042–1045.

7. For a discussion of "comfort items" in stress management for Autistics, see, for example: Taghizadeh, N., Davidson, A., Williams, K., & Story, D. (2015). Autism spectrum disorder (ASD) and its perioperative management. *Pediatric Anesthesia, 25*(11), 1076–1084.

8. Luke, L., Clare, I. C., Ring, H., Redley, M., & Watson, P. (2012). Decision-making difficulties experienced by adults with autism spectrum conditions. *Autism, 16*(6), 612–621.

9. https://algedra.com.tr/en/blog/importance-of-interior-design-for-autism.

10. https://www.vice.com/en/article/8xk854/fitted-sheets-suck.

11. https://www.discovermagazine.com/health/this-optical-illusion-could-help-to -diagnose-autism.

12. https://www.monster.com/career-advice/article/autism-hiring-initiatives-tech.

13. Baker, E. K., & Richdale, A. L. (2017). Examining the behavioural sleep-wake rhythm in adults with autism spectrum disorder and no comorbid intellectual disability. *Journal of Autism and Developmental Disorders, 47*(4), 1207–1222.

14. Galli-Carminati, G. M., Deriaz, N., & Bertschy, G. (2009). Melatonin in treatment of chronic sleep disorders in adults with autism: A retrospective study. *Swiss Medical Weekly, 139*(19–20), 293–296.

15. https://www.businessinsider.com/8-hour-workday-may-be-5-hours-too-long -research-suggests-2017–9.

16. Olsson, L. E., Gärling, T., Ettema, D., Friman, M., & Fujii, S. (2013). Happiness and satisfaction with work commute. *Social Indicators Research, 111*(1), 255–263.

17. Su, J. (2019). *Working Hard and Work Outcomes: The Relationship of Workaholism and Work Engagement with Job Satisfaction, Burnout, and Work Hours*. Normal: Illinois State University.

18. Sato, K., Kuroda, S., & Owan, H. (2020). Mental health effects of long work hours, night and weekend work, and short rest periods. *Social Science & Medicine, 246*, 112774.

19. https://www.instagram.com/_steviewrites/?hl=en.

20. Aday, M. (2011). Special interests and mental health in autism spectrum disorders (No. D. Psych (C)). Deakin University.

21. Kapp, S. K., Steward, R., Crane, L., Elliott, D., Elphick, C., Pellicano, E., & Russell, G. (2019). "People should be allowed to do what they like": Autistic adults' views and experiences of stimming. *Autism, 23*(7), 1782–1792.

22. Rose, M. (2020). Neuroemergent Time: Making Time Make Sense for ADHD & Autistic People. Martarose.com.

23. https://twitter.com/roryreckons/status/1361391295571222530.

24. http://unstrangemind.com/autistic-inertia-an-overview/.

25. Autistic inertia is frequently assumed to be "volitional." See Donnellan, A. M., Hill, D. A., & Leary, M. R. (2013). Rethinking autism: Implications of sensory and movement differences for understanding and support. *Frontiers in Integrative Neuroscience, 6*, 124.

26. https://autistrhi.com/2018/09/28/hacks/.

27. Sedgewick, F., Hill, V., Yates, R., Pickering, L., & Pellicano, E. (2016). Gender differences in the social motivation and friendship experiences of autistic and non-autistic adolescents. *Journal of Autism and Developmental Disorders, 46*(4), 1297–1306.

28. http://rebirthgarments.com/radical-visibility-zine.

29. Sasson, N. J., Faso, D. J., Nugent, J., Lovell, S., Kennedy, D. P., & Grossman, R. B. (2017). Neurotypical Peers are Less Willing to Interact with Those with Autism Based on Thin Slice Judgments. *Scientific Reports, 7*, 40700. https://doi .org/10.1038/srep40700.

30. McAndrew, F. T., & Koehnke, S. S. (2016). On the nature of creepiness. *New Ideas in Psychology*, *43*, 10–15.

31. Leander, N. P., Chartrand, T. L., & Bargh, J. A. (2012). You give me the chills: Embodied reactions to inappropriate amounts of behavioral mimicry. *Psychological Science*, *23*(7), 772–779. Note: many of John Bargh's priming studies have failed replication attempts in recent years. For a discussion of a failed attempt of a related but different series of temperature priming studies, see Lynott, D., Corker, K. S., Wortman, J., Connell, L., Donnellan, M. B., Lucas, R. E., & O'Brien, K. (2014). Replication of "Experiencing physical warmth promotes interpersonal warmth" by Williams and Bargh (2008). *Social Psychology*.

32. Sasson, N. J., & Morrison, K. E. (2019). First impressions of adults with autism improve with diagnostic disclosure and increased autism knowledge of peers. *Autism*, *23*(1), 50–59.

33. YouTuber Sundiata Smith has a video about natural Black hair care for those on the spectrum. You can watch it here: https://www.youtube.com/watch?v=KjsnIG7kvWg.

34. https://www.instagram.com/postmodernism69/?hl=en.

Chapter 7

1. Gayol, G. N. (2004). Codependence: A transgenerational script. *Transactional Analysis Journal*, *34*(4), 312–322.

2. Romualdez, A. M., Heasman, B., Walker, Z., Davies, J., & Remington, A. (2021). "People Might Understand Me Better": Diagnostic Disclosure Experiences of Autistic Individuals in the Workplace. *Autism in Adulthood*.

3. Sasson, N. J., & Morrison, K. E. (2019). First impressions of adults with autism improve with diagnostic disclosure and increased autism knowledge of peers. *Autism*, *23*(1), 50–59.

4. https://www.distractify.com/p/jay-will-float-too-tiktok#:~:text=Source%3A%20TikTok-,Jay%20Will%20Float%20Too's%20Latest%20TikTok,Lesser%2DKnown%20Aspect%20of%20Autism&text=On%20July%2028%2C%20a%20TikTok,grappling%20with%20the%20sheer%20cuteness.

5. https://nicole.substack.com/p/a-little-bit-autistic-a-little-bit.

6. Richards, Z., & Hewstone, M. (2001). Subtyping and subgrouping: Processes for the prevention and promotion of stereotype change. *Personality and Social Psychology Review*, *5*(1), 52–73.

7. https://letsqueerthingsup.com/2019/06/01/fawning-trauma-response/.

8. Martin, K. B., Haltigan, J. D., Ekas, N., Prince, E. B., & Messinger, D. S. (2020). Attachment security differs by later autism spectrum disorder: A prospective study. *Developmental Science*, *23*(5), e12953.

9. Bastiaansen, J. A., Thioux, M., Nanetti, L., van der Gaag, C., Ketelaars, C., Minderaa, R., & Keysers, C. (2011). Age-related increase in inferior frontal gyrus activity and social functioning in autism spectrum disorder. *Biological Psychiatry*, *69*(9), 832–838. doi:10.1016/j.biopsych.2010.11.007. Epub 2011 Feb 18. PMID: 21310395.

10. Lever, A. G., & Geurts, H. M. (2016). Age-related differences in cognition

across the adult lifespan in autism spectrum disorder. *Autism Research, 9*(6), 666–676.

11. Bellini, S. (2006). The development of social anxiety in adolescents with autism spectrum disorders. *Focus on Autism and Other Developmental Disabilities, 21*(3), 138–145.

12. Crompton, C. J., Ropar, D., Evans-Williams, C. V., Flynn, E. G., & Fletcher-Watson, S. (2019). Autistic peer-to-peer information transfer is highly effective. *Autism*, 1362361320919286.

13. https://www.jacobinmag.com/2015/05/slow-food-artisanal-natural -preservatives/.

14. https://poweredbylove.ca/2019/08/19/why-everyone-needs-a-personal-mission -statement-and-four-steps-to-get-started-on-your-own/.

15. Adapted from the blog post above—questions and quoted portions are by Heather R. Morgan; additional writing/prompts are by me.

16. Silberman, S. (2015). *NeuroTribes: The Legacy of Autism and the Future of Neurodiversity*. New York: Penguin. Chapter 5: "Princes of the Air."

17. http://cubmagazine.co.uk/2020/06/autistic-people-the-unspoken-creators-of -our-world/.

18. https://www.wired.com/2015/08/neurotribes-with-steve-silberman/.

19. https://www.cam.ac.uk/research/news/study-of-half-a-million-people-reveals -sex-and-job-predict-how-many-autistic-traits-you-have.

20. https://www.accessliving.org/defending-our-rights/racial-justice/community -emergency-services-and-support-act-cessa/; https://www.nprillinois.org /statehouse/2021-06-02/illinois-begins-to-build-mental-health-emergency -response-system.

21. https://www.imdb.com/title/tt2446192/.

22. Pramaggiore, M. (2015). The taming of the bronies: Animals, autism and fandom as therapeutic performance. *Journal of Film and Screen Media, 9*.

23. Autistic people tend to socialize around shared activities rather than emotional bonding: Orsmond, G. I., Shattuck, P. T., Cooper, B. P., Sterzing, P. R., Anderson, K. A. (2013). Social participation among young adults with an autism spectrum disorder. *Journal of Autism and Developmental Disorders, 43*(11), 2710–2719.

24. Crompton, C. J., Hallett, S., Ropar, D., Flynn, E., & Fletcher-Watson, S. (2020). 'I never realised everybody felt as happy as I do when I am around autistic people': A thematic analysis of autistic adults' relationships with autistic and neurotypical friends and family. *Autism, 24*(6), 1438–1448.

25. Cresswell, L., Hinch, R., & Cage, E. (2019). The experiences of peer relationships amongst autistic adolescents: A systematic review of the qualitative evidence. *Research in Autism Spectrum Disorders, 61*, 45–60.

26. For a quick review of some of the issues with Autism Speaks, see https://www .washingtonpost.com/outlook/2020/02/14/biggest-autism-advocacy-group-is -still-failing-too-many-autistic-people/.

Chapter 8

1. See this article about Autism Speaks's infamous "I Am Autism" PSA: http://content.time.com/time/health/article/0,8599,1935959,00.html.

2. Oliver, Michael (1990). *The Politics of Disablement*. London: Macmillan Education.

3. For a great review of the ways Deaf people have been systematically denied access to sign language and accessible schooling, I recommend Solomon, A. (2012). *Far from the Tree: Parents, Children and the Search for Identity*. New York: Simon & Schuster.

4. The podcast *Fat Outta Hell* has a lot of great coverage on how most public spaces are inaccessible to fat bodies; even something as simple as a restaurant having tables bolted to the floor can mean the space is completely inaccessible to larger people. For an example of how excluding fat patients from medical research leads to pervasive health inequities, see this article in *Nature:* https://www.nature.com/articles/ejcn201457.

5. Uono, S., & Hietanen, J. K. (2015). Eye contact perception in the West and East: A cross-cultural study. *PloS One, 10*(2), e0118094, https://doi.org/10.1371/journal.pone.0118094.

6. Grinker, R. R. (2021). In *Nobody's Normal: How Culture Created the Stigma of Mental Illness*. New York: Norton, 30.

7. Esteller-Cucala, P., Maceda, I., Børglum, A. D., Demontis, D., Faraone, S. V., Cormand, B., & Lao, O. (2020). Genomic analysis of the natural history of attention-deficit/hyperactivity disorder using Neanderthal and ancient Homo sapiens samples. *Scientific Reports, 10*(1), 8622. https://doi.org/10.1038/s41598-020-65322-4.

8. See, for example: Shpigler, H. Y., Saul, M. C., Corona, F., Block, L., Ahmed, A. C., Zhao, S. D., & Robinson, G. E. (2017). Deep evolutionary conservation of autism-related genes. *Proceedings of the National Academy of Sciences, 114*(36), 9653–9658. And Ploeger, A., & Galis, F. (2011). Evolutionary approaches to autism: An overview and integration. *McGill Journal of Medicine: MJM,13*(2).

9. So long as a person is "otherwise qualified to do the job." This is somewhat subjective and does provide room for discrimination to take place. Many job listings for positions that don't otherwise involve physical labor (say, an administrative assistant position) nonetheless state that the employee must be able to lift twenty- to fifty-pound boxes, for example.

10. https://www.un.org/development/desa/disabilities/disability-laws-and-acts-by-country-area.html.

11. Organized by the late Marca Bristo, founder of Access Living Chicago. https://news.wttw.com/2019/09/09/disability-rights-community-mourns-loss-pioneer-marca-bristo.

12. https://www.americanbar.org/groups/crsj/publications/human_rights_magazine_home/human_rights_vol34_2007/summer2007/hr_summer07_hero/#:~:text=In%20Chicago%20in%201984%2C%20people,My%20name%20is%20Rosa%20Parks.%E2%80%9D.

13. https://www.chicagotribune.com/news/ct-xpm-1987-05-27-8702080978-story
.html.

14. The CTA website claims that 71 percent of all train stations are accessible
"with an elevator or ramp." The "or" here is doing a lot of work—many stations
lack elevators and simply have ramps into the station at the ground level, but
offer no way to the train tracks themselves. See https://wheelchairtravel.org
/chicago/public-transportation/.

15. Target and Sobey's are some of the most well-known retailers to adopt sensory-
friendly hours: https://www.consumeraffairs.com/news/target-store-offers
-sensory-friendly-shopping-hours-for-customers-with-autism-120916
.html; https://strategyonline.ca/2019/12/04/sobeys-rolls-out-sensory-friendly
-shopping-nationally/.

16. https://autisticadvocacy.org/wp-content/uploads/2016/06/Autistic-Access
-Needs-Notes-on-Accessibility.pdf.

17. http://ada.ashdownarch.com/?page_id=428#:~:text=Any%20disabled
%20person%20who%20encounters,statutory%20damages%20plus%20attorney
's%20fees.

18. For a full review of how these attitudes shifted from the Middle Ages through
industrialization, I recommend reading *Madness in Civilization* by Andrew
Scull, and the first three chapters of *Nobody's Normal* by Roy Grinker.

19. Mancini, T., Caricati, L., & Marletta, G. (2018). Does contact at work extend
its influence beyond prejudice? Evidence from healthcare settings. *Journal of
Social Psychology, 158*(2), 173–186.

20. Cameron, L., & Rutland, A. (2006). Extended contact through story reading in
school: Reducing children's prejudice toward the disabled. *Journal of Social
Issues, 62* (3), 469–488.

21. Kende, J., Phalet, K., Van den Noortgate, W., Kara, A., & Fischer, R. (2018).
Equality revisited: A cultural meta-analysis of intergroup contact and prejudice.
Social Psychological and Personality Science, 9 (8), 887–895.

22. Most commonly depression or anxiety, though again keep in mind these
numbers are almost certainly an underestimate, given limited mental health
service access. https://www.nami.org/mhstats#:~:text=20.6%25%20of%20U.S.
%20adults%20experienced,2019%20(13.1%20million%20people).

23. https://mhanational.org/issues/2020/mental-health-america-access-care-data
#adults_ami_no_treatment.

24. https://mhanational.org/issues/2020/mental-health-america-access-care-data
#four.

25. https://www.publicsource.org/is-my-life-worth-1000-a-month-the-reality-of
-feeling-undervalued-by-federal-disability-payments/.

26. https://www.specialneedsalliance.org/the-voice/what-happens-when-persons
-living-with-disabilities-marry-2/.

27. https://www.ssa.gov/ssi/text-resources-ussi.htm.

28. Disability benefits eligibility has to be reestablished every six to eighteen
months: https://www.ssa.gov/benefits/disability/work.html#:~:text=Reviewing
%20Your%20Disability.

29. https://www.vox.com/policy-and-politics/2017/5/30/15712160/basic-income-oecd-aei-replace-welfare-state.

30. Metzl, J. M. (2010). *The Protest Psychosis: How Schizophrenia Became a Black Disease.* Boston: Beacon Press.

31. https://psmag.com/education/america-keeps-criminalizing-autistic-children.

32. Reproductive control is exerted over people with disabilities quite commonly: https://www.thedailybeast.com/britney-spears-forced-iud-is-common-in-conservatorships.

Conclusion

1. McAdams, D., & Adler, J. M. "Autobiographical Memory and the Construction of a Narrative Identity: Theory, Research, and Clinical Implications," in Maddux, J. E., & Tagney, J. P. (2010). *Social Psychological Foundations of Clinical Psychology.* New York: Guilford Press.

2. See McAdams, D. P., Josselson, R. E., & Lieblich, A. E. (2006). *Identity and Story: Creating Self in Narrative.* Washington, DC: American Psychological Association.

3. Adler, J. M., Kissel, E. C., & McAdams, D. P. (2006). Emerging from the CAVE: Attributional style and the narrative study of identity in midlife adults. *Cognitive Therapy and Research, 30*(1), 39–51.

4. McAdams, D., & Adler, J. M. "Autobiographical Memory and the Construction of a Narrative Identity Theory, Research, and Clinical Implications," in Maddux, J. E., & Tagney, J. P. (2010). *Social Psychological Foundations of Clinical Psychology.* New York: Guilford Press.

5. Cashin, A., Browne, G., Bradbury, J., & Mulder, A. (2013). The effectiveness of narrative therapy with young people with autism. *Journal of Child and Adolescent Psychiatric Nursing, 26*(1), 32–41.

6. Note that most of the research into narrative therapy in Autistic people focuses on Autistic children or young adults. Some researchers have theorized that narrative therapy is a good fit for Autistic people with high verbal abilities, but those who don't process information in words may not find it suitable. For more on this see Falahi, V., & Karimisani, P. (2016). The effectiveness of Narrative Therapy on improvement of communication and social interaction of children with autism. *Applied Psychological Research Quarterly, 7*(2), 81–104.

7. https://poweredbylove.ca/2017/11/09/your-values-diagram/.

INDEX

reclaiming passions and special interests, 150–55
redemptive self, 254–56, *255*
rediscovering values, 155–59
Regan, Ruti, 5, 143
rejection-sensitive dysphoria, 78–79
relationships. *See* Autistic relationships, cultivating
remote work, 127, 175, 238
repetitive behaviors, 26–27, 33
Rick and Morty (TV series), 37, 133, 134
rigid rules, adherence to, *112,* 129–33
  Andrew's experience, 129–30
  warning signs of high-control groups, 132–33
risks, 28–29
Rock, Chris, 62, 67
Rose Marta, 168–70, 171, 173, 177–78
Rowling, J. K., 59
rudeness, 37, 63

St. Elsewhere (TV series), 67
samefoods, 27
Schaber, Amythest, 5
Schevers, Ky, 131–32
schizophrenia, 11, 37, 72, 145, 238, 246
scripting, 180–81
Scull, Andrew, 246
Seal, Moorea, 164–67, 170
seizure disorders, 16, 28
self-acceptance, 11, 12, 39, 213–14
self-advocacy community, 5, 10, 11, 85–87
self-advocacy organizations, 83, 86–87, 225, 234
self-determination, 44, 45–46
self-diagnosis, 44, 45–46
self-disclosure, 195–200
  affirmations for process, 199–200
  questions to ask, 198–99
self-employment, 127, 175, 238
self-gratitude, 159–63
self-harm of masking. *See* costs of masking
selfishness, 77, 104, 145
self-loathing, 5, 16, 220, 252
self-realization, 44, 45–46, 85–86
self-soothing, 26–27, *55,* 87, 112, 171, 202
self-stigma, 144–45, 184–85
sensory adaptation, 114
sensory avoiders, 70–71
sensory-friendly public spaces, *236–37*
sensory overload, 9, 24, 25, 26, 33, 75, 78, 110, 114–15, 146, 175, 199, *209,* 232
sensory seekers (sensory inattentive types), 69–72
"severely" Autistic, 49, 99–100
severity of Autism symptoms, 99–100
sexism, 87, 241

sex work, 98, 175
shame, 10, 12, 16, 28, 85–86, 101, 102, 141, 145, 152, 160, 214
shutdowns, 7, 33–34, 114, 223
shyness, 7, 54, *56*
sign language, 230–31, 235, 237
Silberman, Steven, 36, 218–19
Simone, Rudy, 7, 54
Singer, Judy, 30–31
"sister conditions," 72
slavery, 65–66, 240
sleep disorders, 174–75
Social Anxiety Disorder, 20, 25, *55,* 110
social chameleons, 56, 57
social exclusion, 5, 6, 8, 230
social media, 87, 153, 165, 196–97, 225–26
social model of disability, 230–31
social norms, 61, 115–16, 232–33
  broadening, 238–40
social value, 81–82, 85
speaking styles and code switching, 63–64
Spears, Britney, 247
special interests, 26, 150–55, 176–77, 218–19
  Clara's experience, 150–51
  Jersey Noah's experience, 153–55
  meetups, 226–27
Special Interest Week, 153–55
specialists and diagnosis, 41–42
spiral time, 177–78
spirited child, 142–43
standing up for yourself, 143, *147,* 190, 191–93, 259, 260
stereotypes, 12, 94–95, 197
  exercise for how they have affected you, *38*
  exercise for reflecting on the need to mask, 95, *95–96*
  media portrayals, 4, 13, 19, 37, 39–40, 67, 133–34
  negative, 63, 105, *106–8,* 110
  reframing, 140–50, *147–49*
  white Autistic boys, 6–7, 33, 35–39
stigma, 11, 15–16, 30, 75, 80, 214, 232, 239
  self-stigma, 144–45, 184–85
stimming, 26–27, 28, 87, 101, 102, 103, 141, 172, 194, 231
Stimtastic, 87, 141, 188
strawberry people, 200–207
stress, 4, 17, *55,* 63, 112, 130, 134, 169, 232. *See also* post-traumatic stress disorder
stress management, 26, 28, 56, 75, 176–77
stubbornness, 77, 143, *144,* 145–46, 159
subclinical Autism, 9, 31–32